# Other Books and Series by Jeff Bowen

*Applications for Enrollment of Chickasaw Newborn Act of 1905*
*Volumes I thru VII*

*Cherokee Intermarried White 1906 Volume I thru X*

*Applications for Enrollment of Creek Newborn Act of 1905*
*Volumes I thru XIV*

*Applications for Enrollment of Choctaw Newborn Act of 1905*
*Volume I, II, III, IV, V, VI, VII, VIII, IX, X, XI & XII*

Visit our website at **www.nativestudy.com** to learn more about these and other books and series by Jeff Bowen

# APPLICATIONS FOR ENROLLMENT OF CHOCTAW NEWBORN ACT OF 1905

## VOLUME XIII

### TRANSCRIBED BY
### JEFF BOWEN

NATIVE STUDY
Gallipolis, Ohio
USA

# Other Books and Series by Jeff Bowen

*1901-1907 Native American Census Seneca, Eastern Shawnee, Miami, Modoc, Ottawa, Peoria, Quapaw, and Wyandotte Indians (Under Seneca School, Indian Territory)*

*1932 Census of The Standing Rock Sioux Reservation with Births And Deaths 1924-1932*

*Census of The Blackfeet, Montana, 1897- 1901 Expanded Edition*

*Eastern Cherokee by Blood, 1906-1910, Volumes I thru XIII*

*Choctaw of Mississippi Indian Census 1929-1932 with Births and Deaths 1924-1931 Volume I*
*Choctaw of Mississippi Indian Census 1933, 1934 & 1937, Supplemental Rolls to 1934 & 1935 with Births and Deaths 1932-1938, and Marriages 1936-1938 Volume II*

*Eastern Cherokee Census Cherokee, North Carolina 1930-1939 Census 1930-1931 with Births And Deaths 1924-1931 Taken By Agent L. W. Page Volume I*
*Eastern Cherokee Census Cherokee, North Carolina 1930-1939 Census 1932-1933 with Births And Deaths 1930-1932 Taken By Agent R. L. Spalsbury Volume II*
*Eastern Cherokee Census Cherokee, North Carolina 1930-1939 Census 1934-1937 with Births and Deaths 1925-1938 and Marriages 1936 & 1938 Taken by Agents R. L. Spalsbury And Harold W. Foght Volume III*

*Seminole of Florida Indian Census, 1930-1940 with Birth and Death Records, 1930-1938*

*Texas Cherokees 1820-1839 A Document For Litigation 1921*

*Choctaw By Blood Enrollment Cards 1898-1914 Volumes I thru XVII*

*Starr Roll 1894 (Cherokee Payment Rolls) Districts: Canadian, Cooweescoowee, and Delaware Volume One*
*Starr Roll 1894 (Cherokee Payment Rolls) Districts: Flint, Going Snake, and Illinois Volume Two*
*Starr Roll 1894 (Cherokee Payment Rolls) Districts: Saline, Sequoyah, and Tahlequah; Including Orphan Roll Volume Three*

*Cherokee Intruder Cases Dockets of Hearings 1901-1909 Volumes I & II*

*Indian Wills, 1911-1921 Records of the Bureau of Indian Affairs Books One thru Seven;*
*Native American Wills & Probate Records 1911-1921*

# Other Books and Series by Jeff Bowen

*Turtle Mountain Reservation Chippewa Indians 1932 Census with Births & Deaths, 1924-1932*

*Chickasaw By Blood Enrollment Cards 1898-1914 Volume I thru V*

*Cherokee Descendants East An Index to the Guion Miller Applications Volume I*
*Cherokee Descendants West An Index to the Guion Miller Applications Volume II (A-M)*
*Cherokee Descendants West An Index to the Guion Miller Applications Volume III (N-Z)*

*Applications for Enrollment of Seminole Newborn Freedmen, Act of 1905*

*Eastern Cherokee Census, Cherokee, North Carolina, 1915-1922, Taken by Agent James E. Henderson     Volume I (1915-1916)*
*Volume II (1917-1918)*
*Volume III (1919-1920)*
*Volume IV (1921-1922)*

*Complete Delaware Roll of 1898*

*Eastern Cherokee Census, Cherokee, North Carolina, 1923-1929, Taken by Agent James E. Henderson     Volume I (1923-1924)*
*Volume II (1925-1926)*
*Volume III (1927-1929)*

*Applications for Enrollment of Seminole Newborn Act of 1905 Volumes I & II*

*North Carolina Eastern Cherokee Indian Census 1898-1899, 1904, 1906, 1909-1912, 1914 Revised and Expanded Edition*

*1932 Hopi and Navajo Native American Census with Birth & Death Rolls (1925-1931) Volume 1 - Hopi*
*1932 Hopi and Navajo Native American Census with Birth & Death Rolls (1930-1932) Volume 2 - Navajo*

*Western Navajo Reservation Navajo, Hopi and Paiute 1933 Census with Birth & Death Rolls 1925-1933*

*Cherokee Citizenship Commission Dockets 1880-1884 and 1887-1889 Volumes I thru V*

Copyright © 2013
by Jeff Bowen

ALL RIGHTS RESERVED
No part of this publication may be reproduced
or used in any form or manner whatsoever
without previous written permission from the
copyright holder or publisher.

Originally published:
Baltimore, Maryland
2013

Reprinted by:

Native Study LLC
Gallipolis, OH
*www.nativestudy.com*
2020

Library of Congress Control Number: 2020918113

ISBN: 978-1-64968-106-5

*Made in the United States of America.*

This series is dedicated to the descendants of the Choctaw newborn listed in these applications.

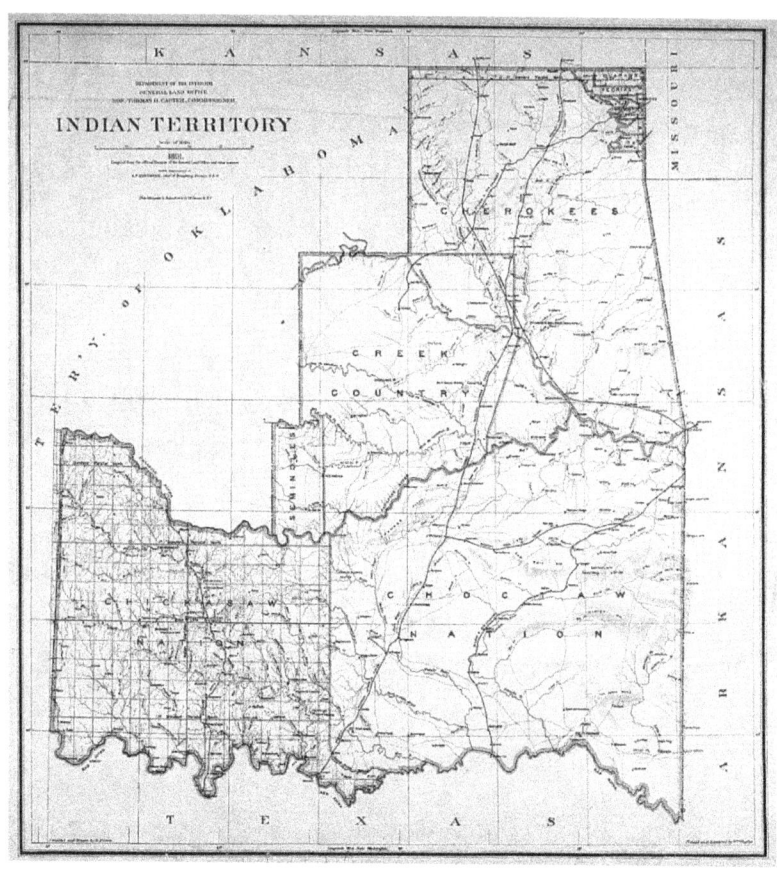

This map of Indian Territory shows how large the Choctaw and Chickasaw Nations' land base was that contained huge deposits of asphalt and coal. Just the size and territory involved was flooded with the "Grafters".

DEPARTMENT OF THE INTERIOR.
Commissioner to the Five Civilized Tribes.

# NOTICE.

## Opening of Land Office at Wewoka,
### IN THE SEMINOLE NATION, INDIAN TERRITORY.

Notice is hereby given that on Monday, September 4, 1905, the Commissioner to the Five Civilized Tribes will establish a land office at Wewoka, in the Seminole Nation, Indian Territory, for the purpose of allowing citizens and freedmen of the Seminole Nation to select allotments of land for their minor children enrolled under the Act of Congress approved March 3, 1905 (33 Stat. L 1060), and for the further purpose of allowing citizens and freedmen of the Seminole Nation, whose allotments are incomplete, to select additional land in order to bring the value of their allotments up to the standard of $309.09, as nearly as may be practicable.

Each child whose enrollment in accordance with the Act of March 3, 1905, has been duly approved by the Secretary of the Interior, is entitled to receive an alllotment of forty acres without regard to the character or value of the land selected.

Selection of allotments for minor children must be made by their citizen or freedmen parents or by a duly appointed guardian, or curator, or by a duly appointed administrator.

TAMS BIXBY,
Commissioner.

Muskogee, Indian Territory,
July 29, 1905.

*This particular notice for the Seminole and Creek Newborn makes mention of the Act of 1905. It is likely that a similar notice was posted in the Choctaw and Chickasaw Nations for the registration of newborn children.*

# DEPARTMENT OF THE INTERIOR,
## Commission to the Five Civilized Tribes.

### Rules and Regulations Governing the Selection of Allotments and the Designation of Homesteads in the Choctaw and Chickasaw Nations.

1. Selections of allotments and designations of homesteads for adult citizens and selections of allotments for adult freedmen must be made in person except as herein otherwise provided.

2. Applications to have land set apart and homesteads designated for duly identified Mississippi Choctaws must be made personally before the Commission to the Five Civilized Tribes. Fathers may apply for their minor children and if the father be dead the mother may apply. Husbands may apply for wives. Applications for orphans, insane persons and persons of unsound mind may be made by duly appointed guardian or curator, and for aged and infirm persons and prisoners by agents duly authorized thereunto by power of attorney, in the discretion of said Commission.

3. At the time of the selection of allotment each citizen and duly identified Mississippi Choctaw shall designate as a homestead out of said selection land equal in value to one hundred and sixty acres of the average allottable land of the Choctaw and Chickasaw Nations, as nearly as may be.

4. Each Choctaw and Chickasaw freedman, at the time of selection shall designate as his or her allotment of the lands of the Choctaw and Chickasaw Nations, land equal in value to forty acres of the average allottable land of the Choctaw and Chickasaw Nations.

5. Citizens, freedmen and identified Mississippi Choctaws who are married, whether they have attained their majority or not, will be regarded as of age for the purpose of making selections.

6. Selections may be made by citizen and freedman parents for unmarried male children under twenty-one years of age and for unmarried female children under eighteen years of age, and a male citizen or freedman may make selection for his wife, if she is entitled to make selection, unless she shall, at the time or previously thereto, protest in writing.

7. Where the father of an unmarried minor citizen, freedman or identified Mississippi Choctaw is a non-citizen, the citizen, freedman or identified Mississippi Choctaw mother of such children must make selection in person in behalf of said children.

8. Selections of allotments and designations of homesteads for minor citizens and selections of allotments for minor freedmen may be made by the citizen father or mother or freedman father or mother, as the case may be, or by a guardian, curator, or an administrator having charge of their estate, in the order named.

9. Selections of allotments and designations of homesteads for citizen, and selections of allotment for freedmen, prisoners, convicts, aged and infirm persons and soldiers and sailors of the United States on duty outside of Indian Territory, may be made by duly appointed agents under power of attorney, and for incompetents by guardians, curators, or other suitable person akin to them.

10. Selections may be made and homesteads designated for duly identified Mississippi Choctaws, who have, within one year after the date of their identification as such, made satisfactory proof of bona fide settlement within the Choctaw-Chickasaw country, at any time within six months after the date of their said identification.

11. Persons authorized to make selections by power of attorney, as provided in rules 2 and 9 hereof, must be the husband or wife, or a relative not further removed than a cousin of the first degree of the person for whom such selection is made.

12. It shall be the duty of the Commission to the Five Civilized Tribes to see that selections of allotments and designations of homesteads for the classes of persons mentioned in rules 2, 6, 7, 8 and 9 hereof, are made for the best interests of such persons.

13. Selections of allotments for citizens, freedmen and identified Mississippi Choctaws who have died subsequent to September 25, 1902, and before making a selection of allotment, shall be made by a duly appointed administrator or executor. If, however, such administrator or executor be not duly and expeditiously appointed, or fails to act promptly when appointed, or for any other cause such selections be not so made within a reasonable and practicable time, the Commission to the Five Civilized Tribes shall designate the lands thus to be allotted.

14. In determining the value of a selection the appraised value of the land selected shall be increased by the appraised value of such pine timber on such land as has heretofore been estimated by the Commission to the Five Civilized Tribes.

15. Selections of allotments may be made only by citizens and freedmen whose enrollment has been approved by the Secretary of the Interior, and by persons duly identified by the Commission to the Five Civilized Tribes as Mississippi Choctaws, and by none others.

16. When a selection of land has been made by a citizen, freedman or identified Mississippi Choctaw, and the land so selected is claimed by a person whose rights as a citizen or freedman have not been finally determined, contest for the land so selected may be instituted by the person claiming the land, formal application for the land being first made as is required by the Rules of Practice in Choctaw and Chickasaw allotment contest cases.

THE COMMISSION TO THE FIVE CIVILIZED TRIBES.
TAMS BIXBY, Chairman.

Muskogee, Indian Territory, March 24, 1903.

---

The above statement published prior to 1905, was established for what was supposed to be a set of guidelines when it came to allotments. But with supplemental agreements and Congressional legislation, time frames as well as rules and regulations often changed and were not the same for every tribe.

# INTRODUCTION

The *Applications for Enrollment of Choctaw Newborn Act of 1905*, National Archive film M-1301, Rolls 50-57, are found under the heading of Applications for Enrollment of the Commission to the Five Civilized Tribes. For this series, I have transcribed the application forms filled out by individuals applying for enrollment in the Five Civilized Tribes under the Dawes Commission. These applications contain considerably more information than stated on the census cards found in series M-1186. M-1301 possesses its own numerical sequence, separate from M-1186. To find each party's roll number you would have to reference M-1186.

The Choctaw as well as the Chickasaw allotments were likely some of the most sought after properties in Indian Territory. There was supposed to be a 25-year restriction on the sale or lease of any Indian lands so as to insure that the owners wouldn't be swindled, but that isn't what happened. This fact is borne out in the Dawes Commission General Allotment Act, of February 8, 1887, Section 5, which "Provides that after an Indian person is allotted land, the United States will hold the land 'in trust [1] for the sole use and benefit of the Indian' (or his heirs if the Indian landowner dies) for a period of 25 years. (Land held in trust by the United States government cannot be sold or in anyway alienated by the Indian landowner, since the United States government considers the underlying ownership of the land held by itself and not the tribe. After the period of trust ends, the Indian landowner is free to sell the land and is free from any encumbrance from the United States.)"[1] Instead, Native Americans were exploited by the devious. The Choctaw and Chickasaw Districts both had huge asphalt and coal deposits, so there was pressure from outsiders to acquire them from the minute they were discovered. After repeated attacks throughout the years and many legislative changes, President "Roosevelt finally signed the Five Tribes Bill at noon on April 26, 1906, the forces seeking to end all restrictions were disappointed. Section 19 removed restrictions from the sale of all inherited land but directed that no full-bloods could sell their land for twenty-five years. The Act also prohibited leases for more than one year without the approval of the Secretary of the Interior."[2]

Angie Debo described the opportunists that wanted these Native American allotments as, "Grafters". The parents of the newborns enumerated within this series would no sooner receive the approval for their child's allotment than there would be someone there with cash in hand holding a new deed or lease for the parents to sign their child's birthright away. Angie Debo said it best, "As the business incapacity of the allottees became apparent, a horde of despoilers fastened themselves upon their property." According to Debo, "The term 'grafter' was applied as a matter of course to dealers in Indian land, and was frankly accepted by them. The speculative fever also affected Government employees so that it was almost impossible to prevent them from making personal investments."[3]

---

[1] General Allotment Act, Act of Feb. 8, 1887 (24 Stat. 388, ch. 119, 25 USCA 331)
[2] The Dawes Commission and the Allotment of the Five Civilized Tribes, 1893-1914 by Kent Carter, pg. 173
[3] And Still the Waters Run, Angie Debo, p. 92.

# INTRODUCTION

According to the Department of Interior in 1905, "It is estimated that there will be added to the final rolls of the citizens and freedmen of the Choctaw and Chickasaw nations the names of 2,000 persons, including 1,500 new-born children to be enrolled under the provisions of the act of Congress approved March 3, 1905."[4]

The quote below explains, in detail, the requirements for qualifying as a newborn Choctaw, "By the act of Congress approved March 3, 1905 (H.R. 17474), entitled 'An act making appropriations for the current and contingent expenses of the Indian Department and for fulfilling treaty stipulations with various Indian tribes for the fiscal year ending June 30, 1906, and for other purposes,' it was provided as follows:

'That the Commission to the Five Civilized Tribes is hereby authorized for sixty days after the date of the approval of this act to receive and consider applications for enrollment of infant children born prior to September twenty-fifth, nineteen hundred and two, and who were living on said date, to citizens by blood of the Choctaw and Chickasaw tribes of Indians whose enrollment has been approved by the Secretary of the Interior prior to the date of the approval of this act; and to enroll and make allotments to such children.'

'That the Commission to the Five Civilized Tribes is authorized for sixty days after the date of the approval of this act to receive and consider applications for enrollment of children born subsequent to September twenty-fifth, nineteen hundred and two, and prior to March fourth, nineteen hundred and five, and who were living on said latter date, to citizens by blood of the Choctaw and Chickasaw tribes of Indians whose enrollment has been approved by the Secretary of the Interior prior to the date of the approval of this act; and to enroll and make allotments to such children.'

"Notice is hereby given that the Commission to the Five Civilized Tribes will, up to and inclusive of midnight, May 2, 1905, receive applications for the enrollment of infant children born prior to September 25, 1902, and who were living on said date, to citizens by blood of the Choctaw and Chickasaw tribes of Indians whose enrollment has been approved by the Secretary of the Interior prior to March 3, 1905."[5]

Following is the scope of these transcriptions: Besides the applications themselves, researchers will find the identities of other individuals within these applications -- doctors, lawyers, mid-wives, and other relatives -- that may help with you genealogical research.

Jeff Bowen
Gallipolis, Ohio
NativeStudy.com

---

[4] Annual Reports of the Department of the Interior For the Fiscal Year Ended June 30, 1905, p. 609.
[5] Annual Reports of the Department of the Interior For the Fiscal Year Ended June 30, 1905, p. 593.

# Applications for Enrollment of Choctaw Newborn
## Act of 1905 Volume XIII

Choc New Born 867
    Thurman Lewis  b. 1-22-05
    Harmon Lewis  b. 5-1-03

United States of America,   )
                                  )
Indian Territory,           ) ss.
                                  )
Central District.           )

    I, Vinson Going, on oath state that I am twenty years of age and a citizen by blood of the Choctaw Nation; that my post offce[sic] address is Smithville, Indian Territory; that I am personally acquainted with Littie Lewis, wife of Simmon[sic] Lewis; that for the last three years said parties have lived within four miles of where I have lived, near Smithville, Indian Territory; that there was born to the said Littie Lewis on or about the first day of May, 1903, a male child; that said child is now living and is said to have been named Harmon Lewis.

                                                        Vinson Going

Subscribed and sworn to before me this 5th day of April, 1905.

                                                        Wirt Franklin
                                                        Notary Public.

United States of America,   )
                                  )
Indian Territory,           ) ss.
                                  )
Central District.           )

    I, Peter Going, on oath state that I am twenty-six years of age and a citizen of the Choctaw Nation; that my post office address is Smithville, Indian Territory, that I am personally acquainted with Littie Lewis, wife of Simmon Lewis; that for the last three years said parties have lived within four miles of where I live near Smithville, Indian Territory; that there was born to the said Littie Lewis on or about the first day of May, 1903, a male child; that said child is now living and is said to have been named Harmon Lewis.

                                                        Peter Going

Subscribed and sworn to before me this 5th day of April, 1905.

                                                        Wirt Franklin
                                                        Notary Public.

# Applications for Enrollment of Choctaw Newborn
## Act of 1905 Volume XIII

**BIRTH AFFIDAVIT.**

## DEPARTMENT OF THE INTERIOR.
## COMMISSION TO THE FIVE CIVILIZED TRIBES.

---

**IN RE APPLICATION FOR ENROLLMENT,** as a citizen of the Choctaw Nation, of Harmon Lewis, born on the 1st day of May, 1903

Name of Father: Simmon Lewis     a citizen of the Choctaw Nation.
Name of Mother: Littie Lewis     a citizen of the Choctaw Nation.

Postoffice    Smithville, I.T.

---

**AFFIDAVIT OF MOTHER.**

UNITED STATES OF AMERICA, Indian Territory, }
Central     DISTRICT. }

I, Littie Lewis, on oath state that I am 19 years of age and a citizen by blood, of the Choctaw Nation; that I am the lawful wife of Simmon Lewis, who is a citizen, by blood of the Choctaw Nation; that a male child was born to me on 1st day of May, 1903; that said child has been named Harmon Lewis, and was living March 4, 1905. *and that the said wife who attended me is dead*

                               her
                     Littie x Lewis
Witnesses To Mark:      mark
    { Vester W Rose
    { Robert Anderson

Subscribed and sworn to before me this 5th day of April, 1905

                         Wirt Franklin
                           Notary Public.

---

**BIRTH AFFIDAVIT.**

## DEPARTMENT OF THE INTERIOR.
## COMMISSION TO THE FIVE CIVILIZED TRIBES.

---

**IN RE APPLICATION FOR ENROLLMENT,** as a citizen of the Choctaw Nation, of Thurman Lewis, born on the 22nd day of January, 1905

Name of Father: Simmon Lewis     a citizen of the Choctaw Nation.
Name of Mother: Littie Lewis     a citizen of the Choctaw Nation.

Postoffice    Smithville, Ind.Ter.

# Applications for Enrollment of Choctaw Newborn
## Act of 1905 Volume XIII

**AFFIDAVIT OF MOTHER.**

UNITED STATES OF AMERICA, Indian Territory,  
Central DISTRICT.

I, Littie Lewis, on oath state that I am 19 years of age and a citizen by blood, of the Choctaw Nation; that I am the lawful wife of Simmon Lewis, who is a citizen, by blood of the Choctaw Nation; that a male child was born to me on 22nd day of January, 1905; that said child has been named Thurman Lewis, and was living March 4, 1905.

                                  her  
                           Littie x Lewis

Witnesses To Mark:             mark  
  Vester W Rose  
  Robert Anderson

Subscribed and sworn to before me this 5th day of April, 1905

                          Wirt Franklin  
                          Notary Public.

**AFFIDAVIT OF ATTENDING PHYSICIAN OR MID-WIFE.**

UNITED STATES OF AMERICA, Indian Territory,  
Central DISTRICT.

I, Narsie Benjamin, a mid-wife, on oath state that I attended on Mrs. Littie Lewis, wife of Simmon Lewis on the 22nd day of January, 1905; that there was born to her on said date a male child; that said child was living March 4, 1905, and is said to have been named Thurman Lewis

                                  her  
                           Narsie x Benjamin

Witnesses To Mark:             mark  
  Robert Anderson  
  Vester W Rose

Subscribed and sworn to before me this 5th day of April, 1905

                          Wirt Franklin  
                          Notary Public.

# Applications for Enrollment of Choctaw Newborn
## Act of 1905   Volume XIII

Choc New Born 868
    Phoebe Clay   b. 5-24-03
    Henry Clay   b. 2-16-05

---

7- 5340      7- 13730
BIRTH AFFIDAVIT.

### DEPARTMENT OF THE INTERIOR.
### COMMISSION TO THE FIVE CIVILIZED TRIBES.

---

IN RE APPLICATION FOR ENROLLMENT, as a citizen of the    Choctaw    Nation, of Henry Clay    , born on the  16  day of  February  , 1905

Name of Father: Andrew Clay        a citizen of the   Choctaw   Nation.
Name of Mother: Louisa Clay        a citizen of the   Choctaw   Nation.

                Postoffice   Ti   I.T.

---

### AFFIDAVIT OF MOTHER.

UNITED STATES OF AMERICA, Indian Territory, }
    Central              DISTRICT. }

    I,  Louisa Clay  , on oath state that I am  25  years of age and a citizen by blood  , of the  Choctaw  Nation; that I am the lawful wife of  Andrew Clay  , who is a citizen, by blood  of the  Choctaw  Nation; that a  male  child was born to me on  16  day of  February  , 1905; that said child has been named Henry Clay  , and was living March 4, 1905.

                                    her
                            Louisa  x  Clay
Witnesses To Mark:            mark
    { Chas T. Difendafer
      OL Johnson

    Subscribed and sworn to before me this  10  day of   April   , 1905

                          OL Johnson
                              Notary Public.

# Applications for Enrollment of Choctaw Newborn
## Act of 1905 Volume XIII

### AFFIDAVIT OF ATTENDING PHYSICIAN OR MID-WIFE.

UNITED STATES OF AMERICA, Indian Territory,  
Central DISTRICT.

I, Nancy Brown, a midwife, on oath state that I attended on Mrs. Louisa Clay, wife of Andrew Clay on the 16 day of February, 1905; that there was born to her on said date a male child; that said child was living March 4, 1905, and is said to have been named Henry Clay

                                           her  
                                    Nancy x Brown  
Witnesses To Mark:            mark  
   { Chas T. Difendafer  
     OL Johnson

Subscribed and sworn to before me this 10 day of April, 1905

                                OL Johnson  
                                Notary Public.

7-5340        7-13730  
BIRTH AFFIDAVIT.

### DEPARTMENT OF THE INTERIOR.
### COMMISSION TO THE FIVE CIVILIZED TRIBES.

IN RE APPLICATION FOR ENROLLMENT, as a citizen of the Choctaw Nation, of Phoebe Clay, born on the 24 day of May, 1903

Name of Father: Andrew Clay      a citizen of the Choctaw Nation.  
Name of Mother: Louisa Clay      a citizen of the Choctaw Nation.

                         Postoffice   Ti, I.T.

### AFFIDAVIT OF MOTHER.

UNITED STATES OF AMERICA, Indian Territory,  
Central DISTRICT.

I, Louisa Clay, on oath state that I am 25 years of age and a citizen by blood, of the Choctaw Nation; that I am the lawful wife of Andrew Clay, who is a citizen, by blood of the Choctaw Nation; that a female child was born to me on 24 day of May, 1903; that said child has been named Phoebe Clay, and was living March 4, 1905.

                                    her  
                               Louisa x Clay  
                                mark

# Applications for Enrollment of Choctaw Newborn
## Act of 1905   Volume XIII

Witnesses To Mark:
   { Chas T. Difendafer
     OL Johnson

    Subscribed and sworn to before me this   10   day of   April   , 1905

                            OL Johnson
                            Notary Public.

**AFFIDAVIT OF ATTENDING PHYSICIAN OR MID-WIFE.**

UNITED STATES OF AMERICA, Indian Territory, }
   Central                 DISTRICT. }

    I,   Nancy Brown   , a   midwife   , on oath state that I attended on Mrs.   Louisa Clay   , wife of   Andrew Clay   on the   24   day of   May   , 1903; that there was born to her on said date a   female   child; that said child was living March 4, 1905, and is said to have been named Phoebe Clay

                            her
                       Nancy x Brown
Witnesses To Mark:          mark
   { Chas T. Difendafer
     OL Johnson

    Subscribed and sworn to before me this   10   day of   April   , 1905

                            OL Johnson
                            Notary Public.

---

Choc New Born 869
    Arbon Blackburn Potter   b. 7-26-04

Applications for Enrollment of Choctaw Newborn
Act of 1905   Volume XIII

**NEW-BORN AFFIDAVIT.**

Number..............

...Choctaw Enrolling Commission...

IN THE MATTER OF THE APPLICATION FOR ENROLLMENT, as a citizen of the Choctaw Nation, of   Olburn Potter

born on the   26   day of _____July_____ 190 4

Name of father   R. H. Potter          a citizen of   Choctaw
Nation final enrollment No. ——
Name of mother   Minnie Potter (nee Davis)   a citizen of   Choctaw
Nation final enrollment No.   9323

Postoffice   Hartshorne, Ind Ter

**AFFIDAVIT OF MOTHER.**

UNITED STATES OF AMERICA
INDIAN TERRITORY
   Central       DISTRICT

I   Minnie Potter (nee Davis)   , on oath state that I am   21   years of age and a citizen by   blood   of the   Choctaw   Nation, and as such have been placed upon the final roll of the   Choctaw   Nation, by the Honorable Secretary of the Interior my final enrollment number being   9323  ; that I am the lawful wife of   R. H. Potter   , who is a   non   citizen of the   Choctaw   Nation, and as such has   not  been placed upon the final roll of said Nation by the Honorable Secretary of the Interior, his final enrollment number being   ——   and that a   male   child was born to me on the   26$^{th}$   day of   July   190 4; that said child has been named   Olburn Potter   , and is now living.

Minnie Potter nee Davis

Witnesseth.
   Must be two    ⎫   John Pulcher
   Witnesses who  ⎬
   are Citizens.  ⎭   J D Chastain

Subscribed and sworn to before me this   6$^{th}$   day of   March   190 5

Wm J Hulsey
Notary Public.

My commission expires:   1908

# Applications for Enrollment of Choctaw Newborn
# Act of 1905 Volume XIII

## AFFIDAVIT OF ATTENDING PHYSICIAN OR MIDWIFE

UNITED STATES OF AMERICA
INDIAN TERRITORY
Central          DISTRICT

I, Lizzie Scott    a    midwife on oath state that I attended on Mrs. Minnie Potter (nee Davis) wife of R H Potter on the 26<sup>th</sup> day of July, 190 4, that there was born to her on said date a male child, that said child is now living, and is said to have been named Olburn Potter

Witness to mark                                her
John Pulcher                           Lizzie x Scott          M.D.
J D Chastain                                 mark

Subscribed and sworn to before me this, the 6<sup>th</sup> day of March 190 5

WITNESSETH:                           Wm J Hulsey    Notary Public.
Must be two witnesses { John Pulcher
who are citizens      { JD Chastain

We hereby certify that we are well acquainted with Lizzie Scott a midwife and know she to be reputable and of good standing in the community.

John Pulcher

JD Chastain                           ___X___  ___X___

BIRTH AFFIDAVIT.

### DEPARTMENT OF THE INTERIOR.
### COMMISSION TO THE FIVE CIVILIZED TRIBES.

IN RE APPLICATION FOR ENROLLMENT, as a citizen of the Choctaw Nation, of Arbon Blackburn Potter, born on the 26 day of July, 1904

Name of Father: R. H. Potter          a citizen of the Choctaw Nation.
Name of Mother: Minnie Potter (nee Davis)    a citizen of the Choctaw Nation.

Postoffice    Hartshorne, Ind Terry.

# Applications for Enrollment of Choctaw Newborn
## Act of 1905 Volume XIII

**AFFIDAVIT OF MOTHER.**

UNITED STATES OF AMERICA, Indian Territory, }
Central          DISTRICT.

I,   Minnie Potter (nee Davis)   , on oath state that I am   21   years of age and a citizen by   Blood   , of the   Choctaw   Nation; that I am the lawful wife of   R. H. Potter   , who is a citizen, by Marriage   of the   Choctaw   Nation; that a   Male   child was born to me on   26$^{th}$   day of   Jul   , 1904; that said child has been named   Arbon Blackburn Potter   , and was living March 4, 1905.

                                                    Minnie Potter   (nee Davis)
Witnesses To Mark:
{

Subscribed and sworn to before me this   8$^{th}$   day of   April   , 1905

                                                  W.R. Patterson
                                                  Notary Public.

---

**AFFIDAVIT OF ATTENDING PHYSICIAN OR MID-WIFE.**

UNITED STATES OF AMERICA, Indian Territory, }
Central          DISTRICT.

I,   Lizzie Scott   , a   midwife   , on oath state that I attended on Mrs.   Minnie Potter (nee Davis)   , wife of   R. H. Potter   on the   26$^{th}$   day of   July   , 1904; that there was born to her on said date a   Male   child; that said child was living March 4, 1905, and is said to have been named   Arbon Blackburn Potter
                                                  her
                                            Lizzie x Scott
Witnesses To Mark:                      mark
{ John Pulcher
  William Bee

Subscribed and sworn to before me this   8$^{th}$   day of   April   , 1905

                                              W.R. Patterson
                                              Notary Public.

## Applications for Enrollment of Choctaw Newborn
## Act of 1905   Volume XIII

Choc New Born 870
J. H. Rayburn Harris  b. 12-8-03
Jack L. Harris  b. 2-13-05

Choctaw 3924.

Muskogee, Indian Territory, April 15, 1905.

Amelia Harris,
  Caddo, Indian Territory.

Dear Madam:

Receipt is hereby acknowledged of the affidavits of Amelia Harris and LeRoy Long to the birth of J. H. Rayburn Harris; also the affidavits of Amelia Harris and William Graves to the birth of Jack L. Harris, children of Amelia and Jack L. Harris (deceased), December 8, 1903 and February 13, 1905, respectively, and the same have been filed with our records as applications for the enrollment of said children.

Respectfully,

Chairman.

**BIRTH AFFIDAVIT.**
### DEPARTMENT OF THE INTERIOR.
### COMMISSION TO THE FIVE CIVILIZED TRIBES.

**IN RE APPLICATION FOR ENROLLMENT,** as a citizen of the   Choctaw   Nation, of J. H. Rayburn Harris   , born on the 8th   day of   December   , 1903

Name of Father: Jack L. Harris         a citizen of the   Choctaw   Nation.
Name of Mother: Amelia Harris         a citizen of the   Choctaw   Nation.

Postoffice   Caddo, Indian Territory

**AFFIDAVIT OF MOTHER.**

UNITED STATES OF AMERICA, Indian Territory,
  Central            DISTRICT.

I,   Amelia Harris   , on oath state that I am   27   years of age and a citizen by   blood   , of the   Choctaw   Nation; that I am the lawful wife of   Jack L. Harris, deceased   , who is a citizen, by   marriage   of the   Choctaw   Nation; that a   male   child was born to me on   8th   day of   December   , 1903;

10

## Applications for Enrollment of Choctaw Newborn
## Act of 1905 Volume XIII

that said child has been named    J. H. Rayburn Harris    , and was living March 4, 1905.

Amelia Harris

Witnesses To Mark:
{

Subscribed and sworn to before me this 8th day of  April  , 1905

J L Rappolee
Notary Public.

---

**AFFIDAVIT OF ATTENDING PHYSICIAN OR MID-WIFE.**

UNITED STATES OF AMERICA, Indian Territory, }
Central                DISTRICT.

I, LeRoy Long, a Physician, on oath state that I attended on Mrs. Amelia Harris, wife of Jack L Harris, deceased on the 8th day of December, 1903; that there was born to her on said date a male child; that said child was living March 4, 1905, and is said to have been named J. H. Rayburn Harris

LeRoy Long

Witnesses To Mark:
{

Subscribed and sworn to before me this 11<sup>th</sup> day of April, 1905

Brooks Fort
Notary Public.

Com Ex 3/6/07

---

## Affidavit of Attending Physician or Midwife

UNITED STATES OF AMERICA, }
  INDIAN TERRITORY, }
Central   DISTRICT

I, LeRoy Long       a    Practicing Physician on oath state that I attended on Mrs. Amelia Harris    wife of Jack L Harris on the 8<sup>th</sup> day of December, 190 3, that there was born to her on said date a male child, that said child is now living, and is said to have been named John H.R. Harris

LeRoy Long       M. D.

## Applications for Enrollment of Choctaw Newborn
## Act of 1905   Volume XIII

Subscribed and sworn to before me this the 13<sup>th</sup> day of Feby 1905

Com Ex 3/6/07

Brooks Fort
Notary Public.

WITNESSETH:

Must be two witnesses who are citizens and know the child. { F Manning
Gertrude Crutchfield

We hereby certify that we are well acquainted with Dr Le Roy Long a Physician and know him to be reputable and of good standing in the community.

Must be two citizen witnesses. { F Manning
Gertrude Crutchfield

# NEW BORN AFFIDAVIT

No ............

## CHOCTAW ENROLLING COMMISSION

IN THE MATTER OF THE APPLICATION FOR ENROLLMENT as a citizen of the Choctaw Nation, of   John H. R. Harris   born on the 8<sup>th</sup> day of December 190 3

Name of father  Jack L Harris   a citizen of  Choctaw   Nation, final enrollment No.  365

Name of mother  Amelia Harris   a citizen of  Choctaw   Nation, final enrollment No.  11019

Caddo I.T.   Postoffice.

### AFFIDAVIT OF MOTHER

UNITED STATES OF AMERICA
INDIAN TERRITORY
DISTRICT   Central

I  Amelia Harris  , on oath state that I am  26  years of age and a citizen by  blood  of the  Choctaw  Nation, and as such have been placed upon the final roll of the  Choctaw  Nation, by the Honorable Secretary of the Interior my final enrollment number being  11019  ; that I am the lawful wife of  Jack L Harris  , who

# Applications for Enrollment of Choctaw Newborn
## Act of 1905   Volume XIII

is a citizen of the   Choctaw   Nation, and as such has been placed upon the final roll of said Nation by the Honorable Secretary of the Interior, his final enrollment number being 365   and that a   Male   child was born to me on the   8$^{th}$   day of   December   190 3; that said child has been named   John H. R. Harris   , and is now living.

WITNESSETH:                                                                  Amelia Harris
Must be two witnesses { F Manning
who are citizens         { Gertrude Crutchfield

Subscribed and sworn to before me this, the   8$^{th}$   day of   February   , 190 5

A.E. Folsom
Notary Public.

My Commission Expires:
9 Jan 1905[sic]

# NEW BORN AFFIDAVIT

No ............

## CHOCTAW ENROLLING COMMISSION

IN THE MATTER OF THE APPLICATION FOR ENROLLMENT   as   a   citizen   of   the   Choctaw Nation, of   Jack L. Harris Jr   born on the   13$^{th}$   day of   February   190 5

Name of father   Jack L Harris   a citizen of   Choctaw   Nation, final enrollment No.   365
Name of mother   Amelia Harris   a citizen of   Choctaw   Nation, final enrollment No.   11019

Caddo I.T.                                                   Postoffice.

**AFFIDAVIT OF MOTHER**

UNITED STATES OF AMERICA }
   INDIAN TERRITORY              }
DISTRICT        Central              }

I   Amelia Harris   , on oath state that I am   27   years of age and a citizen by   blood   of the   Choctaw   Nation, and as such have been placed upon the final roll of the   Choctaw   Nation, by the Honorable Secretary of the Interior my final enrollment number being   11019   ; that I am the lawful wife of   Jack L Harris   , who is a citizen of the   Choctaw   Nation, and as such has been placed upon the final roll

## Applications for Enrollment of Choctaw Newborn
## Act of 1905  Volume XIII

of said Nation by the Honorable Secretary of the Interior, his final enrollment number being 365 and that a Male child was born to me on the 13th day of February 190 5; that said child has been named Jack L Harris Jr, and is now living.

            Amelia Harris

WITNESSETH:
Must be two witnesses who are citizens { Edward E Pitchlynn / F Manning

Subscribed and sworn to before me this, the 10th day of March, 190 5

          A.E. Folsom
            Notary Public.

My Commission Expires:
Jan 9-1909

---

### *Affidavit of Attending Physician or Midwife*

UNITED STATES OF AMERICA,  
 INDIAN TERRITORY,  
 Central  DISTRICT

I, Will Graves a Osteopath on oath state that I attended on Mrs. Amelia Harris wife of Jack L Harris on the 13th day of February, 190 5, that there was born to her on said date a male child, that said child is now living, and is said to have been named Jack L Harris Jr

         William Graves D.O.   ~~M.D.~~

Subscribed and sworn to before me this the 10th day of Feby 1905

          A.E. Folsom
            Notary Public.

WITNESSETH:
Must be two witnesses who are citizens and know the child. { Edward E Pitchlynn / F Manning

We hereby certify that we are well acquainted with Dr William Graves a Osteopath and know him to be reputable and of good standing in the community.

         Must be two citizen witnesses. { Edward E Pitchlynn / F Manning

# Applications for Enrollment of Choctaw Newborn
## Act of 1905 Volume XIII

BIRTH AFFIDAVIT.

### DEPARTMENT OF THE INTERIOR.
### COMMISSION TO THE FIVE CIVILIZED TRIBES.

---

IN RE APPLICATION FOR ENROLLMENT, as a citizen of the Choctaw Nation, of Jack L. Harris, born on the 13th day of Feb., 1905

Name of Father: Jack L. Harris     a citizen of the Choctaw Nation.
Name of Mother: Amelia Harris     a citizen of the Choctaw Nation.

Postoffice    Caddo, Ind., Ter.,

---

### AFFIDAVIT OF MOTHER.

UNITED STATES OF AMERICA, Indian Territory, }
    Central              DISTRICT. }

I, Amelia Harris, on oath state that I am 27 years of age and a citizen by blood, of the Choctaw Nation; that I am the lawful wife of Jack L. Harris, deceased, who is a citizen, by marriage of the Choctaw Nation; that a male child was born to me on 13th day of Feb., 1905; that said child has been named Jack L. Harris, and was living March 4, 1905.

                                         Amelia Harris

Witnesses To Mark:
{

Subscribed and sworn to before me this 8th day of April, 1905

                                       J L Rappolee
                                         Notary Public.

---

### AFFIDAVIT OF ATTENDING PHYSICIAN OR MID-WIFE.

UNITED STATES OF AMERICA, Indian Territory, }
    Central              DISTRICT. }

I, William Graves, a Physician, on oath state that I attended on Mrs. Amelia Harris, wife of Jack L Harris, deceased on the 13th day of Feb., 1905; that there was born to her on said date a male child; that said child was living March 4, 1905, and is said to have been named Jack L. Harris

                                     William Graves

Witnesses To Mark:
{

## Applications for Enrollment of Choctaw Newborn
## Act of 1905   Volume XIII

Subscribed and sworn to before me this 8th   day of   April   , 1905

J L Rappolee
Notary Public.

---

Choc New Born 871
    Dora Eunice Folsom   b.   11-17-02
    Junier[sic] Wade Folsom   b.   10-29-04

Choctaw 452.

Muskogee, Indian Territory, April 15, 1905.

Wade Folsom,
    Dixie, Indian Territory.

Dear Sir:

    Receipt is hereby acknowledged of the affidavits of Maude A. Folsom and F. M. Jackson to the birth of Dora Eunice Folsom; also the affidavits of Maude A. Folsom and L. J. Cranfill to the birth of Junier Wade Folsom, children of Maude A. and Wade Folsom, November 17, 1902 and October 29, 1904, respectively, and the same have been filed with our records as applications for the enrollment of said children.

Respectfully,

Chairman.

7-NB-871

Muskogee, Indian Territory, July 12, 1905.

Wade Folsom,
    Dixie, Indian Territory.

Dear Sir:

    Receipt is hereby acknowledged of your letter of July 6, 1905, asking if your two children Dora Unice[sic] and Junier Wade Folsom have been approved.

## Applications for Enrollment of Choctaw Newborn
## Act of 1905 Volume XIII

In reply to your letter you are advised that the names of your children Dora Eunice and Junier Wade Folsom have been placed upon a schedule of citizens by blood of the Choctaw Nation which has been forwarded the Secretary of the Interior. You will be notified when their enrollment is approved by the Department.

Respectfully,

Commissioner.

BIRTH AFFIDAVIT.

DEPARTMENT OF THE INTERIOR.
**COMMISSION TO THE FIVE CIVILIZED TRIBES.**

IN RE APPLICATION FOR ENROLLMENT, as a citizen of the Choctaw Nation, of Dora Eunice Folsom , born on the 17 day of Nov , 1902

Name of Father: Wade Folsom　　a citizen of the Choctaw Nation.
Name of Mother: Maude A Folsom　　a citizen of the Choctaw Nation.

Postoffice　Dixie Ind. Ter.

AFFIDAVIT OF MOTHER.

UNITED STATES OF AMERICA, Indian Territory,
Southern　　　　　　　DISTRICT.

I, Maude A Folsom , on oath state that I am 31 years of age and a citizen by Intermarriage , of the Choctaw Nation; that I am the lawful wife of Wade Folsom , who is a citizen, by Blood of the Choctaw Nation; that a Female child was born to me on 17 day of Nov , 1902; that said child has been named Dora Eunice Folsom , and was living March 4, 1905.

Maude A Folsom

Witnesses To Mark:

Subscribed and sworn to before me this 28 day of March , 1905

U. T. Rexroat
Notary Public.

# Applications for Enrollment of Choctaw Newborn
## Act of 1905 Volume XIII

### AFFIDAVIT OF ATTENDING PHYSICIAN OR MID-WIFE.

UNITED STATES OF AMERICA, Indian Territory, }
Southern DISTRICT.

I, F. M. Jackman, a Physician, on oath state that I attended on Mrs. Maude A Folsom, wife of Wade Folsom on the 17 day of Nov, 1902; that there was born to her on said date a Female child; that said child was living March 4, 1905, and is said to have been named Dora Eunice Folsom

F.M. Jackman

Witnesses To Mark:
{

Subscribed and sworn to before me this 30 day of March, 1905

C M Inge
Notary Public.

---

**BIRTH AFFIDAVIT.**

### DEPARTMENT OF THE INTERIOR.
### COMMISSION TO THE FIVE CIVILIZED TRIBES.

---

IN RE APPLICATION FOR ENROLLMENT, as a citizen of the Choctaw Nation, of Junier Wade Folsom, born on the 29 day of Oct, 1904

Name of Father: Wade Folsom    a citizen of the Choctaw Nation.
Name of Mother: Maude A Folsom    a citizen of the Choctaw Nation.

Postoffice    Dixie Ind. Ter.

---

### AFFIDAVIT OF MOTHER.

UNITED STATES OF AMERICA, Indian Territory, }
Southern DISTRICT.

I, Maude A Folsom, on oath state that I am 31 years of age and a citizen by Intermarriage, of the Choctaw Nation; that I am the lawful wife of Wade Folsom, who is a citizen, by Blood of the Choctaw Nation; that a male child was born to me on Oct day of 29, 1904; that said child has been named Junier Wade Folsom, and was living March 4, 1905.

Maude A Folsom

Witnesses To Mark:
{

# Applications for Enrollment of Choctaw Newborn
## Act of 1905 Volume XIII

Subscribed and sworn to before me this 29 day of March, 1905

A M Hightower
Notary Public.

### AFFIDAVIT OF ATTENDING PHYSICIAN OR MID-WIFE.

UNITED STATES OF AMERICA, Indian Territory,  
Southern DISTRICT.

I, L J Cranfill M.D., a Physician, on oath state that I attended on Mrs. Maude A Folsom, wife of Wade Folsom on the Oct day of 29, 1904; that there was born to her on said date a Male child; that said child was living March 4, 1905, and is said to have been named Junier Wade Folsom

L J Cranfill M.D.

Witnesses To Mark:

Subscribed and sworn to before me this 29 day of March, 1905

A M Hightower
Notary Public.

---

Choc New Born 872
    Ola Edith Perry  b. 2-16-05

9-NB-285.

Muskogee, Indian Territory, May 17, 1905.

Thomas Elmer Perry,
    Caney, Kansas.

Dear Sir:

Referring to the application for the enrollment of your infant child, Ola Edith Perry, born February 16, 1905, it is noted from the affidavits heretofore filed with the Commission that your wife claims to be a Chickasaw by blood.

## Applications for Enrollment of Choctaw Newborn
## Act of 1905   Volume XIII

    If this is correct you will please state when, where and under what name she was listed for enrollment, the names of her parents and other members of her family for whom application was made at the same time, and if she has selected an allotment, give her roll number as the same appears on her allotment certificate.

                        Respectfully,

                                        Chairman.

---

                        9-NB-285.

            Muskogee, Indian Territory, May 20, 1905.

Thomas Elmer Perry,
    Caney, Kansas.

Dear Sir:

    Referring to the application for the enrollment of your infant child, Ola Edith Perry, born February 16, 1905, it is noted from the affidavits heretofore filed with the Commission that your wife claims to be a Chickasaw by blood.

    If this is correct you will please state when, where and under what name she was listed for enrollment, the names of her parents and other members of her family for whom application was made at the same time, and if she has selected an allotment, give her roll number as the same appears on her allotment certificate. If she was married before your marriage to her, please give the name of her former husband, the names and dates of birth of her children, if any, by such former marriage.

                        Respectfully,

                                        Chairman.

---

                        7-2551

            Muskogee, Indian Territory, June 8, 1905.

Thomas L. Perry,
    Kaney[sic], Kansas.

Dear Sir:

    Receipt is hereby acknowledged of your letter of June 2, 1905, stating that your wife is Choctaw instead of Chickasaw by blood and that she was enrolled as Cornelia C. Walker.

## Applications for Enrollment of Choctaw Newborn
## Act of 1905  Volume XIII

    In reply to your letter you advised that this information has enabled us to identify her upon our records as an enrolled citizen by blood of the Choctaw Nation and the affidavits heretofore forwarded to the birth of your child Ola Edith Perry have been filed with our records as an application for her enrollment.

Respectfully,

Chairman.

*(The letter dated May 20, 1905, above, given again.)*

*(The letter below typed as given.)*

(Copy)

Caney Kans.

June 2, 1905.

Commission to the Five Civilized Tribes Five,
    Muskogee, I. T.

Dear :-

    I will now and. in regard to the letter received Sat: of you. Stating the mistake made in the filling out of the affidavet of (Ola Edith Perry) for enrollment. The mistake being wheather or not my wife was a Chickasaw or Choctaw by blood. She is a Choctaw by blood. And was enrolled as (Cornelia C. Walker). She has never been married before this time. Her father's name is (Tandy. K. Walker) her Sister (Rebecca N. Walker) this is all of the family that is to be enrolled. Her enrollment number is

(7171)

    Hoping this will fix things all O. K. I will close.

Respt.

Thomas Elmer Perry.

Caney

Kans.

# Applications for Enrollment of Choctaw Newborn
## Act of 1905  Volume XIII

9-3

Muskogee, Indian Territory, April 11, 1905.

Thomas Elmer Perry,
    Caney, Kansas.

Dear Sir:

    Receipt is hereby acknowledged of the affidavits of Cornelia C. Perry and Ira B. Chadwick to the birth of Ola Edith Perry, daughter of Thomas and Cornelia C. Perry, February 16, 1905, and the same have been filed with our records as an application for the enrollment of said child.

                    Respectfully,

                    Commissioner in Charge.

---

*(The letter below typed as given.)*

Caney Kan

Mar 22 1905

Commission of the five Tribes
    Ardmore I. T.

Sirs will you Please send me a birth afidavid as I have an infant child that I want to inRole as a citizen of the Chickashaw Nation. will it be nessary for me to come in Pearson to inrole the child or can I Just fill out the affidavid and sent it in to the Land Office.

My wife is on the Regular Roles of the Chickashaw Nation and have filed My wife Madin name was Cornelia C. Walker. she filed as Walker.

Please let me here frome you soon

I get my mail at Caney
    Kan.

           Yours truly

              Elmer Perry.

## Applications for Enrollment of Choctaw Newborn
## Act of 1905 Volume XIII

**BIRTH AFFIDAVIT.**

### DEPARTMENT OF THE INTERIOR.
### COMMISSION TO THE FIVE CIVILIZED TRIBES.

IN RE APPLICATION FOR ENROLLMENT, as a citizen of the Chickasaw Nation, of Ola Edith Perry, born on the 16" day of February, 1905

Name of Father: Thomas Elmer Perry     a citizen of the Chickasaw Nation.
Name of Mother: Cornealia[sic] C Perry     a citizen of the Chickasaw Nation.

Postoffice    Caney Kansas

**AFFIDAVIT OF MOTHER.**

State of Kansas   ss
County of Montgomery.

I, Cornelia C. Perry, on oath state that I am 20 years of age and a citizen by blood, of the Chickasaw Nation; that I am the lawful wife of Thomas Elmer Perry, who is a citizen, by marriage of the Chickasaw Nation; that a Female child was born to me on 16$^{th}$ day of February, 1905; that said child has been named Ola Edith Perry, and was living March 4, 1905.

Cornelia C Perry

Witnesses To Mark:
   { R.A. Park    TYRO, KANS.
   { E A Denney    TYRO, KANS.

Subscribed and sworn to before me this 5th day of April, 1905

C A Pocock
Notary Public.
My Com Ex 2/23/1909

**AFFIDAVIT OF ATTENDING PHYSICIAN OR MID-WIFE.**

State of Kansas   ss
County of Montgomery.

I, Ira B Chadwick, a physician, on oath state that I attended on Mrs. Cornelia C Perry, wife of Thomas Elmer Perry on the 16$^{th}$ day of February, 1905; that there was born to her on said date a female child; that said child was living March 4, 1905, and is said to have been named Ola Edith Perry

Ira B Chadwick M.D.

# Applications for Enrollment of Choctaw Newborn
## Act of 1905 Volume XIII

Witnesses To Mark:
- D.S. Alexander
- M.E. Pocock

Subscribed and sworn to before me this 5th day of April, 1905

C A Pocock
Notary Public.
My Com Ex 2/23/1909

---

Choc New Born 873
Lula Bell Costilow  b. 11-6-03

7-504

Muskogee, Indian Territory, April 15, 1905.

Elijah Costilow,
Lukfata, Indian Territory.

Dear Sir:

Receipt is hereby acknowledged of the affidavits of Jennie Costilow and Amanda Butler to the birth of Lula Bell Costilow, daughter of Elijah and Jennie Costilow, November 6, 1903, and the same have been filed with our records as an application for the enrollment of said child.

Respectfully,

Chairman.

**BIRTH AFFIDAVIT.**

### DEPARTMENT OF THE INTERIOR.
### COMMISSION TO THE FIVE CIVILIZED TRIBES.

**IN RE APPLICATION FOR ENROLLMENT,** as a citizen of the Choctaw Nation, of Lula Bell Costilow, born on the 6 day of November, 1903

Name of Father: Elijah Costilow    a citizen of the Choctaw Nation.
Name of Mother: Jennie Costilow    a citizen of the Choctaw Nation.

Postoffice    LUKFATA IND TER

# Applications for Enrollment of Choctaw Newborn
# Act of 1905 Volume XIII

**AFFIDAVIT OF MOTHER.**

UNITED STATES OF AMERICA, Indian Territory,
Central DISTRICT.

I, Jennie Costilow, on oath state that I am 26 years of age and a citizen by Blood, of the Choctaw Nation; that I am the lawful wife of Elijah Costilow, who is a citizen, by Intermarriage of the Choctaw Nation; that a Female child was born to me on 6th day of November, 1903; that said child has been named Lula Bell Costilow, and was living March 4, 1905.

Jennie Costilow

Witnesses To Mark:

Subscribed and sworn to before me this 10th day of April, 1905

J.W. Costilow
Notary Public.

**AFFIDAVIT OF ATTENDING PHYSICIAN OR MID-WIFE.**

UNITED STATES OF AMERICA, Indian Territory,
Central DISTRICT.

I, Amanda Butler, a midwife, on oath state that I attended on Mrs. Jennie Costilow, wife of Elijah Costilow on the 6th day of November, 1903; that there was born to her on said date a Female child; that said child was living March 4, 1905, and is said to have been named Lula Bell Costilow

her
Amanda x Butler
mark

Witnesses To Mark:
D S Miller
W A Julius

Subscribed and sworn to before me this 10th day of April, 1905

J.W. Costilow
Notary Public.

## Applications for Enrollment of Choctaw Newborn
## Act of 1905 Volume XIII

Choc New Born 874
  Jane Anderson  b. 2-21-04

**BIRTH AFFIDAVIT.**

## DEPARTMENT OF THE INTERIOR.
## COMMISSION TO THE FIVE CIVILIZED TRIBES.

IN RE APPLICATION FOR ENROLLMENT, as a citizen of the    Choctaw    Nation, of Jane Anderson   , born on the 21st  day of  February  , 1905

Name of Father: Colbert Anderson    a citizen of the  Choctaw  Nation.
Name of Mother: Maggie Anderson   a citizen of the  Choctaw  Nation.

Postoffice    Lukfata, Ind. Ter.

### AFFIDAVIT OF MOTHER.

UNITED STATES OF AMERICA, Indian Territory, }
      Central             DISTRICT.

I,  Maggie Anderson   , on oath state that I am  30  years of age and a citizen by  blood  , of the  Choctaw  Nation; that I am the lawful wife of Colbert Anderson  , who is a citizen, by blood  of the  Choctaw  Nation; that a  female  child was born to me on  21st  day of  February  , 1905; that said child has been named  Jane Anderson  , and was living March 4, 1905.

                                    her
                            Maggie x Anderson
Witnesses To Mark:              mark
  { Robert Anderson
  { Vester W Rose

Subscribed and sworn to before me this  12th  day of    April    , 1905

                            Wirt Franklin
                              Notary Public.

### AFFIDAVIT OF ATTENDING PHYSICIAN OR MID-WIFE.

UNITED STATES OF AMERICA, Indian Territory, }
      Central             DISTRICT.

    I,  Casey Ward    , a   mid-wife    , on oath state that I attended on Mrs.  Maggie Anderson    , wife of  Colbert Anderson    on the 21st  day of

26

## Applications for Enrollment of Choctaw Newborn
## Act of 1905   Volume XIII

February    , 1905; that there was born to her on said date a    female    child; that said child was living March 4, 1905, and is said to have been named Jane Anderson

Witnesses To Mark:
{ Robert Anderson
{ Vester W Rose

her
Casey x Ward
mark

Subscribed and sworn to before me this  12th  day of   April   , 1905

Wirt Franklin
Notary Public.

---

Choc New Born 875
  Elliot[sic] McKinney  b. 1-18-04

$W^m O.B.$

**COMMISSIONERS:**
TAMS BIXBY,
THOMAS B. NEEDLES,
C.R. BRECKINBRIDGE.

**DEPARTMENT OF THE INTERIOR,**
**COMMISSIONER TO THE FIVE CIVILIZED TRIBES.**

REFER IN REPLY TO THE FOLLOWING:

7-NB-875.

WM. O. BEALL
Secretary

ADDRESS ONLY THE
COMMISSION TO THE FIVE CIVILIZED TRIBES.

Muskogee, Indian Territory, June 1, 1905.

John McKinney,
  Lukfatah, Indian Territory.

Dear Sir:

    Referring to the application for the enrollment of your infant child, Elliott McKinney, born January 18, 1904, it is noted from the affidavits heretofore filed in this office that you were the only one in attendance upon your wife at the time of birth of the applicant.

    In this event it will be necessary that you file in this office the affidavits of two persons, who have actual knowledge of the facts that the child was born, the date of his birth; that he was living on March 4, 1905, and that Eliza McKinney is his mother.

    The affidavit of Jimmie Jones to these facts has been filed. It will, therefore, be necessary that you secure a similar affidavit from another person.

# Applications for Enrollment of Choctaw Newborn
## Act of 1905   Volume XIII

Respectfully,

T.B. Needles
Commissioner in Charge.

---

7-NB-875
7-NB-875

Muskogee, Indian Territory, July 28, 1905.

John McKinney,
Lukfata, Indian Territory.

Dear Sir:

Your attention is called to a communication addressed to you by the Commission to the Five Civilized Tribes, under date of June 1, 1905, in which you were requested to furnish additional evidence in the matter of the enrollment of your child, Elliot[sic] McKinney, born January 18, 1904.

In said letter you were advised that it was necessary for the enrollment of the child that you furnish this office with the affidavit of one person who is disinterested and not related to the applicant, and who has actual knowledge of the facts, that the child was born, the date of his birth, that he was living March 4, 1905, and that Eliza McKinney is his mother. No reply to this letter has been received.

The matter should receive your immediate attention as no further action can be taken relative to the enrollment of the applicant until the evidence requested is supplied.

Respectfully,

Commissioner.

---

7-NB-875.

Muskogee, Indian Territory, September 18, 1905.

John McKinney,
Lukfata, Indian Territory.

Dear Sir:

Receipt is hereby acknowledged of the joint affidavit of yourself and your wife Eliza McKinney relative to the birth of your minor son and the same has been filed with the records of this office in the matter of the enrollment of said child as a citizen by blood of the Choctaw Nation.

## Applications for Enrollment of Choctaw Newborn
## Act of 1905 Volume XIII

You are advised that the name of your said son has been placed upon a partial roll of new born citizens by blood of the Choctaw Nation opposite number 1495, which said partial roll has been forwarded the Honorable Secretary of the Interior for approval.

As soon as the same is approved you will be notified.

Respectfully,

Acting Commissioner.

---

Affidavit
Lukfata Ind Ter
Sept 9th 1905

Commission to the Five Civilized Tribes Five Muskogee Ind Terr.

This is to certify that on or about January 18th 1904 There was a male child born to John M$^c$Kinney and Eliza M$^c$Kinney of Lukfata Ind Terr. and know that he is still living. And I do so certify.

                                                                                       her

Witness Lenas Wesley    John M$^c$Kinney and Eliza x M$^c$Kinney
                                                                                              mark

Sworn to before me this 9th day of September 1905.

W.P. Wilson
Notary Public.

My commission expires December 1st 1905.

---

| | |
|---|---|
| United States of America, | ) |
| | ) |
| Indian Territory, | ) ss. |
| | ) |
| Central District. | ) |

I, Jimmie Jones, on oath state that I am twenty-two years of age and a citizen by blood of the Choctaw Nation; that I am personally acquainted with Eliza McKinney, wife of John McKinney, and have known said parties nearly all my life; that I know of my own knowledge that there was born to the Eliza McKinney on or about the 18th day of January, 1904, a male child; that said child is now living and is said to have been named Elliott McKinney, and that the way I know the circumstances attending the birth of said child is that for several years prior to the birth of said child I had lived in the same house with said parties, but had removed there from at the time of the birth of said child; and that I am well acquainted with said child and know said child to be the son of said Eliza McKinney and John McKinney.

                                                    Jimmie Jones

## Applications for Enrollment of Choctaw Newborn
## Act of 1905   Volume XIII

Subscribed and sworn to before me this 12th day of April, 1905.

                      Wirt Franklin
                      Notary Public.

---

**BIRTH AFFIDAVIT.**

### DEPARTMENT OF THE INTERIOR.
### COMMISSION TO THE FIVE CIVILIZED TRIBES.

---

**IN RE APPLICATION FOR ENROLLMENT**, as a citizen of the Choctaw Nation, of Elliott McKinney, born on the 18th day of January, 1904

Name of Father: John McKinney     a citizen of the Choctaw Nation.
Name of Mother: Eliza McKinney     a citizen of the Choctaw Nation.

                Postoffice    Lukfatah[sic], Ind. Ter.

*Child present. WF*

### AFFIDAVIT OF MOTHER.

**UNITED STATES OF AMERICA, Indian Territory,**
**Central DISTRICT.**

I, Eliza McKinney, on oath state that I am about 28 years of age and a citizen by blood, of the Choctaw Nation; that I am the lawful wife of John McKinney, who is a citizen, by blood of the Choctaw Nation; that a male child was born to me on 18th day of January, 1904; that said child has been named Elliott McKinney, and was living March 4, 1905. *and that no physician or mid-wife attended me at the birth of said child*

                    her
              Eliza x McKinney
Witnesses To Mark:      mark
   Robert Anderson
   Vester W Rose

    Subscribed and sworn to before me this 12th day of April, 1905

                Wirt Franklin
                Notary Public.

# Applications for Enrollment of Choctaw Newborn
# Act of 1905 Volume XIII

### AFFIDAVIT OF ATTENDING PHYSICIAN OR MID-WIFE.

UNITED STATES OF AMERICA, Indian Territory, }
Central   DISTRICT. }

I, John McKinney, ~~a~~ ................., on oath state that I attended on Mrs. Eliza McKinney, ~~wife of~~ *my wife* on the 18th day of January, 1904; that there was born to her on said date a male child; that said child was living March 4, 1905, and ~~is said to have~~ *has* been named Elliott McKinney; *and that no one else was present when said child was born*

Witnesses To Mark:
{ Robert Anderson
{ Vester W Rose

his
John x McKinney
mark

Subscribed and sworn to before me this 12th day of April, 1905

Wirt Franklin
Notary Public.

---

Choc New Born 876
   Jeff LeFlore   b. 3-2-03

BIRTH AFFIDAVIT.
### DEPARTMENT OF THE INTERIOR.
### COMMISSION TO THE FIVE CIVILIZED TRIBES.

IN RE APPLICATION FOR ENROLLMENT, as a citizen of the Choctaw Nation, of Jeff Le Flore, born on the 2nd day of March, 1903

Name of Father: Watson Le Flore      a citizen of the Choctaw Nation.
Name of Mother: Silway Edwards       a citizen of the Choctaw Nation.

Postoffice   Noah Ind. Ter.

# Applications for Enrollment of Choctaw Newborn
## Act of 1905   Volume XIII

### AFFIDAVIT OF MOTHER.

UNITED STATES OF AMERICA, Indian Territory, }
Central                          DISTRICT.

I, Silway Edwards, on oath state that I am 21 years of age and a citizen by blood, of the Choctaw Nation; that I am ~~not~~ the lawful wife of Watson Le Flore, deceased, who ~~is~~ ~~was~~ a citizen, by blood of the Choctaw Nation; that a male child was born to me on 2nd day of March, 1903; that said child has been named Jeff Le Flore, and was living March 4, 1905.

                                                           her
                                        Silway  x  Edwards

Witnesses To Mark:                          mark
{ Robert Anderson
{ Vester W Rose

Subscribed and sworn to before me this 5th day of April, 1905

                                        Wirt Franklin
                                            Notary Public.

---

### AFFIDAVIT OF ATTENDING PHYSICIAN OR MID-WIFE.

UNITED STATES OF AMERICA, Indian Territory, }
Central                          DISTRICT.

I, Louisa Edwards, a midwife, on oath state that I attended on Mrs. Silway Edwards ~~not~~, wife of Watson Le Flore on the 2nd day of March, 1903; that there was born to her on said date a male child; that said child was living March 4, 1905, and is said to have been named Jeff Le Flore

                                        Louisa Edwards

Witnesses To Mark:
{

Subscribed and sworn to before me this 5th day of April, 1905

                                        Wirt Franklin
                                          Notary Public.

## Applications for Enrollment of Choctaw Newborn
## Act of 1905 Volume XIII

Choc New Born 877
Reason Oklahambi b. 1-21-05

---

7--NB--877

Muskogee, Indian Territory, June 1, 1905.

Mary Oklahambi,
Goodwater, Indian Territory.

Dear Madam:

Referring to your application for the enrollment of your infant child, Reason Oklahambi, born January 21, 1905, it is noted from the affidavits heretofore filed in this office that no physician or midwife was in attendance upon you at the time of the birth of the applicant.

In this event it will be necessary that the affidavits of two persons who are disinterested, and not related to the applicant, who have actual knowledge of the facts that the child was born, the date of his birth; that he was living on March 4, 1905, and that you are his mother be filed in this office.

The affidavit of Simeon Byington to these facts has been filed. It will, therefore, be necessary that you secure a similar affidavit from another person.

This matter should receive your immediate attention as no further action can be taken relative to the enrollment of your child until the Commission has been furnished with this information.

Respectfully,

Chairman.

---

7-NB-877

Muskogee, Indian Territory, July 28, 1905.

Mary Oklahambi,
Goodwater, Indian Territory.

Dear Madam:

Your attention is called to a communication addressed to you by the Commission to the Five Civilized Tribes under date of June 1, 1905, in which you were requested to furnish additional evidence in the matter of the enrollment of your infant child, Reason Oklahambi, born January 21, 1905.

## Applications for Enrollment of Choctaw Newborn
## Act of 1905   Volume XIII

In said letter you were advised that it was necessary for the enrollment of the child that you furnish this office with the affidavit of one person who is disinterested and not related to the applicant, and who has actual knowledge of the facts, that the child was born, the date of his birth, that he was living March 4, 1905, and that your[sic] are his mother. No reply to this letter has been received.

The matter should receive your immediate attention as no further action can be taken relative to the enrollment of said child until the evidence requested has been supplied.

Respectfully,

Commissioner.

# NEW BORN AFFIDAVIT

No ............

## CHOCTAW ENROLLING COMMISSION

**IN THE MATTER OF THE APPLICATION FOR ENROLLMENT** as a citizen of the Choctaw Nation, of   Rayson[sic] Oklahambi   born on the $21^{st}$ day of   January   190 5

Name of father   John Scott   a citizen of   Choctaw   Nation, final enrollment No. ............
Name of mother   Mary Oklahambi   a citizen of   Choctaw   Nation, final enrollment No. ............

Norwood, I.T.
Postoffice.

**AFFIDAVIT OF MOTHER**

UNITED STATES OF AMERICA }
   INDIAN TERRITORY
DISTRICT   Central

I   Mary Oklahambi   , on oath state that I am   18   years of age and a citizen by   Blood   of the   Choctaw   Nation, and as such have been placed upon the final roll of the   Choctaw   Nation, by the Honorable Secretary of the Interior my final enrollment number being ............ ; that I am the lawful wife of   "not married"   , who is a citizen of the ............ Nation, and as such has been placed upon the final roll of said Nation by the Honorable Secretary of the Interior, his final enrollment number being

## Applications for Enrollment of Choctaw Newborn
## Act of 1905  Volume XIII

................and that a  Male  child was born to me on the  21  day of  January  190 5; that said child has been named  Rayson Oklahambi  , and is now living.

WITNESSETH:                                    Mary Oklahambi

Must be two witnesses ⎰ Arlington King
who are citizens      ⎱ J E Harris

Subscribed and sworn to before me this, the  13ᵗʰ  day of  March  , 190 5

W A Shoney
Notary Public.

My Commission Expires:  Jan 10, 1909

### Affidavit of Attending Physician or Midwife

UNITED STATES OF AMERICA, ⎱
INDIAN TERRITORY,         ⎰
Central       DISTRICT

I,  Simeon Byington  a  attendant on oath state that I attended on Mrs. Mary Oklahambi  wife of ................ on the  21ˢᵗ  day of January  , 190 5, that there was born to her on said date a  male child, that said child is now living, and is said to have been named  Rayson Oklahambi

Simeon Byington  ~~M. D~~.

Subscribed and sworn to before me this the  13ᵗʰ  day of  March  1905

W.A. Shoney
Notary Public.

WITNESSETH:

Must be two witnesses    ⎰ Arlington King
who are citizens and     ⎱ J E Harris
know the child.

We hereby certify that we are well acquainted with  Simeon Byington  a~~n~~ attendant  and know  him  to be reputable and of good standing in the community.

Must be two citizen ⎰ Arlington King
witnesses.          ⎱ J E Harris

## Applications for Enrollment of Choctaw Newborn
## Act of 1905    Volume XIII

**BIRTH AFFIDAVIT.**

### DEPARTMENT OF THE INTERIOR.
### COMMISSION TO THE FIVE CIVILIZED TRIBES.

**IN RE APPLICATION FOR ENROLLMENT,** as a citizen of the Choctaw Nation, of Reason Oklahambi, born on the 21st day of January, 1905

Name of Father: John Scott    a citizen of the Choctaw Nation.
Name of Mother: Mary Oklahambi    a citizen of the Choctaw Nation.

Postoffice    Goodwater, Ind. Ter.

### AFFIDAVIT OF MOTHER.

**UNITED STATES OF AMERICA, Indian Territory,**
**Central    DISTRICT.**

I, Mary Oklahambi, on oath state that I am 19 years of age and a citizen by blood, of the Choctaw Nation; that I am *not* the lawful wife of John Scott, who is a citizen, by blood of the Choctaw Nation; that a male child was born to me on 21st day of January, 1905; that said child has been named Reason Oklahambi, and was living March 4, 1905. *and that no physician or mid-wife attended me when said child was born*

Mary Oklahambi

Witnesses To Mark:

Subscribed and sworn to before me this 10th day of April, 1905

Wirt Franklin
Notary Public.

### AFFIDAVIT OF ATTENDING PHYSICIAN OR MID-WIFE.

**UNITED STATES OF AMERICA, Indian Territory,**
**Central    DISTRICT.**

*was present with*
I, Simeon Byington, ~~a~~ ................., on oath state that I ~~attended on~~ ~~Mrs.~~ Mary Oklahambi *not*, wife of John Scott on the 21st day of January, 1905; that there was born to her on said date a male child; that said child was living March 4, 1905, and is said to have been named Reason Oklahambi

Simeon Byington

## Applications for Enrollment of Choctaw Newborn
## Act of 1905  Volume XIII

Witnesses To Mark:

{

Subscribed and sworn to before me this 10th day of April , 1905

Wirt Franklin
Notary Public.

---

Choc New Born 878
  Winston Dyer  b. 4-14-04

United States of America, )
)
Indian Territory, ) ss.
)
Central District. )

I, Willis Tushka, on oath state that I am twenty-two years of age and a citizen by blood of the Choctaw Nation; that I am personally acquainted with Maggie Dyer and her husband, Louis Dyer, and have known said parties all my life; that there was born to the said Maggie Dyer on or about the 14th day of April, 1904, a male child; that said child is now living and is said to have been named Winston Dyer.

Willis Tushka

Subscribed and sworn to before me this 10th day of April, 1905.

Wirt Franklin
Notary Public.

---

**BIRTH AFFIDAVIT.**

### DEPARTMENT OF THE INTERIOR.
### COMMISSION TO THE FIVE CIVILIZED TRIBES.

---

**IN RE APPLICATION FOR ENROLLMENT,** as a citizen of the    Choctaw    Nation, of Winston Dyer    , born on the 14th  day of  April , 1904

Name of Father: Louis Dyer            a citizen of the   Choctaw    Nation.
Name of Mother: Maggie Dyer           a citizen of the   Choctaw    Nation.

## Applications for Enrollment of Choctaw Newborn
## Act of 1905 Volume XIII

Postoffice   Norwood, Ind. Ter.

---

### AFFIDAVIT OF MOTHER.

UNITED STATES OF AMERICA, Indian Territory, }
Central            DISTRICT.

I,   Maggie Dyer   , on oath state that I am   26   years of age and a citizen by blood   , of the   Choctaw   Nation; that I am the lawful wife of   Louis Dyer   , who is a citizen, by   blood   of the   Choctaw   Nation; that a   male   child was born to me on   14th   day of   April   , 1904; that said child has been named   Winston Dyer   , and was living March 4, 1905. *and that no physician or mid-wife attended me at the birth of said child.*

                                      her
                              Maggie x Dyer
Witnesses To Mark:             mark
 { Robert Anderson
  Vester W Rose

Subscribed and sworn to before me this   10th   day of   April   , 1905

                              Wirt Franklin
                              Notary Public.

---

### AFFIDAVIT OF ATTENDING PHYSICIAN OR MID-WIFE.

UNITED STATES OF AMERICA, Indian Territory, }
Central            DISTRICT.

I,   Louis Dyer   , a~~~~~~~, on oath state that I attended on Mrs.   Maggie Dyer   , ~~wife of~~ *my wife* on the   14th day of   April   , 1904; that there was born to her on said date a   male   child; that said child was living March 4, 1905, and is said to have been named   Winston Dyer   *and that no one else was present when said child was born*

                              Louis Dyer
Witnesses To Mark:
 {

Subscribed and sworn to before me this   10th   day of   April   , 1905

                              Wirt Franklin
                              Notary Public.

Applications for Enrollment of Choctaw Newborn
Act of 1905 Volume XIII

# NEW BORN AFFIDAVIT

No ........

## CHOCTAW ENROLLING COMMISSION

IN THE MATTER OF THE APPLICATION FOR ENROLLMENT as a citizen of the Choctaw Nation, of Winston Dyer born on the 14th day of April 1904

Name of father Louis Dyer a citizen of Choctaw Nation, final enrollment No. 3186
Name of mother Maggie Harley Dyer a citizen of Choctaw Nation, final enrollment No. 3312

Norwood I.T. Postoffice.

**AFFIDAVIT OF MOTHER**

UNITED STATES OF AMERICA
INDIAN TERRITORY
DISTRICT  Central

I  Maggie Harley Dyer , on oath state that I am 26 years of age and a citizen by blood of the Choctaw Nation, and as such have been placed upon the final roll of the Choctaw Nation, by the Honorable Secretary of the Interior my final enrollment number being 3312 ; that I am the lawful wife of Louis Dyer , who is a citizen of the Choctaw Nation, and as such has been placed upon the final roll of said Nation by the Honorable Secretary of the Interior, his final enrollment number being 3186 and that a Male child was born to me on the 14th day of April 1904; that said child has been named Winston Dyer , and is now living.

WITNESSETH:  Maggie Harley Dyer
Must be two witnesses  Walter C Harris
who are citizens  Ed Kirby

Subscribed and sworn to before me this, the 13th day of March , 1905

W.A. Shoney
Notary Public.

My Commission Expires: Jan 10, 1909

## Applications for Enrollment of Choctaw Newborn
## Act of 1905   Volume XIII

United States of America, )
)
Indian Territory, )
)
Central District. )

  I, William Barnett, on oath state that I am fifty years of age and a citizen by blood of the Choctaw Nation; that I am personally acquainted with Maggie Dyer, and her husband, Louis Dyer, and have known said parties for more than twenty years; that I have lived within three miles of them since their marriage, about four years ago; that there was born to the said Maggie Dyer on the 14th day of April, 1904, a male child; that said child is now living and is said to have been named Winston Dyer.

his<br>
William x Barnett<br>
mark

Subscribed and sworn to before me this 10<sup>th</sup> day of April, 1905.

Wirt Franklin<br>
Notary Public.

Witnesses to mark.
  Robert Anderson
      Vester W. Rose

---

### *Affidavit of Attending Physician or Midwife*

UNITED STATES OF AMERICA, )
 INDIAN TERRITORY, )
Central  DISTRICT )

  I, Louis Dyer  a~n~  attendant on oath state that I attended on Mrs. Maggie Harley-Dyer my wife of ............. on the 14<sup>th</sup> day of April, 1904, that there was born to her on said date a male child, that said child is now living, and is said to have been named Winston Dyer

Louis Dyer  <s>M. D.</s>

Subscribed and sworn to before me this the 13 day of March 1905

W A Shoney<br>
Notary Public.

WITNESSETH:
 Must be two witnesses
 who are citizens and
 know the child.
{ Walter C Harris
 Ed Kirby

## Applications for Enrollment of Choctaw Newborn
## Act of 1905   Volume XIII

We hereby certify that we are well acquainted with   Louis Dyer
a~ attendant    and know    him   to be reputable and of good standing in the community.

Must be two citizen witnesses. { Walter C Harris
Ed Kirby

---

Choc New Born 879
   Isom Ward  b. 1-1-03

**BIRTH AFFIDAVIT.**

### DEPARTMENT OF THE INTERIOR.
### COMMISSION TO THE FIVE CIVILIZED TRIBES.

**IN RE APPLICATION FOR ENROLLMENT**, as a citizen of the   Choctaw   Nation, of Isom Ward   , born on the 1st   day of   January   , 1903

Name of Father: William S. Ward      a citizen of the  Choctaw   Nation.
Name of Mother: Sillan Ward         a citizen of the  Choctaw   Nation.

Postoffice   Idabel, Ind. Ter

**AFFIDAVIT OF MOTHER.**

UNITED STATES OF AMERICA, Indian Territory,
   Central        DISTRICT.

I,  Sillan Ward   , on oath state that I am  44   years of age and a citizen by blood   , of the   Choctaw   Nation; that I am the lawful wife of  William S. Ward , who is a citizen, by blood   of the   Choctaw   Nation; that a   male   child was born to me on   1st   day of   January   , 1903; that said child has been named Isom Ward   , and was living March 4, 1905.

                        her
               Sillan  x  Ward
Witnesses To Mark:          mark
{ Vester W Rose
  Robert Anderson

41

# Applications for Enrollment of Choctaw Newborn
## Act of 1905   Volume XIII

Subscribed and sworn to before me this 10th day of April, 1905

                      Wirt Franklin
                      Notary Public.

**AFFIDAVIT OF ATTENDING PHYSICIAN OR MID-WIFE.**

UNITED STATES OF AMERICA, Indian Territory, }
   Central                  DISTRICT. }

    I, Sally Kuniatubbee, a mid-wife, on oath state that I attended on Mrs. Sillan Ward, wife of William S Ward on the 1st day of January, 1903; that there was born to her on said date a male child; that said child was living March 4, 1905, and is said to have been named Isom Ward

                              her
                      Sally x Kuniatubbee
Witnesses To Mark:     mark
  { Vester W Rose
  { Robert Anderson

Subscribed and sworn to before me this 10th day of April, 1905

                      Wirt Franklin
                      Notary Public.

---

<u>Choc New Born 880</u>
    Elsie McAfee   b. 2-4-03

United States of America, )
                             )
Indian Territory          ) ss.
                             )
Central District.         )

    I, Joe Hotinlubbee, on oath state that I am twenty-eight years of age and a citizen by blood of the Choctaw Nation; that my post office address is Idabel, Indian Territory; that I am a brother of Sena McAfee, deceased, formerly the wife of Frank McAfee, and I know of my own knowledge that on or about the 4th day of February, 1903, there was born to the said Sena McAfee a female child; that said child is now living and has been named Elsie McAfee.

                    Joe Hotinlubbee

## Applications for Enrollment of Choctaw Newborn
## Act of 1905 Volume XIII

Subscribed and sworn to before me this 11th day of April, 1905.

Wirt Franklin
Notary Public.

United States of America, )
)
Indian Territory ) ss.
)
Central District. )

I, Moses William, on oath state that I am twenty-two years of age and a citizen by blood of the Choctaw Nation; that my post office address is Garvin, Indian Territory; that I was personally acquainted with Sena McAfee, deceased, formerly the wife of Frank McAfee, and have known said parties all my life; and of late years have lived within one and one half miles of where they have lived near Garvin, Indian Territory; that I visited them at their home quite often; and that I know of my own knowledge that on or about the 4th of February, 1903, there was born to the said Sena McAfee a female child; that said child is now living and is said to have been named Elsie McAfee.

Moses William

Subscribed and sworn to before me this 11th day of April, 1905.

Wirt Franklin
Notary Public.

**BIRTH AFFIDAVIT.**

**DEPARTMENT OF THE INTERIOR.**
**COMMISSION TO THE FIVE CIVILIZED TRIBES.**

IN RE APPLICATION FOR ENROLLMENT, as a citizen of the Choctaw Nation, of Elsie McAfee , born on the 4th day of February , 1903

Name of Father: Frank McAfee           a citizen of the   Choctaw   Nation.
Name of Mother: Sena McAfee           a citizen of the   Choctaw   Nation.

Postoffice    Idabel, Ind. Ter.

# Applications for Enrollment of Choctaw Newborn
## Act of 1905 Volume XIII

**AFFIDAVIT OF MOTHER.**

UNITED STATES OF AMERICA, Indian Territory,
Central DISTRICT.

I, Frank McAfee, on oath state that I am 35 years of age and a citizen by blood, of the Choctaw Nation; that I ~~am~~ was the lawful ~~wife~~ husband of Sena McAfee, deceased, who ~~is~~ was a citizen, by blood of the Choctaw Nation; that a female child was born to ~~me us~~ on 4th day of February, 1903; that said child has been named Elsie McAfee, and was living March 4, 1905. *and that I attended my said wife at the birth of said child and that no one else was present*

Frank M<sup>c</sup>Afee

Witnesses To Mark:

Subscribed and sworn to before me this 11th day of April, 1905

Wirt Franklin
Notary Public.

---

Choc New Born 881
　　Johnson Kaniatobe *(b.)* 1-16-02

7-NB-881

Muskogee, Indian Territory, September 8, 1905.

Sam Kaniatobe,
　　Kullitucklo, Indian Territory.

Dear Sir:

　　Replying to your letter of September 5th, you are advised that on August 22, 1905, the Secretary of the Interior approved the enrollment of your minor child, Johnson Kaniatobe, as a new-born citizen by blood of the Choctaw Nation, and the name of the child appears upon the roll of such citizens, opposite number 1376.

　　The child is now entitled to an allotment and selection of the same should be made at the land office of the nation in which the prospective allotment is located.

## Applications for Enrollment of Choctaw Newborn
## Act of 1905 Volume XIII

Respectfully,

Acting Commissioner.

*(The affidavit below typed as given.)*

\* AFFIDAVIT. \*

United States of America,

Indian Territory, ss.

Central District.

    I, Edward Dwight on oath state that I am 39 years of age and a citizen by blood Choctaw Nation; that a male child was born to the Sela James on 16 day of Nov. 190 2 . and that said child has been named Johnson Kaniatobe and was living March 4, 1905.
    I have been known Sam Kaniatobe and Sela James for about 15 years, I have live with 4 mile S.E. where they live.

Edward Dwight

Subscribed and sworn to before me this the 14 day of June 1905.

John Simpson
Notary Public.

7-NB-881.

Muskogee, Indian Territory, June 7, 1905.

Sam Kaniatobe,
    Kullitukle[sic], Indian Territory.

Dear Sir:

    Referring to the application for the enrollment of Johnson Kaniatobe, born November 16, 1902, it is noted from the affidavits heretofore filed in this office that the mother of the applicant, Sela James, is dead.

    In this event it will be necessary for you to file in this office the affidavits of two persons who are disinterested and are not related to the applicant, who have actual knowledge of the facts; that the child was born, the date of his birth, that he was living on March 4, 1905 and that Sela James was his mother.

## Applications for Enrollment of Choctaw Newborn
## Act of 1905   Volume XIII

      The affidavit of Silena Ward heretofore filed in this office does not fulfill these requirements in that she is a person that is related to the applicant.

      This matter should receive immediate attention as no further action can be taken until these affidavits re filed with the Commission.

                              Respectfully,

                                                        Commissioner in Charge.

7 NB 881

Muskogee, Indian Territory, June 19, 1905.

Sam Kaniatobe,
        Idabel, Indian Territory.

Dear Sir:

      Receipt is hereby acknowledged of the affidavits of Edward Dwight and Joe Hotinlobbe to the birth of Johnson Kaniatobe, son of Sela James, November 16, 1902, and the same have been filed with our records in the matter of the enrollment of said child.

                              Respectfully,

                                                Chairman.

| | |
|---|---|
| United States of America, | ) |
| | ) |
| Indian Territory | ) ss. |
| | ) |
| Central District. | ) |

      I, Silena Ward, on oath state that I am eighteen years of age and a citizen by blood of the Choctaw Nation; that I am personally acquainted with Sela James, who is my cousin; that I was present with the said Sela James on the 16th day of November, 1902, when there was born to her a male child, which child has been named Johnson Kaniatobe and is now living; and that the father of said child is Sam Kaniatobe; and that the said Sela James is now dead.                her
                                        Silena  x  Ward
                                          mark

# Applications for Enrollment of Choctaw Newborn
# Act of 1905 Volume XIII

Subscribed and sworn to before me this 10th day of April, 1905.

                                              Wirt Franklin
                                              Notary Public.

Witnesses to mark.
Robert Anderson
Vester W Rose

---

*(The affidavit below typed as given.)*

                                              * Affidavit. *

United States of America, |
Indian Territory, |ss.
Central District. |

     I, Joe Hotinlobbe on oath state that I am 29 years of age and a citizen by blood Choctaw Nation; that a male child was born to the Sela James on 16 day of Nov. 190 2 . and that said child has been named Johnson Kaniatobe and was living March 4, 1905.
     I have been known for this Sam Kaniatobe and Sela James for about 20 years, I have live with 7 mile West where they live.

                                            Joe Hotinlobbe

Subscribed and sworn to before me this the 14th day of June 1905.

                                            John Simpson
                                            Notary Public.

---

**BIRTH AFFIDAVIT.**
                            **DEPARTMENT OF THE INTERIOR.**
                  **COMMISSION TO THE FIVE CIVILIZED TRIBES.**

     **IN RE APPLICATION FOR ENROLLMENT,** as a citizen of the Choctaw Nation, of Johnson Kaniatobe , born on the 16th day of November , 1902

Name of Father: Sam Kaniatobe      a citizen of the Choctaw Nation.
Name of Mother: Sela James      a citizen of the Choctaw Nation.

                                Postoffice     Kullituklo, Ind. Ter.

# Applications for Enrollment of Choctaw Newborn
## Act of 1905 Volume XIII

### AFFIDAVIT OF MOTHER.

UNITED STATES OF AMERICA, Indian Territory,  
Central DISTRICT.

I, Sam Kaniatobe, on oath state that I am 60 years of age and a citizen by blood, of the Choctaw Nation; that I ~~am the lawful wife of~~ *was not the lawful husband of Sela James, deceased*, who ~~is~~ *was* a citizen, by blood of the Choctaw Nation; that a male child was born to ~~me~~ *her* on *the* 16th day of November, 1902; that said child has been named Johnson Kaniatobe, and was living March 4, 1905.

                          his  
                         Sam x Kaniatobe  
Witnesses To Mark:           mark  
  { Robert Anderson  
    Vester W Rose

Subscribed and sworn to before me this 10th day of April, 1905

                                    Wirt Franklin  
                                      Notary Public.

---

### AFFIDAVIT OF ATTENDING PHYSICIAN OR MID-WIFE.

UNITED STATES OF AMERICA, Indian Territory,  
Central DISTRICT.

I, Sally Kaniatobe, a mid-wife, on oath state that I attended on Mrs. Sela James *not*, wife of Sam Kaniatobe on the 16th day of November, 1902; that there was born to her on said date a male child; that said child was living March 4, 1905, and is said to have been named Johnson Kaniatobe

                         her  
                      Sally x Kaniatobe  
Witnesses To Mark:       mark  
  { Robert Anderson  
    Vester W Rose

Subscribed and sworn to before me this 10th day of April, 1905

                                    Wirt Franklin  
                                      Notary Public.

## Applications for Enrollment of Choctaw Newborn
## Act of 1905  Volume XIII

Choc New Born 882
Maudie Stanford  b. 6-16-03

**NEW-BORN AFFIDAVIT.**

Number................

...Choctaw Enrolling Commission...

IN THE MATTER OF THE APPLICATION FOR ENROLLMENT, as a citizen of the Choctaw Nation, of Maude[sic] Stanford born on the 16th day of June 190 3

Name of father  Henry Stanford        a citizen of   Choctaw
Nation final enrollment No.  597
Name of mother  Sallie Stanford        a citizen of ..............
Nation final enrollment No.  13555

Postoffice   Idabel IT

**AFFIDAVIT OF MOTHER.**

UNITED STATES OF AMERICA
INDIAN TERRITORY
Central       DISTRICT

I   Sallie Stanford   , on oath state that I am 19 years of age and a citizen by blood of the Choctaw Nation, and as such have been placed upon the final roll of the Choctaw Nation, by the Honorable Secretary of the Interior my final enrollment number being   13555 ; that I am the lawful wife of   Henry C Stanford   , who is a citizen of the   Choctaw   Nation, and as such has been placed upon the final roll of said Nation by the Honorable Secretary of the Interior, his final enrollment number being   597   and that a   female   child was born to me on the   16th   day of  June   190 3; that said child has been named   Maude Stanford   , and is now living.

Sallie Stanford

Witnesseth.
Must be two  } S.E. Morris
Witnesses who
are Citizens.     J B McFarland

Subscribed and sworn to before me this   21   day of  Jan   190 5

W.A. Shoney
Notary Public.

My commission expires:  Jan 10, 1909

49

**Applications for Enrollment of Choctaw Newborn
Act of 1905 Volume XIII**

## AFFIDAVIT OF ATTENDING PHYSICIAN OR MIDWIFE

UNITED STATES OF AMERICA
INDIAN TERRITORY
   Central       DISTRICT

I, Carrie Scribner    a    midwife on oath state that I attended on Mrs. Sallie Stanford    wife of  Henry C Stanford on the 16$^{th}$  day of  June  , 190 3 , that there was born to her on said date a    female child, that said child is now living, and is said to have been named  Maude Stanford

Mrs Carrie Scribner

Subscribed and sworn to before me this, the  21$^{st}$    day of Jan    190 5

WITNESSETH:                                W.A. Shoney    Notary Public.
Must be two witnesses  { S.E. Morris
who are citizens          { J B M$^c$Farland

We hereby certify that we are well acquainted with    Carrie Scribner a    midwife    and know    her    to be reputable and of good standing in the community.

S.E. Morris    _____

J B M$^c$Farland    _____

BIRTH AFFIDAVIT.

**DEPARTMENT OF THE INTERIOR.
COMMISSION TO THE FIVE CIVILIZED TRIBES.**

IN RE APPLICATION FOR ENROLLMENT, as a citizen of the    Choctaw    Nation, of Maudie Stanford    , born on the  16th  day of  June  , 1903

Name of Father: Henry C. Stanford    a citizen of the  Choctaw    Nation.
Name of Mother: Sallie E. Stanford    a citizen of the  Choctaw    Nation.

Postoffice    Idabel, Ind. Ter.

# Applications for Enrollment of Choctaw Newborn
## Act of 1905   Volume XIII

**AFFIDAVIT OF MOTHER.**

UNITED STATES OF AMERICA, Indian Territory, }
Central                DISTRICT.

I, Sallie E. Stanford, on oath state that I am 19 years of age and a citizen by blood, of the Choctaw Nation; that I am the lawful wife of Henry C. Stanford, who is a citizen, by marriage of the Choctaw Nation; that a female child was born to me on 16th day of June, 1903; that said child has been named Maudie Stanford, and was living March 4, 1905.

Sallie E. Stanford

Witnesses To Mark:
{

Subscribed and sworn to before me this 12th day of April, 1905

Wirt Franklin
Notary Public.

---

**AFFIDAVIT OF ATTENDING PHYSICIAN OR MID-WIFE.**

UNITED STATES OF AMERICA, Indian Territory, }
Central                DISTRICT.

I, Elizar Jones, a Midwife, on oath state that I attended on Mrs. Sallie E. Stanford, wife of Henry C. Stanford on the 16 day of June, 1903; that there was born to her on said date a Female child; that said child was living March 4, 1905, and is said to have been named Maudie Stanford

Elizar Jones

Witnesses To Mark:
{

Subscribed and sworn to before me this 12 day of April, 1905

*(Name Illegible)*
Notary Public.

# Applications for Enrollment of Choctaw Newborn
## Act of 1905  Volume XIII

Choc New Born 883
    Florence Stewart  b.  11-23-03

---

7-NB-883.

Muskogee, Indian Territory, June 2, 1905.

Levi Stewart,
    Kullituklo, Indian Territory.

Dear Sir:

    Referring to the application for the enrollment of your infant child, Florence Stewart, born November 23, 1903, it is noted from the affidavits heretofore filed in this office that you attended upon your wife at the time of birth of the applicant.

    If there was no one else in attendance excepting yourself it will be necessary that you file in this office the affidavits of two persons, who are disinterested and not related to the applicant, who have actual knowledge of the facts that the child was born, the date of her birth; that she was living on March 4, 1905, and that Annie Stewart is her mother.

        Respectfully,

                [sic]

---

7 NB 883

Muskogee, Indian Territory, June 26, 1905.

Levi Stewart,
    Kullituklo, Indian Territory.

Dear Sir:

    Receipt is hereby acknowledged of your letter of June 22, 1905, asking for blanks for the affidavits of two disinterested persons who have knowledge of the birth of your child Florence Stewart and the same are enclosed herewith in compliance with your request.

        Respectfully,

KB 2-26                              Chairman.

## Applications for Enrollment of Choctaw Newborn
## Act of 1905 Volume XIII

7-NB-883

Muskogee, Indian Territory, August 19, 1905.

Levi Stewart,
    Kullituklo, Indian Territory.

Dear Sir:

    On June 2, 1905, the Commission to the Five Civilized Tribes addressed a letter to you advising you that it would be necessary, in the matter of the enrollment of your daughter, Florence Stewart, born November 23, 1903, as a citizen by blood of the Choctaw Nation, for you to furnish this office with the affidavits of two disinterested persons as to the birth of said child. Said affidavits to set forth said child's name, the date of her birth, the names of her parents and whether or not she was living on March 4, 1905. Said affidavits have not as yet been filed.

    You are therefore again requested to file the same with this office and are advised that until said affidavits are furnished the rights of your said daughter Florence Stewart as a citizen by blood of the Choctaw Nation can not be finally determined.

Respectfully,

Acting Commissioner.

7-NB-883
23-139

Muskogee, Indian Territory, August 28, 1906.

Hon. Green McCurtain,
    Principal Chief, Choctaw Nation,
        Kinta, Indian Territory.

Dear Sir:-

    Receipt is hereby acknowledged of your letter of August 20, 1906, in which you state that you have received a letter from L. A. Stewart, of Kullituklo, Indian Territory, who advises you that he has two children whose names do not appear upon the approved roll of citizens of the Choctaw Nation. One of these, Florence Stewart, was born November 23, 1903, and the other, Ed Stewart, was born January 12, 1906.

    In reply you are advised that the name of Florence Stewart, child of Levi and Annie Stewart, has been placed upon a schedule of new born citizens of the Choctaw Nation under the Act of Congress approved March 3, 1905, which has been forwarded to

## Applications for Enrollment of Choctaw Newborn
## Act of 1905 Volume XIII

the Secretary of the Interior, and he will be notified when her enrollment is approved by the Department.

It further appears that Ed Stewart, child of Levi and Annie Stewart, has been enrolled as a minor citizen of the Choctaw Nation under the Act of Congress approved April 26, 1906, and his enrollment was approved by the Secretary of the Interior August 6, 1906.

Respectfully,

Acting Commissioner.

DEPARTMENT OF THE INTERIOR,
COMMISSIONER TO THE FIVE CIVILIZED TRIBES.

Mena, Arkansas, May 31, 1906.

In the matter of the enrollment of Florence Stewart, Choctaw New Born, card Number 883:

Testimony taken five miles west of Kullituklo, Indian Territory, May 3, 1906.

MINNIE JACKSON?[sic], being duly sworn, testified as follows:

BY THE COMMISSIONER:

Q What is your name? A Minnie Jackson.
Q How old are you? A About 36.
Q What is your post office address? A Kullituklo, I. T.
Q Are you a citizen of the Choctaw Nation?
A I am an applicant for enrollment as an intermarried citizen of thr[sic] Choctaw Nation.
Q Are you acquainted with Levi and Annie Stewart? A Yes, sir.
Q How long have you known them?
A I have been knowing Levi about 15 years and Annie about 5 years
Q Have they any children? A Two.
Q What is the name of the oldest? A Florence.
Q Is Florence a boy or girl? A Girl.
Q When was Florence born?
A She was born in November 1903; she will be three years old this next coming November.
Q Do you know the day of the month the child was born?
A No, I never saw it until it was about a week old when the mother brought it to my house to stay all night when her husband was gone.
Q Is the child living at this date?
A She was about a week ago, I have not heard anything about her being dead.

## Applications for Enrollment of Choctaw Newborn
## Act of 1905   Volume XIII

Q Have you any interest, directly or indirectly, in any estate this child may have by virtue of its enrollment as a citizen by blood of the Choctaw Nation blood of the Choctaw Nation?
A No, it don't make any difference to me.

Witness Excused.

---

Testimony taken at Kullituklo, Indian Territory, May 4, 1906.

WILSON A. SHONEY, being duly sworn, testified as follows:

BY THE COMMISSIONER:

Q What is your name? A Wilson A. Shoney.
Q What is your post office address? A Kullituklo, I. T.
Q How old are you? A 33.
Q Are you acquainted with Levi Stewart? A Yes, sir.
Q What is his wife's name? A Annie Steward, formerly Collins.
Q Have they children? A Yes, sir.
Q How many? A Why, I think they have two.
Q Were either one of these children born prior to September 25, 1902?
A They were both born after September 25, 1902.
Q What is the name of the oldest one? A Florence.
Q Do you know either the year, the month or the season of the year that Florence Stewart was born? A No, sir.
Q You swear as a matter of fact that Florence Stewart was born after September 25, 1902? A Yes, sir.
Q How long have you known Levi and Annie Stewart?
A I have known them about 10 or 15 years, ever since I was old enough to know anybody.
Q Are you intimately acquainted with them?
A With Levi, not with his wife.
Q Was this child Florence Stewart born near where you reside?
A Yes, sir, in about a mile and a half.
Q You have frequently seen the child have you? A Yes, sir.
Q Judging from the appearance of the child, about how old is she?
A I suppose she is about 2 years old, two and a little past, because I saw the child and registered her at Idabel; she was a great big child then and that has been over a year ago.
Q Were you a member of the Choctaw enrolling Commission that enrolled new borns in the years '04 and '05? A Yes, sir.
Q What sex is Florence Stewart? A Female.
Q Are her parents citizens by blood of the Choctaw Nation?
A Yes, sir
Q Was Florence Stewart living March 4, 1905?
A Yes, sir, and is living now; I saw her about two weeks ago at church.

# Applications for Enrollment of Choctaw Newborn
## Act of 1905   Volume XIII

Witness Excused.

---

W. P. Covington on oath states that the above and foregoing is a full, true and cirrect[sic] transcript of his stenographic notes taken in said case on dates and at places set forth.

W.P. Covington

Subscribed and sworn to before me this 9th day of June 1906

Lacey P Bobo
Notary Public.

---

## AFFIDAVIT OF ATTENDING PHYSICIAN OR MIDWIFE

UNITED STATES OF AMERICA
INDIAN TERRITORY
Central   DISTRICT

I, Levi Stewart   a   attendant on oath state that I attended on Mrs. Anna Stewart   wife of Levi Stewart on the 23$^{rd}$ day of Nov, 190 3, that there was born to her on said date a female child, that said child is now living, and is said to have been named Florence Stewart

Levi Stewart

Subscribed and sworn to before me this, the   21   day of Jan   190 5

WITNESSETH:                                        W.A. Shoney     Notary Public.
Must be two witnesses   { Benson Maytobe
who are citizens           Willington Haiskonabbe

We hereby certify that we are well acquainted with   Levi Stewart a   attendant   and know   him   to be reputable and of good standing in the community.

Benson Maytobe   _____

Willington Haiskonabbe   _____

## Applications for Enrollment of Choctaw Newborn
## Act of 1905  Volume XIII

**NEW-BORN AFFIDAVIT.**

Number...............

**...Choctaw Enrolling Commission...**

IN THE MATTER OF THE APPLICATION FOR ENROLLMENT, as a citizen of the Choctaw Nation, of Florence Stewart

born on the 23$^{rd}$ day of __Nov__ 190 3

Name of father  Levi Stewart     a citizen of   Choctaw
Nation final enrollment No.  2450
Name of mother  Annie Stewart *known as Collins*   a citizen of   Choctaw
Nation final enrollment No.  2935

Postoffice   Kullituklo I.T.

**AFFIDAVIT OF MOTHER.**

UNITED STATES OF AMERICA
INDIAN TERRITORY
 Central       DISTRICT

I   Annie Stewart  known as Collins   , on oath state that I am 20  years of age and a citizen by  blood  of the  Choctaw  Nation, and as such have been placed upon the final roll of the  Choctaw  Nation, by the Honorable Secretary of the Interior my final enrollment number being   2935  ; that I am the lawful wife of  Levi Stewart  , who is a citizen of the  Choctaw  Nation, and as such has been placed upon the final roll of said Nation by the Honorable Secretary of the Interior, his final enrollment number being   2450   and that a   female   child was born to me on the  23$^{rd}$  day of  Nov   190 3; that said child has been named  Florence Stewart  , and is now living.

                                                    her
                                     Annie Stewart  x
Witnesseth.                                   mark

Must be two Witnesses who are Citizens.   Benson Maytobe
                      Willington Haiskonabbe

Subscribed and sworn to before me this  21   day of  Jan    190 5

                                  W.A. Shoney
                                           Notary Public.
My commission expires:  Jan 10, 1909

# Applications for Enrollment of Choctaw Newborn
## Act of 1905 Volume XIII

**BIRTH AFFIDAVIT.**

## DEPARTMENT OF THE INTERIOR.
## COMMISSION TO THE FIVE CIVILIZED TRIBES.

---

IN RE APPLICATION FOR ENROLLMENT, as a citizen of the Choctaw Nation, of Florence Stewart, born on the 23rd day of November, 1903

Name of Father: Levi Stewart     a citizen of the Choctaw Nation.
Name of Mother: Annie Stewart     a citizen of the Choctaw Nation.

           Postoffice    Kullituklo, Ind. Ter.

---

### AFFIDAVIT OF MOTHER.

UNITED STATES OF AMERICA, Indian Territory, }
     Central            DISTRICT. }

     I, Annie Stewart, on oath state that I am 21 years of age and a citizen by blood, of the Choctaw Nation; that I am the lawful wife of Levi Stewart, who is a citizen, by blood of the Choctaw Nation; that a female child was born to me on 23rd day of November, 1903; that said child has been named Florence Stewart, and was living March 4, 1905. *and that no physician or mid-wife attended me at the birth of said child*

                              her
                           Annie x Stewart
Witnesses To Mark:          mark
    { Robert Anderson
    { Vester W Rose

     Subscribed and sworn to before me this 12th day of April, 1905

                         Wirt Franklin
                         Notary Public.

---

### AFFIDAVIT OF ATTENDING PHYSICIAN OR MID-WIFE.

UNITED STATES OF AMERICA, Indian Territory, }
     Central            DISTRICT. }

     I, Levi Stewart, a ..................., on oath state that I attended on Mrs. Annie Stewart, ~~wife of~~ *my wife* on the 23rd day of November, 1903; that there was born to her on said date a female child; that said child was living March 4, 1905, and is said to have been named Florence Stewart *and that no one else was present when said child was born.*

# Applications for Enrollment of Choctaw Newborn
## Act of 1905 Volume XIII

Levi Stewart

Witnesses To Mark:
{

Subscribed and sworn to before me this 12th day of April , 1905

Wirt Franklin
Notary Public.

---

Choc New Born 884
Leo Herndon  b. 5-16-03

**BIRTH AFFIDAVIT.**

## DEPARTMENT OF THE INTERIOR.
## COMMISSION TO THE FIVE CIVILIZED TRIBES.

**IN RE APPLICATION FOR ENROLLMENT,** as a citizen of the Choctaw Nation, of Leo Herndon , born on the 16th day of May , 1903

Name of Father: Sidney J Herndon     a citizen of the Choctaw Nation.
Name of Mother: Emma J Herndon    a citizen of the Choctaw Nation.

Postoffice   Idabel, Ind. Ter.

**AFFIDAVIT OF MOTHER.**

UNITED STATES OF AMERICA, Indian Territory, }
Central           DISTRICT.

I, Emma J Herndon , on oath state that I am 26 years of age and a citizen by blood , of the Choctaw Nation; that I am the lawful wife of Sidney J Herndon , who is a citizen, by marriage of the Choctaw Nation; that a male child was born to me on 16th day of May , 1903; that said child has been named Leo Herndon , and was living March 4, 1905.

Emma J Herndon

Witnesses To Mark:
{

# Applications for Enrollment of Choctaw Newborn
## Act of 1905   Volume XIII

Subscribed and sworn to before me this 12th day of April, 1905

                                    Wirt Franklin
                                    Notary Public.

---

**AFFIDAVIT OF ATTENDING PHYSICIAN OR MID-WIFE.**

UNITED STATES OF AMERICA, Indian Territory, }
   Central                     DISTRICT. }

I, Viney Frazier, a mid-wife, on oath state that I attended on Mrs. Emma J Herndon, wife of Sidney J Herndon on the 16th day of May, 1903; that there was born to her on said date a male child; that said child was living March 4, 1905, and is said to have been named Leo Herndon

                                  her
                             Viney x Frazier
Witnesses To Mark:           mark
 { Robert Anderson
   Vester W Rose

Subscribed and sworn to before me this 12th day of April, 1905

                                    Wirt Franklin
                                    Notary Public.

---

Choc New Born 885
    Carl Jones  b. 11-21-04

**BIRTH AFFIDAVIT.**

**DEPARTMENT OF THE INTERIOR.**
**COMMISSION TO THE FIVE CIVILIZED TRIBES.**

IN RE APPLICATION FOR ENROLLMENT, as a citizen of the Choctaw Nation, of Carl Jones, born on the 21st day of November, 1904

Name of Father: B. W. Jones         a citizen of the United States Nation.
Name of Mother: Josephine Jones    a citizen of the Choctaw Nation.

                       Postoffice    Garvin, Ind. Ter.

# Applications for Enrollment of Choctaw Newborn
## Act of 1905 Volume XIII

### AFFIDAVIT OF MOTHER.

UNITED STATES OF AMERICA, Indian Territory, }
Central            DISTRICT. }

I, Josephine Jones, on oath state that I am 20 years of age and a citizen by blood, of the Choctaw Nation; that I am the lawful wife of B. W. Jones, who is a citizen, ~~by~~ ............ of the United States Nation; that a male child was born to me on 21st day of November, 1904; that said child has been named Carl Jones, and was living March 4, 1905.

Josephine Jones

Witnesses To Mark:
{

Subscribed and sworn to before me this 12th day of April, 1905

Wirt Franklin
Notary Public.

---

### AFFIDAVIT OF ATTENDING PHYSICIAN OR MID-WIFE.

UNITED STATES OF AMERICA, Indian Territory, }
Central District       DISTRICT. }

I, B. L. Denison, a Physician, on oath state that I attended on Mrs. Josephine Jones, wife of B. W. Jones on the 21st day of November, 1904; that there was born to her on said date a male child; that said child was living March 4, 1905, and is said to have been named Carl Jones

B.L. Denison M.D.

Witnesses To Mark:
{

Subscribed and sworn to before me this 12th day of April, 1905

Wirt Franklin
Notary Public.

# Applications for Enrollment of Choctaw Newborn
## Act of 1905   Volume XIII

Choc New Born 886
   Smallwood King   b. 8-21-03

**NEW-BORN AFFIDAVIT.**

　　　　　Number..............

...Choctaw Enrolling Commission...

　　　IN THE MATTER OF THE APPLICATION FOR ENROLLMENT, as a citizen of the Choctaw　　　Nation, of　　　　Smallwood King

born on the   21   day of __August__   190 3

Name of father   Arlington King　　　　a citizen of   Choctaw
Nation final enrollment No. 3273
Name of mother   Zona Byington  *now King*　　a citizen of   Choctaw
Nation final enrollment No. 2754

　　　　　　　　　　　　　Postoffice　　Goodwater I.T.

**AFFIDAVIT OF MOTHER.**

UNITED STATES OF AMERICA
INDIAN TERRITORY
   Central      DISTRICT

　　　　I   Zona Byington (now King)　　　　, on oath state that I am   24   years of age and a citizen by   blood   of the   Choctaw   Nation, and as such have been placed upon the final roll of the   Choctaw   Nation, by the Honorable Secretary of the Interior my final enrollment number being   2754 ; that I am the lawful wife of   Arlington King   , who is a citizen of the   Choctaw   Nation, and as such has been placed upon the final roll of said Nation by the Honorable Secretary of the Interior, his final enrollment number being   3273   and that a   Male   child was born to me on the 21$^{st}$   day of   August   190 3; that said child has been named   Smallwood King   , and is now living.

　　　　　　　　　　　　Zona Byington King

Witnesseth.
   Must be two　⎫   Moody Byington
   Witnesses who ⎬
   are Citizens.　⎭   Simmon Byington

　　Subscribed and sworn to before me this   21    day of   Jan    190 5

　　　　　　　　　　W.A. Shoney
　　　　　　　　　　　　　Notary Public.
My commission expires:

# Applications for Enrollment of Choctaw Newborn
## Act of 1905 Volume XIII

## AFFIDAVIT OF ATTENDING PHYSICIAN OR MIDWIFE

UNITED STATES OF AMERICA
INDIAN TERRITORY
Central DISTRICT

I, Maimie ~~James~~ Byington a midwife on oath state that I attended on Mrs. Zona Byington now wife of Arlington King on the 21$^{st}$ day of August, 1903, that there was born to her on said date a male child, that said child is now living, and is said to have been named Smallwood King

Maimie Byington x her mark

Subscribed and sworn to before me this, the 21 day of Jan 1905

WITNESSETH:                    W.A. Shoney     Notary Public.
Must be two witnesses    Moody Byington
who are citizens            Simmon Byington

We hereby certify that we are well acquainted with Maimie Byington a midwife and know her to be reputable and of good standing in the community.

Moody Byington                _____

Simmon Byington              _____

BIRTH AFFIDAVIT.

### DEPARTMENT OF THE INTERIOR.
### COMMISSION TO THE FIVE CIVILIZED TRIBES.

IN RE APPLICATION FOR ENROLLMENT, as a citizen of the Choctaw Nation, of Smallwood King, born on the 21st day of August, 1903

Name of Father: Arlington King        a citizen of the Choctaw Nation.
Name of Mother: Zona King             a citizen of the Choctaw Nation.

Postoffice   Goodwater, Ind. Ter.

# Applications for Enrollment of Choctaw Newborn
# Act of 1905   Volume XIII

### AFFIDAVIT OF MOTHER.

UNITED STATES OF AMERICA, Indian Territory, }
Central                 DISTRICT.

    I, Zona King, on oath state that I am 24 years of age and a citizen by blood, of the Choctaw Nation; that I am the lawful wife of Arlington King, who is a citizen, by blood of the Choctaw Nation; that a male child was born to me on 21st day of August, 1903; that said child has been named Smallwood King, and was living March 4, 1905.

                                        her
                                  Zona x King
Witnesses To Mark:                mark
  { Robert Anderson
    Vester W Rose

    Subscribed and sworn to before me this 12th day of April, 1905

                                Wirt Franklin
                                Notary Public.

---

### AFFIDAVIT OF ATTENDING PHYSICIAN OR MID-WIFE.

UNITED STATES OF AMERICA, Indian Territory, }
Central                 DISTRICT.

    I, Sissie Harley, a mid-wife, on oath state that I attended on Mrs. Zona King, wife of Arlington King on the 21st day of August, 1903; that there was born to her on said date a male child; that said child was living March 4, 1905, and is said to have been named Smallwood King

                                        her
                                Sissie x Harley
Witnesses To Mark:                mark
  { Robert Anderson
    Vester W Rose

    Subscribed and sworn to before me this 12th day of April, 1905

                                Wirt Franklin
                                Notary Public.

Applications for Enrollment of Choctaw Newborn
Act of 1905 Volume XIII

Choc New Born 887
Clyde Jones  b. 5-5-04

# NEW BORN AFFIDAVIT

No ................

## CHOCTAW ENROLLING COMMISSION

IN THE MATTER OF THE APPLICATION FOR ENROLLMENT as a citizen of the Choctaw Nation, of Clyde Jones born on the $5^{th}$ day of May 190 4

Name of father  John Dickerson   a citizen of "non citizen"  Nation, final enrollment No. ———
Name of mother  Hannah Jones   a citizen of  Choctaw  Nation, final enrollment No. 2251

Garvin I T   Postoffice.

*(The affidavit below typed as given.)*

United States of America
Indian Territory
Central District

I Salina LeFlore on oath, states that I am 42 years of age and a citizen by blood of the Choctaw Nation, that I am personally acquainted with Hannah Jones who is a citizen by blood, Choctaw Nation and as such has been placed on the Roll of the Choctaw Nation by the Honorable Sec. of the Interior, her final Roll No. being 2251 and that said Hannah Jones, is of an unsound mind from child up, and that a male child was born to her on the $5^{th}$ day of May, 1904, and that said child has been named Clyde Jones and is now living.

Witnesses                                   her
Susan Austin                         Salina x LeFlore
James LeFlore                               mark

Subscribed and sworn to before me this the $16^{th}$ day of Feb. 1905

                                    W.A. Shoney
My Com Expires                      Notary Public.
    Jan 10, 1909

## Applications for Enrollment of Choctaw Newborn
## Act of 1905 Volume XIII

*Affidavit of Attending Physician or Midwife*

UNITED STATES OF AMERICA,
   INDIAN TERRITORY,
Central     DISTRICT

I, Nellie Hall a midwife ~~not married~~ on oath state that I attended on Mrs. Hannah Jones wife of John Dickerson on the 5th day of May, 1904, that there was born to her on said date a male child, that said child is now living, and is said to have been named Clyde Jones

                her
Nellie x Hall     ~~M.D.~~
      mark

Subscribed and sworn to before me this the 16th day of Feb 1905

                W.A. Shoney
                    Notary Public.

WITNESSETH:
Must be two witnesses who are citizens and know the child.
{ Susan Austin
  James LeFlore

We hereby certify that we are well acquainted with Nellie Hall a midwife and know her to be reputable and of good standing in the community.

Must be two citizen witnesses.
{ Susan Austin
  James LeFlore

---

BIRTH AFFIDAVIT.

### DEPARTMENT OF THE INTERIOR.
### COMMISSION TO THE FIVE CIVILIZED TRIBES.

---

IN RE APPLICATION FOR ENROLLMENT, as a citizen of the Choctaw Nation, of Clyde Jones, born on the 5th day of May, 1904

Name of Father: John Dickerson     a citizen of the United States Nation.
Name of Mother: Hannah Jones     a citizen of the Choctaw Nation.

            Postoffice    Garvin, Ind. Ter.

# Applications for Enrollment of Choctaw Newborn
## Act of 1905   Volume XIII

*Child present WJ*

**AFFIDAVIT OF MOTHER.**

UNITED STATES OF AMERICA, Indian Territory, }
Central                    DISTRICT.

    I, Hannah Jones, on oath state that I am 25 years of age and a citizen by blood, of the Choctaw Nation; that I am *not* the lawful wife of John Dickerson, who is a citizen, ~~by~~ ............. of the United States Nation; that a male child was born to me on 5th day of May, 1904; that said child has been named Clyde Jones, and was living March 4, 1905.

                                          her
                                  Hannah x Jones
Witnesses To Mark:                mark
  { Robert Anderson
    Vester W Rose

    Subscribed and sworn to before me this 12th day of April, 1905

                                    Wirt Franklin
                                    Notary Public.

---

**AFFIDAVIT OF ATTENDING PHYSICIAN OR MID-WIFE.**

UNITED STATES OF AMERICA, Indian Territory, }
Central                    DISTRICT.

    I, Nellie Hall, a mid-wife, on oath state that I attended on Mrs. Hannah Jones, ~~wife of~~ ............. on the 5th day of May, 1904; that there was born to her on said date a male child; that said child was living March 4, 1905, and is said to have been named Clyde Jones

                                        her
                                  Nellie x Hall
Witnesses To Mark:                mark
  { Robert Anderson
    Vester W Rose

    Subscribed and sworn to before me this 12th day of April, 1905

                                    Wirt Franklin
                                    Notary Public.

## Applications for Enrollment of Choctaw Newborn
## Act of 1905   Volume XIII

Choc New Born 888
         Ed Wilson   b. 2-28-03

United States of America,   )
                            )
Indian Territory,           )   ss.
                            )
Central District.           )

     I, Singlin Forbit, on oath state that I am about forty years of age and a citizen by blood of the Choctaw Nation; that my post office address is Smithville, Indian Territory; that I am personally acquainted with Taby Wilson, wife of Norwood Wilson, and have known said parties for about seven years; that on or about the 28th day of February, 1903, there was born to the said Taby Wilson a male child; that said child is now living and is said to have been named Ed Wilson.

                                    his
                            Singlin x Forbit
                                  mark

Subscribed and sworn to before me this 7th day of April, 1905.

                                          Wirt Franklin
                                             Notary Public.

Witnesses to make.
     Robert Anderson
     Vester W Rose

United States of America,   )
                            )
Indian Territory,           )   ss.
                            )
Central District.           )

     I, Charles Wilson, on oath state that I am twenty-six years of age and a citizen by blood of the Choctaw Nation; that my post office address is Hatfield, Arkansas; that I am personally acquainted with Taby Wilson, wife of Norwood Wilson, and have known said parties all my life; that on or about the 28th day of February, 1903, there was born to the said Taby Wilson a male child; that said child is now living and is said to have been named Ed Wilson.

                                          Charles Wilson

Subscribed and sworn to before me this 7th day of April, 1905.

                                          Wirt Franklin
                                             Notary Public.

## Applications for Enrollment of Choctaw Newborn
## Act of 1905 Volume XIII

**BIRTH AFFIDAVIT.**

**DEPARTMENT OF THE INTERIOR.**
**COMMISSION TO THE FIVE CIVILIZED TRIBES.**

IN RE APPLICATION FOR ENROLLMENT, as a citizen of the Choctaw Nation, of Ed Wilson, born on the 28th day of February, 1903

Name of Father: Norwood Wilson a citizen of the Choctaw Nation.
Name of Mother: Taby Wilson a citizen of the Choctaw Nation.

Postoffice Smithville, Ind. Ter.

**AFFIDAVIT OF MOTHER.**

UNITED STATES OF AMERICA, Indian Territory,
Central DISTRICT.

I, Taby Wilson, on oath state that I am about 40 years of age and a citizen by blood, of the Choctaw Nation; that I am the lawful wife of Norwood Wilson, who is a citizen, by blood of the Choctaw Nation; that a male child was born to me on 28th day of February, 1903; that said child has been named Ed Wilson, and was living March 4, 1905. *and that no physician or mid-wife attended me at the birth of said child*

                         her
                     Taby x Wilson
Witnesses To Mark:      mark
   { Robert Anderson
   { Vester Rose

Subscribed and sworn to before me this 7th day of April, 1905

                  Wirt Franklin
                  Notary Public.

Choc New Born 889
     Somlin Bohanan b. 7-16-03

# Applications for Enrollment of Choctaw Newborn
## Act of 1905   Volume XIII

COMMISSIONERS:
TAMS BIXBY,
THOMAS B. NEEDLES,
C.R. BRECKINBRIDGE.

WM. O. BEALL
Secretary

**DEPARTMENT OF THE INTERIOR,**
**COMMISSIONER TO THE FIVE CIVILIZED TRIBES.**

$W^m O.B.$

REFER IN REPLY TO THE FOLLOWING:

7-NB-889.

ADDRESS ONLY THE
COMMISSION TO THE FIVE CIVILIZED TRIBES.

Muskogee, Indian Territory, June 2, 1905.

Jesse Bohanan,
    Smithville, Indian Territory.

Dear Sir:

    Referring to the application for the enrollment of your infant child, Somlin Bohanan, born July 16, 1903, it is noted from the affidavits heretofore filed in this office that the midwife, who attended upon your wife at the time of birth of the applicant, is dead.

    In this event it will be necessary that you file in this office the affidavits of two persons, who are disinterested and not related to the applicant, who have actual knowledge of the facts that the child was born, the date of his birth; that he was living on March 4, 1905, and that Sophia Bohanan is his mother.

    The affidavit of Amy Bohanan to these facts has been filed. It will, therefore, be necessary that you secure a similar affidavit from another person.

                   Respectfully,
                     T. B. Needles
                     Commissioner in Charge.

7 NB 889

Muskogee, Indian Territory, June 24, 1905.

Jesse Bohanan,
    Smithville, Indian Territory.

Dear Sir:

    Receipt is hereby acknowledged of the affidavit of Thomas Watson to the birth of Somlin Bohanan, son of Jesse and Sophia Bohanan, July 16, 1903, and the same has been filed in the matter of the enrollment of said child.

                   Respectfully,

                         Chairman.

# Applications for Enrollment of Choctaw Newborn
## Act of 1905   Volume XIII

United States of America
Indian Territory
Central District
Affidavit of Acquaintance

I Thomas Watson on oath state that I am 45 years of age and a citizen by blood of the Choctaw Nation, that my post office address is Smithville, Indian Territory, that I am not related to the applicant, who is a citizen by blood of the Choctaw Nation, that I am personally acquainted with Sophia Bohanan, wife of Jesse Bohanan who is a citizen by blood of the Choctaw Nation, and that a male child was born to Sophie[sic] Bohanan on the 16$^{th}$ day of July 1903, and that said male child has been named Somlin Bohanan and that said Somlin Bohanan was living on the 4$^{th}$ day of March 1905 and is now living; and I have personal knowledge that Sophie Bohanan is the mother of said Somlin Bohanan.

Thomas Watson

Subscribed and sworn to before me this 19$^{th}$ day of June 1905

W.H. McKinney
My Commission expires March 30 1909                    Notary Public.

United States of America, )
)
Indian Territory,         )  ss.
)
Central District.         )

I, Amy Bohanan, on oath state that I am about thirty-five years of age and a citizen by blood of the Choctaw Nation; that my post office address is Smithville, Indian Territory; that I am personally acquainted with Sophia Bohanan, wife of Jesse Bohanan; that I have known said parties for many years; that for several years last past said parties have lived within one mile of where I have lived, near Smithville, Indian Territory; that on the 16th day of July, 1903, there was born to the said Sophia Bohanan a male child; that said child is now living and is said to have been named Somlin Bohanan.

her
Amy x Bohanan
mark

Subscribed and sworn to before me this 5th day of April, 1905.

Wirt Franklin
Witnesses to mark.                    Notary Public.
    Robert Anderson
    Vester Rose

# Applications for Enrollment of Choctaw Newborn
## Act of 1905   Volume XIII

BIRTH AFFIDAVIT.

**DEPARTMENT OF THE INTERIOR.**
**COMMISSION TO THE FIVE CIVILIZED TRIBES.**

---

IN RE APPLICATION FOR ENROLLMENT, as a citizen of the Choctaw Nation, of Somlin Bohanan, born on the 16th day of July, 1903

Name of Father: Jesse Bohanan    a citizen of the Choctaw Nation.
Name of Mother: Sophia Bohanan    a citizen of the Choctaw Nation.

Postoffice   Smithville, Ind. Ter.

---

**AFFIDAVIT OF MOTHER.**

UNITED STATES OF AMERICA, Indian Territory, }
    Central            DISTRICT.             }

I, Sophia Bohanan, on oath state that I am 28 years of age and a citizen by blood, of the Choctaw Nation; that I am the lawful wife of Jesse Bohanan, who is a citizen, by blood of the Choctaw Nation; that a male child was born to me on 16th day of July, 1903; that said child has been named Somlin Bohanan, and was living March 4, 1905. *and that the mid-wife who attended me at the birth of said child is dead.*   her
                                      Sophia x Bohanan
Witnesses To Mark:                       mark
  { Robert Anderson
  { Vester Rose

Subscribed and sworn to before me this 5th day of April, 1905

Wirt Franklin
Notary Public.

---

**AFFIDAVIT OF ATTENDING PHYSICIAN OR MID-WIFE.**

UNITED STATES OF AMERICA, Indian Territory, }
    Central            DISTRICT.             }

                                                                *am the husband of*
I, Jesse Bohanan, ~~a~~ _____, on oath state that I ~~attended on~~ Mrs. Sophia Bohanan, ~~wife of~~ *that* on the 16th day of July, 1903; that there was born to her on said date a male child; that said child was living March 4, 1905, and ~~is said to have~~ *has* been named Somlin Bohanan

## Applications for Enrollment of Choctaw Newborn
## Act of 1905   Volume XIII

Witnesses To Mark:
{ Robert Anderson
{ Vester Rose

Jesse x Bohanan
his mark

Subscribed and sworn to before me this 5th day of April, 1905

Wirt Franklin
Notary Public.

---

Choc New Born 890
Grincy Norlett[sic]   b. 9-25-03

COMMISSIONERS:
TAMS BIXBY,
THOMAS B. NEEDLES,
C.R. BRECKINBRIDGE.

WM. O. BEALL
Secretary

**DEPARTMENT OF THE INTERIOR,**
**COMMISSIONER TO THE FIVE CIVILIZED TRIBES.**

$W^m O.B.$

REFER IN REPLY TO THE FOLLOWING:

7-NB-890.

ADDRESS ONLY THE
COMMISSION TO THE FIVE CIVILIZED TRIBES.

Muskogee, Indian Territory, June 1, 1905.

Adam Narlett,
　　　Smithville, Indian Territory.

Dear Sir:

　　Referring to the application for the enrollment of your infant child, Grincy Narlett, born September 25, 1903, it is noted from the affidavits heretofore filed in this office that you attended upon you[sic] wife at the time of birth of the applicant.

　　If there was no one else in attendance excepting yourself it will be necessary that you file in this office the affidavits of two persons, who are disinterested and not related to the applicant, who have actual knowledge of the facts that the child was born, the date of his birth; that he was living on March 4, 1905, and that Emma Narlett is his mother.

　　The affidavit of Simpson Wilson, heretofore filed in this office, does not fulfill the requirement, in that it does not give the date of the applicant's birth.

Respectfully,
T.B. Needles
Commissioner in Charge.

# Applications for Enrollment of Choctaw Newborn
## Act of 1905   Volume XIII

7-NB-890

Muskogee, Indian Territory, July 28, 1905.

Adam Narlett,
Smithville, Indian Territory.

Dear Sir:

Your attention is called to a communication addressed to you by the Commission to the Five Civilized Tribes, under date of June 1, 1905, in which you were requested to supply additional evidence in the matter of the enrollment of your infant child, Grincy Narlett born September 25, 1903.

In said letter you were advised that if you were the only one in attendance upon your wife at the time of the birth of the applicant it would be necessary that you furnish the affidavits of two persons who are disinterested and not related to said child, and who have actual knowledge of the facts, that the child was born, the date of his birth, that he was living March 4, 1905, and that Emma Narlett is his mother; you were also advised that affidavit of Simpson Wilson to these facts had heretofore been filed in this office and that a similar affidavit of one other person was required. No reply to this letter has been received.

The matter should receive your immediate attention as no further action can be taken relative to the enrollment of your child until the evidence requested is supplied.

Respectfully,

Commissioner.

7-NB-890

Muskogee, Indian Territory, August 4, 1905.

Ada[sic] Narlett,
Smithville, Indian Territory.

Dear Madam:

Receipt is hereby acknowledged of your letter of July 27, 1905, transmitting affidavits of Thomas Nolen, Jr. and Hilbon N. McCoy to the birth of Grincy Narlett, September 25, 1903, and the same have been filed with the records in the matter of the enrollment of said child.

## Applications for Enrollment of Choctaw Newborn
## Act of 1905   Volume XIII

Respectfully,

Commissioner.

United States of America,
Indian Territory
Central District

Affidavit of Acquaintance

I, Hilbon N. M$^c$Coy on oath state that I am 46 years of age and a citizen by blood of the Choctaw Nation and that I am acquainted with Emma Narlett wife of Adam Narlett, who is a citizen by blood of the Choctaw Nation and that a male child was born to her on the 25$^{th}$ day of September 1903, and the male child has been named Grincy Narlett and the said child was living March 5, 1905 and Emma Narlett is own mother of the said Grincy Narlett. I am not related and have no interest in the applicant.

Hilbon N. M$^c$Coy

Subscribed and sworn to before me this 27 day of July 1905.

W.H. M$^c$Kinney
My Commission expires March 30-1909      Notary Public.

United States of America,
Indian Territory
Central District

Affidavit of Acquaintance

I Thomas Nolen Jr on oath state that I am _____ years of age and a citizen by blood of the Choctaw Nation and that I am acquainted with Emma Narlett, wife of Adam Narlett, who is a citizen by blood of the Choctaw Nation, and that a male child was born to her on the 25 day of September 1903, and the said child has been named Grincy Narlett, and the said child was living on March 4, 1905, and that Emma Narlett is own mother of the said Grincy Narlett.
I am not related and have no interest in the applicant.

Thomas Nolen Jr

Subscribed and sworn to before me this 27 day of July 1905.

W.H. M$^c$Kinney
My Commission expires March 30-1909      Notary Public.

# Applications for Enrollment of Choctaw Newborn
## Act of 1905  Volume XIII

United States of America, )
)
Indian Territory, ) ss.
)
Central District. )

I, Simpson Wilson, on oath state that I am thirty eight years of age and a citizen by blood of the Choctaw Nation; that I am personally acquainted with Emma Narlett, wife of Adam Narlett; that I have known said parties about twenty years; that there was born to the said Emma Narlett during the month of September, 1903, a male child; and that said child is now living and is said to have been named Grincy Narlett.

Simpson Wilson

Subscribed and sworn to before me this 4th day of April, 1905.

Wirt Franklin
Notary Public.

Witness.

----------------------------------

----------------------------------

**BIRTH AFFIDAVIT.**

### DEPARTMENT OF THE INTERIOR.
### COMMISSION TO THE FIVE CIVILIZED TRIBES.

IN RE APPLICATION FOR ENROLLMENT, as a citizen of the Choctaw Nation, of Grincy Narlett, born on the 25th day of September, 1903

Name of Father: Adam Narlett    a citizen of the Choctaw Nation.
Name of Mother: Emma Narlett    a citizen of the Choctaw Nation.

Postoffice   Smithville Ind Ter

*Child present WF*

**AFFIDAVIT OF MOTHER.**

UNITED STATES OF AMERICA, Indian Territory,
Central    DISTRICT.

I, Emma Narlett, on oath state that I am about 25 years of age and a citizen by blood, of the Choctaw Nation; that I am the lawful wife of Adam Narlett, who is a citizen, by blood of the Choctaw Nation; that

## Applications for Enrollment of Choctaw Newborn
## Act of 1905   Volume XIII

a   male   child was born to me on   25th   day of   September   , 1903; that said child has been named   Grincy Narlett   , and was living March 4, 1905. *and that no physician or mid wife attended me at the birth of said child.*

                her
              Emma x Narlett
Witnesses To Mark:       mark
 { Vester W Rose
   Robert Anderson

  Subscribed and sworn to before me this   4th  day of   April   , 1905

             Wirt Franklin
             Notary Public.

---

**AFFIDAVIT OF ATTENDING PHYSICIAN OR MID-WIFE.**

**UNITED STATES OF AMERICA, Indian Territory,** }
 Central      **DISTRICT.**

  I,   Adam Narlett   , ~~a~~ ............, on oath state that I attended on Mrs.   Emma Narlett   *my* , wife ~~of~~ ............ on the   25th   day of September   , 1903; that there was born to her on said date a   male   child; that said child was living March 4, 1905, and ~~is said to have~~ *has* been named   Grincy Narlett; *and that no one else was present when said child was born*

             his
            Adam x Narlett
Witnesses To Mark:      mark
 { Vester W Rose
   Robert Anderson

  Subscribed and sworn to before me this   4th  day of   April   , 1905

             Wirt Franklin
             Notary Public.

---

Choc New Born 891
  Semiah John  b. 2-24-05

# Applications for Enrollment of Choctaw Newborn
## Act of 1905  Volume XIII

7-NB-891

Muskogee, Indian Territory, August 2, 1905.

William H. McKinney,
Octavia, Indian Territory.

Dear Sir:

Receipt is hereby acknowledged of your letter of July 25, 1905, asking the status of the enrollment of Simih[sic] John, child of Lena John as a citizen by blood of the Choctaw Nation.

In reply to your letter you are advised that on July 22, 1905, the Secretary of the Interior approved the enrollment of Semah[sic] John, child of Museton and Lena John, as a citizen by blood of the Choctaw Nation, and selection of allotment may now be made in accordance with the rules and regulations governing the selection of allotments and the designation of homesteads in the Choctaw and Chickasaw Nations.

Respectfully,

Commissioner.

**BIRTH AFFIDAVIT.**

### DEPARTMENT OF THE INTERIOR.
### COMMISSION TO THE FIVE CIVILIZED TRIBES.

IN RE APPLICATION FOR ENROLLMENT, as a citizen of the Choctaw Nation, of Semiah John, born on the 24th day of February, 1905

Name of Father: Museton John    a citizen of the Choctaw Nation.
Name of Mother: Lena John       a citizen of the Choctaw Nation.

Postoffice  Bethel, Ind. Ter.

**AFFIDAVIT OF MOTHER.**

UNITED STATES OF AMERICA, Indian Territory, }
    Central        DISTRICT.

I, Lena John, on oath state that I am 25 years of age and a citizen by blood, of the Choctaw Nation; that I am the lawful wife of Museton John, who is a citizen, by blood of the Choctaw Nation; that a female child was born to me on 24th day of February, 1905; that said child has been named Semiah John, and was living March 4, 1905.

## Applications for Enrollment of Choctaw Newborn
## Act of 1905   Volume XIII

Lena John

Witnesses To Mark:
{

Subscribed and sworn to before me this 5th day of April, 1905

Wirt Franklin
Notary Public.

---

**AFFIDAVIT OF ATTENDING PHYSICIAN OR MID-WIFE.**

UNITED STATES OF AMERICA, Indian Territory, }
    Central                         DISTRICT. }

I, Mary King, a mid wife, on oath state that I attended on Mrs. Lena John, wife of Museton John on the 24th day of February, 1905; that there was born to her on said date a female child; that said child was living March 4, 1905, and is said to have been named Semiah John

        her
Mary x King
        mark

Witnesses To Mark:
{ Vester W Rose
{ Robert Anderson

Subscribed and sworn to before me this 5th day of April, 1905

Wirt Franklin
Notary Public.

---

Choc New Born 892
    Eliza Jefferson b. 5-6-04
    Cain Jefferson b. 5-6-04

# Applications for Enrollment of Choctaw Newborn
## Act of 1905   Volume XIII

BIRTH AFFIDAVIT.

### DEPARTMENT OF THE INTERIOR.
### COMMISSION TO THE FIVE CIVILIZED TRIBES.

IN RE APPLICATION FOR ENROLLMENT, as a citizen of the Choctaw Nation, of Cain Jefferson, born on the 6th day of May, 1904

Name of Father: Edson Jefferson   a citizen of the Choctaw Nation.
Name of Mother: Sealy Jefferson   a citizen of the Choctaw Nation.

Postoffice   Smithville, Ind. Ter.

### AFFIDAVIT OF MOTHER.

UNITED STATES OF AMERICA, Indian Territory,
Central DISTRICT.

I, Sealy Jefferson, on oath state that I am 29 years of age and a citizen by blood, of the Choctaw Nation; that I am the lawful wife of Edson Jefferson, who is a citizen, by blood of the Choctaw Nation; that a male child was born to me on 6th day of May, 1904; that said child has been named Cain Jefferson, and was living March 4, 1905.

          her
Sealy x Jefferson
          mark

Witnesses To Mark:
{ V.W. Rose
{ Robert Anderson

Subscribed and sworn to before me this 5th day of April, 1905

Wirt Franklin
Notary Public.

### AFFIDAVIT OF ATTENDING PHYSICIAN OR MID-WIFE.

UNITED STATES OF AMERICA, Indian Territory,
Central DISTRICT.

I, Louina Plumbbi, a mid-wife, on oath state that I attended on Mrs. Sealy Jefferson, wife of Edson Jefferson on the 6th day of May, 1904; that there was born to her on said date a male child; that said child was living March 4, 1905, and is said to have been named Cain Jefferson

          her
Louina x Plumbbi
          mark

# Applications for Enrollment of Choctaw Newborn
# Act of 1905   Volume XIII

Witnesses To Mark:
 { V.W. Rose
   Robert Anderson

Subscribed and sworn to before me this 5th day of April , 1905

Wirt Franklin
Notary Public.

---

**BIRTH AFFIDAVIT.**

## DEPARTMENT OF THE INTERIOR.
## COMMISSION TO THE FIVE CIVILIZED TRIBES.

---

**IN RE APPLICATION FOR ENROLLMENT,** as a citizen of the Choctaw Nation, of Eliza Jefferson , born on the 6th day of May , 1904

Name of Father: Edson Jefferson       a citizen of the Choctaw Nation.
Name of Mother: Sealy Jefferson       a citizen of the Choctaw Nation.

Postoffice   Smithville, Ind. Ter.

---

**AFFIDAVIT OF MOTHER.**

UNITED STATES OF AMERICA, Indian Territory, }
Central                 DISTRICT.

I, Sealy Jefferson , on oath state that I am 29 years of age and a citizen by blood , of the Choctaw Nation; that I am the lawful wife of Edson Jefferson , who is a citizen, by blood of the Choctaw Nation; that a female child was born to me on 6th day of May , 1904; that said child has been named Eliza Jefferson , and was living March 4, 1905.

 her
Sealy x Jefferson
 mark

Witnesses To Mark:
 { V.W. Rose
   Robert Anderson

Subscribed and sworn to before me this 5th day of April , 1905

Wirt Franklin
Notary Public.

## Applications for Enrollment of Choctaw Newborn
## Act of 1905 Volume XIII

**AFFIDAVIT OF ATTENDING PHYSICIAN OR MID-WIFE.**

UNITED STATES OF AMERICA, Indian Territory, } 
Central DISTRICT. }

I, Louina Plumbbi, a mid-wife, on oath state that I attended on Mrs. Sealy Jefferson, wife of Edson Jefferson on the 6th day of May, 1904; that there was born to her on said date a female child; that said child was living March 4, 1905, and is said to have been named Eliza Jefferson

             her
          Louina x Plumbbi
            mark

Witnesses To Mark:
{ V.W. Rose
{ Robert Anderson

   Subscribed and sworn to before me this 5th day of April, 1905

          Wirt Franklin
          Notary Public.

---

Choc New Born 893
  Silas Baker b. 4-26-03

**BIRTH AFFIDAVIT.**
        DEPARTMENT OF THE INTERIOR.
      **COMMISSION TO THE FIVE CIVILIZED TRIBES.**

**IN RE APPLICATION FOR ENROLLMENT,** as a citizen of the Choctaw Nation, of Silas Baker, born on the 26th day of April, 1903

Name of Father: Wesley Baker     a citizen of the Choctaw Nation.
Name of Mother: Judy Baker      a citizen of the Choctaw Nation.

      Postoffice  Bethel, Ind. Ter.

# Applications for Enrollment of Choctaw Newborn
# Act of 1905   Volume XIII

### AFFIDAVIT OF MOTHER.

UNITED STATES OF AMERICA, Indian Territory, }
Central            DISTRICT.

I, Judy Baker, on oath state that I am about 48 years of age and a citizen by blood, of the Choctaw Nation; that I am the lawful wife of Wesley Baker, who is a citizen, by blood of the Choctaw Nation; that a male child was born to me on 26th day of April, 1903; that said child has been named Silas Baker, and was living March 4, 1905.

                       her
                       Judy x Baker

Witnesses To Mark:            mark
{ Robert Anderson
  Vester W Rose

Subscribed and sworn to before me this 5th day of April, 1905

                     Wirt Franklin
                     Notary Public.

### AFFIDAVIT OF ATTENDING PHYSICIAN OR MID-WIFE.

UNITED STATES OF AMERICA, Indian Territory, }
Central            DISTRICT.

I, Nantie Baker, a mid-wife, on oath state that I attended on Mrs. Judy Baker, wife of Wesley Baker on the 26th day of April, 1903; that there was born to her on said date a male child; that said child was living March 4, 1905, and is said to have been named Silas Baker

                       her
                       Nantie x Baker

Witnesses To Mark:            mark
{ Robert Anderson
  Vester W Rose

Subscribed and sworn to before me this 5th day of April, 1905

                     Wirt Franklin
                     Notary Public.

# Applications for Enrollment of Choctaw Newborn
## Act of 1905 Volume XIII

Choc New Born 894
    Abner Going  b. 2-24[sic]-04

$W^m O.B.$

COMMISSIONERS:
TAMS BIXBY,
THOMAS B. NEEDLES,
C.R. BRECKINBRIDGE.

WM. O. BEALL
Secretary

DEPARTMENT OF THE INTERIOR,
COMMISSIONER TO THE FIVE CIVILIZED TRIBES.

REFER IN REPLY TO THE FOLLOWING:

7-NB-894.

ADDRESS ONLY THE
COMMISSION TO THE FIVE CIVILIZED TRIBES.

Muskogee, Indian Territory, May 31, 1905.

Gibson Going,
    Smithville, Indian Territory.

Dear Sir:

    There is enclosed you herewith for execution application for the enrollment of your infant child, Abner Going.

    In the affidavits of January 21, 1905, heretofore filed in this office, the date of the applicant's birth is given as February 23, 1904, while in those of April 5, 1905, the date of birth if given as February 24, 1904. In the enclosed application the date of birth is left blank. Please insert the correct date and, when the affidavits are properly executed, return them to this office.

    In having these affidavits executed care should be exercised to see that all names are written in full, as they appear in the body of the affidavit, and in the event that either of the persons signing the affidavit are unable to write, signatures by mark must be attested by two witnesses. Each affidavit must be executed before a Notary Public and the notarial seal and signature of the officer must be attached to each separate affidavit.

                                      Respectfully,
                                        Tams Bixby

VR 31-14.                                     Chairman.

## Applications for Enrollment of Choctaw Newborn
## Act of 1905   Volume XIII

7 NB 894

Muskogee, Indian Territory, June 27, 1905.

Gibson Going,
    Smithville, Indian Territory.

Dear Sir:

    Receipt is hereby acknowledged of the affidavits of Sophia Going and Louina Impalumbe to the birth of Abner Going, son of Gibson and Sophia Going, February 23, 1904, and the same have been filed with our records in the matter of the enrollment of said child. matter of the enrollment of said child.

Respectfully,

Chairman.

---

**BIRTH AFFIDAVIT.**

**DEPARTMENT OF THE INTERIOR.**
**COMMISSION TO THE FIVE CIVILIZED TRIBES.**

IN RE APPLICATION FOR ENROLLMENT, as a citizen of the    Choctaw    Nation, of Abner Going    , born on the 24th[sic]    day of February    , 1904

Name of Father: Gibson Going    a citizen of the   Choctaw   Nation.
Name of Mother: Sophia Going    a citizen of the   Choctaw   Nation.

Postoffice    Smithville, Ind Ter

---

**AFFIDAVIT OF MOTHER.**

UNITED STATES OF AMERICA, Indian Territory,
Central    DISTRICT.

    I,   Sophia Going   , on oath state that I am  35   years of age and a citizen by blood   , of the   Choctaw    Nation; that I am the lawful wife of   Gibson Going   , who is a citizen, by blood   of the    Choctaw    Nation; that a   male   child was born to me on   24th   day of   February   , 1904; that said child has been named   Abner Going   , and was living March 4, 1905.

                           her
                      Sophia x Going
Witnesses To Mark:         mark
    { Robert Anderson
      Vester W Rose

## Applications for Enrollment of Choctaw Newborn
## Act of 1905   Volume XIII

Subscribed and sworn to before me this   5th   day of    April        , 1905

                                          Wirt Franklin
                                          Notary Public.

---

**AFFIDAVIT OF ATTENDING PHYSICIAN OR MID-WIFE.**

UNITED STATES OF AMERICA, Indian Territory, ⎱
   Central                  DISTRICT. ⎰

    I,   Louina Plumbbi         , a   mid-wife      , on oath state that I attended on Mrs.   Sophia Going     , wife of    Gibson Going    on the 24th   day of    February , 1904; that there was born to her on said date a    male    child; that said child was living March 4, 1905, and is said to have been named   Abner Going

                                        her
                               Louina  x  Plumbbi
Witnesses To Mark:                  mark
  ⎱ Robert Anderson
  ⎰ Vester W Rose

Subscribed and sworn to before me this   5th   day of    April        , 1905

                                          Wirt Franklin
                                          Notary Public.

---

**NEW-BORN AFFIDAVIT.**

        Number..................

...Choctaw Enrolling Commission...

---

    IN THE MATTER OF THE APPLICATION FOR ENROLLMENT, as a citizen of the Choctaw           Nation, of            Abner Going

born on the   23   day of    February        190 4

Name of father   Gibson Going             a citizen of    Choctaw
Nation final enrollment No.   1091
Name of mother   Sophia Going            a citizen of    Choctaw
Nation final enrollment No.   1092

                                Postoffice       Smithville I.T.

# Applications for Enrollment of Choctaw Newborn
## Act of 1905 Volume XIII

### AFFIDAVIT OF MOTHER.

UNITED STATES OF AMERICA
INDIAN TERRITORY
Central DISTRICT

I Sophia Going , on oath state that I am 34 years of age and a citizen by Blood of the Choctaw Nation, and as such have been placed upon the final roll of the Choctaw Nation, by the Honorable Secretary of the Interior my final enrollment number being 1092 ; that I am the lawful wife of Gibson Going , who is a citizen of the Choctaw Nation, and as such has been placed upon the final roll of said Nation by the Honorable Secretary of the Interior, his final enrollment number being 1091 and that a Male child was born to me on the 23 day of February 190 4; that said child has been named Abner Going , and is now living.

                                                her
                                      Sophia x Going
Witnesseth.                               mark

Must be two Witnesses who are Citizens.
    Peter Going
    Vinson Going

Subscribed and sworn to before me this 21 day of Jan 190 5

                                      C L Lester
                                                Notary Public.

My commission expires: Oct 15-1905

## AFFIDAVIT OF ATTENDING PHYSICIAN OR MIDWIFE

UNITED STATES OF AMERICA
INDIAN TERRITORY
Central DISTRICT

I, Peter Going a ..................................................
on oath state that I attended on Mrs. Sophia Going wife of Gibson Going on the 23 day of February , 190 4 , that there was born to her on said date a male child, that said child is now living, and is said to have been named Abner Going

                                       Peter Going
Subscribed and sworn to before me this, the 21 day of Jan 190 5

WITNESSETH:                            C L Lester        Notary Public.

Must be two witnesses who are citizens
    Osborne Going
    Peter Going

## Applications for Enrollment of Choctaw Newborn
## Act of 1905   Volume XIII

We hereby certify that we are well acquainted with     Peter Going   a   Choctaw citizen   and know   him   to be reputable and of good standing in the community.

    Osborne Going                         Vinson Going

    Peter Going                             _____

**BIRTH AFFIDAVIT.**

### DEPARTMENT OF THE INTERIOR.
### COMMISSION TO THE FIVE CIVILIZED TRIBES.

IN RE APPLICATION FOR ENROLLMENT, as a citizen of the    Choctaw    Nation, of  Abner Going    , born on the  23   day of  February   , 1904

Name of Father: Gibson Going         a citizen of the   Choctaw   Nation.
Name of Mother: Sophia Going       a citizen of the   Choctaw   Nation.

                    Postoffice    Smithville, Ind Ter

**AFFIDAVIT OF MOTHER.**

UNITED STATES OF AMERICA, Indian Territory, }
    Central                  DISTRICT. }

I,  Sophia Going   , on oath state that I am  35   years of age and a citizen by blood   , of the   Choctaw   Nation; that I am the lawful wife of   Gibson Going   , who is a citizen, by blood   of the   Choctaw   Nation; that a   male   child was born to me on  23   day of  February   , 1904; that said child has been named  Abner Going   , and was living March 4, 1905.

                                her
                        Sophia  x  Going
Witnesses To Mark:            mark
  { Thomas Watson
  { George Watson

Subscribed and sworn to before me this  19 day of   June   , 1905

                        W.H. M<sup>c</sup>Kinney
My commission expires March 30-1909       Notary Public.

## Applications for Enrollment of Choctaw Newborn
## Act of 1905   Volume XIII

**AFFIDAVIT OF ATTENDING PHYSICIAN OR MID-WIFE.**

UNITED STATES OF AMERICA, Indian Territory, }
Central                 DISTRICT.

I, Louina Impalumbi, a mid-wife, on oath state that I attended on Mrs. Sophia Going, wife of Gibson Going on the 23 day of February, 1904; that there was born to her on said date a male child; that said child was living March 4, 1905, and is said to have been named Abner Going

                                          her
                              Louina x Impalumbi
Witnesses To Mark:              mark
  { Larsen Watson
    Wickens M$^c$Coy

Subscribed and sworn to before me this 19 day of June, 1905

                                      W.H. M$^c$Kinney
My commission expires March 30-1909        Notary Public.

---

Choc New Born 895
    Sarah E. T. Garrison  b. 1-14-03

**BIRTH AFFIDAVIT.**
## DEPARTMENT OF THE INTERIOR.
## COMMISSION TO THE FIVE CIVILIZED TRIBES.

**IN RE APPLICATION FOR ENROLLMENT,** as a citizen of the Choctaw Nation, of Sarah E. T. Garrison, born on the 14th day of January, 1903

Name of Father: Lafayette O. Garrison    a citizen of the Choctaw Nation.
Name of Mother: Effie M. Garrison      a citizen of the Choctaw Nation.

                      Postoffice    Idabel, Ind. Ter.

# Applications for Enrollment of Choctaw Newborn
## Act of 1905   Volume XIII

### AFFIDAVIT OF MOTHER.

UNITED STATES OF AMERICA, Indian Territory, }
Central           DISTRICT.

I, Effie M. Garrison, on oath state that I am 27 years of age and a citizen by blood, of the Choctaw Nation; that I am the lawful wife of Lafayette O. Garrison, who is a citizen, by marriage of the Choctaw Nation; that a female child was born to me on 14th day of January, 1903; that said child has been named Sarah E. T. Garrison, and was living March 4, 1905.

Effie M. Garrison

Witnesses To Mark:
{

Subscribed and sworn to before me this 11th day of April, 1905

Wirt Franklin
Notary Public.

---

### AFFIDAVIT OF ATTENDING PHYSICIAN OR MID-WIFE.

UNITED STATES OF AMERICA, Indian Territory, }
Central           DISTRICT.

I, W. B. Long, a physician, on oath state that I attended on Mrs. Effie M. Garrison, wife of Lafayette O. Garrison on the 14th day of January, 1903; that there was born to her on said date a female child; that said child was living March 4, 1905, and is said to have been named Sarah E. T. Garrison

W.B. Long

Witnesses To Mark:
{

Subscribed and sworn to before me this 11th day of April, 1905

Wirt Franklin
Notary Public.

## Applications for Enrollment of Choctaw Newborn
## Act of 1905   Volume XIII

Choc New Born 896
Ollie Lee Gibbs   b. 7-27-04

7-NB-896

Muskogee, Indian Territory, January 30, 1906.

Lizzie Gibbs,
Glover, Indian Territory.

Dear Madam:

Replying to that portion of your letter in which you ask relative to the enrollment of your child, born December last you are advised that inder[sic] the act of Congress approved March 3, 1905, there is no provision for the enrollment of children born subsequent to March 3, 1905.

Respectfully,

Acting Commissioner.

**BIRTH AFFIDAVIT.**
### DEPARTMENT OF THE INTERIOR.
### COMMISSION TO THE FIVE CIVILIZED TRIBES.

IN RE APPLICATION FOR ENROLLMENT, as a citizen of the   Choctaw   Nation, of Ollie Lee Gibbs   , born on the  27th  day of  July  , 1904

Name of Father: Fred Gibbs        a citizen of the United States Nation.
Name of Mother: Lizzie Gibbs       a citizen of the   Choctaw   Nation.

Postoffice   Glover, Ind. Ter.

**AFFIDAVIT OF MOTHER.**

UNITED STATES OF AMERICA, Indian Territory,
Central               DISTRICT.

I,  Lizzie Gibbs  , on oath state that I am  21  years of age and a citizen by blood  , of the  Choctaw  Nation; that I am the lawful wife of  Fred Gibbs  , who is a citizen, ~~by~~ ............. of the  United States ~~Nation~~; that a  male  child was born to me on  27th  day of  July  , 1904; that said child has been named Ollie Lee Gibbs  , and was living March 4, 1905.

Lizzie Gibbs

## Applications for Enrollment of Choctaw Newborn
## Act of 1905  Volume XIII

Witnesses To Mark:
{

Subscribed and sworn to before me this 11th day of April, 1905

Wirt Franklin
Notary Public.

---

**AFFIDAVIT OF ATTENDING PHYSICIAN OR MID-WIFE.**

UNITED STATES OF AMERICA, Indian Territory, }
Central                    DISTRICT.          }

I, Lena Lewis, a mid-wife, on oath state that I attended on Mrs. Lizzie Gibbs, wife of Fred Gibbs on the 27th day of July, 1904; that there was born to her on said date a male child; that said child was living March 4, 1905, and is said to have been named Ollie Lee Gibbs

Lena Lewis

Witnesses To Mark:
{

Subscribed and sworn to before me this 11th day of April, 1905

Wirt Franklin
Notary Public.

---

Choc New Born 897
    Mabel Lewis  b. 2-23-05
    Annie Belle Lewis  b. 3-1-03

---

BIRTH AFFIDAVIT.
**DEPARTMENT OF THE INTERIOR.**
**COMMISSION TO THE FIVE CIVILIZED TRIBES.**

---

IN RE APPLICATION FOR ENROLLMENT, as a citizen of the Choctaw Nation, of Mabel Lewis, born on the 23rd day of February, 1905

Name of Father: David Lewis     a citizen of the Choctaw Nation.
Name of Mother: Lena Lewis     a citizen of the Choctaw Nation.

## Applications for Enrollment of Choctaw Newborn
## Act of 1905 Volume XIII

Postoffice Glover, Ind. Ter.

**AFFIDAVIT OF MOTHER.**

UNITED STATES OF AMERICA, Indian Territory, }
Central DISTRICT.

I, Lena Lewis, on oath state that I am 26 years of age and a citizen by blood, of the Choctaw Nation; that I am the lawful wife of David Lewis, who is a citizen, by blood of the Choctaw Nation; that a female child was born to me on 23rd day of February, 1905; that said child has been named Mabel Lewis, and was living March 4, 1905.

Lena Lewis

Witnesses To Mark:
{

Subscribed and sworn to before me this 11th day of April, 1905

Wirt Franklin
Notary Public.

**AFFIDAVIT OF ATTENDING PHYSICIAN OR MID-WIFE.**

UNITED STATES OF AMERICA, Indian Territory, }
Central DISTRICT.

I, Lizzie Gibbs, a mid-wife, on oath state that I attended on Mrs. Lena Lewis, wife of David Lewis on the 23rd day of February, 1905; that there was born to her on said date a female child; that said child was living March 4, 1905, and is said to have been named Mabel Lewis

Lizzie Gibbs

Witnesses To Mark:
{

Subscribed and sworn to before me this 11th day of April, 1905

Wirt Franklin
Notary Public.

## Applications for Enrollment of Choctaw Newborn
## Act of 1905 Volume XIII

BIRTH AFFIDAVIT.

### DEPARTMENT OF THE INTERIOR.
### COMMISSION TO THE FIVE CIVILIZED TRIBES.

---

IN RE APPLICATION FOR ENROLLMENT, as a citizen of the Choctaw Nation, of Annie Belle Lewis, born on the 1st day of March, 1903

Name of Father: David Lewis     a citizen of the Choctaw Nation.
Name of Mother: Lena Lewis     a citizen of the Choctaw Nation.
Postoffice Glover, Ind. Ter.

---

**AFFIDAVIT OF MOTHER.**

UNITED STATES OF AMERICA, Indian Territory, }
Central     DISTRICT.

    I, Lena Lewis, on oath state that I am 26 years of age and a citizen by blood, of the Choctaw Nation; that I am the lawful wife of David Lewis, who is a citizen, by blood of the Choctaw Nation; that a female child was born to me on 1st day of March, 1903; that said child has been named Annie Belle Lewis, and was living March 4, 1905.

                                          Lena Lewis

Witnesses To Mark:
{

    Subscribed and sworn to before me this 11th day of April, 1905.

                                          Wirt Franklin
                                          Notary Public.

---

**AFFIDAVIT OF ATTENDING PHYSICIAN OR MID-WIFE.**

UNITED STATES OF AMERICA, Indian Territory, }
Central     DISTRICT.

    I, Lizzie Gibbs, a mid-wife, on oath state that I attended on Mrs. Lena Lewis, wife of David Lewis on the 1st day of March, 1903; that there was born to her on said date a female child; that said child was living March 4, 1905, and is said to have been named Annie Belle Lewis

                                          Lizzie Gibbs

Witnesses To Mark:
{

## Applications for Enrollment of Choctaw Newborn
## Act of 1905   Volume XIII

Subscribed and sworn to before me this 11th  day of  April  , 1905

Wirt Franklin<br>Notary Public.

---

Choc New Born 898
    Lillian Aline White   b. 10-27-03

7-NB-898.<br>Muskogee, Indian Territory, May 31, 1905.

John R. White,
    Idabel, Indian Territory.

Dear Sir:

    There is enclosed you herewith for execution application for the enrollment of your infant child, Lillian Aline White.

    In the application filed in this office on April 17, 1905, the date of the applicant's birth is given as October 27, 1904, while in those filed on April 26, 1905, it is given as October 27, 1903. In the enclosed application the date of birth is left blank. Please insert the correct date and, when the affidavits are properly executed, return them to this office.

    In having these affidavits executed care should be exercised to see that all names are written in full, as they appear in the body of the affidavit, and in the event that either of the persons signing the affidavit are unable to write, signatures by mark must be attested by two witnesses. Each affidavit must be executed before a Notary Public and the notarial seal and signature of the officer must be attached to each separate affidavit.

Respectfully,

VR 31-13.                                                                                  [sic]

Applications for Enrollment of Choctaw Newborn
Act of 1905   Volume XIII

7-NB-898.

Muskogee, Indian Territory, June 10, 1905.

John R. White,
    Idabel, Indian Territory.

Dear Sir:

    Receipt is hereby acknowledged of the affidavits of Lena White and Call Adams to the birth of Lillian Aline White, daughter of John R. and Lena White, October 27, 1903, and the same have been filed with our records in the matter of the enrollment of said child.

                    Respectfully,

                                    Commissioner in Charge.

# NEW BORN AFFIDAVIT

No ..................

## CHOCTAW ENROLLING COMMISSION

IN THE MATTER OF THE APPLICATION FOR ENROLLMENT as a citizen of the Choctaw Nation, of   Lillian Aline White   born on the 27th day of  October   190 3

Name of father   John R White   a citizen of   Choctaw   Nation, final enrollment No.  506
Name of mother   Lena White   a citizen of   Choctaw   Nation, final enrollment No.  1902

Idabel I.T.   Postoffice.

### AFFIDAVIT OF MOTHER

UNITED STATES OF AMERICA
    INDIAN TERRITORY
DISTRICT   Central

    I   Lena White   , on oath state that I am   29   years of age and a citizen by   blood   of the   Choctaw   Nation, and as such have been placed upon the final roll of the   Choctaw   Nation, by the Honorable Secretary of the Interior my final

## Applications for Enrollment of Choctaw Newborn
## Act of 1905  Volume XIII

enrollment number being 1902 ; that I am the lawful wife of John R White , who is a citizen of the Choctaw Nation, and as such has been placed upon the final roll of said Nation by the Honorable Secretary of the Interior, his final enrollment number being 506 and that a female child was born to me on the 27$^{th}$ day of October 190 3; that said child has been named Lillian Aline White , and is now living.

WITNESSETH:  Lena White
Must be two witnesses { Richard C Denson
who are citizens  Henry C Stanford

Subscribed and sworn to before me this, the 6$^{th}$ day of Feb , 190 5

W.A. Shoney
Notary Public.

My Commission Expires: Jan 10, 1909

---

## AFFIDAVIT OF ATTENDING PHYSICIAN OR MIDWIFE

UNITED STATES OF AMERICA
INDIAN TERRITORY
Central DISTRICT

I, Caledonia Adams a midwife on oath state that I attended on Mrs. Lena White wife of John R White on the 27$^{th}$ day of October , 190 3 , that there was born to her on said date a female child, that said child is now living, and is said to have been named Lillian A White

her
Caledonia x Adams
mark

Subscribed and sworn to before me this, the 24 day of Jan 190 5

WITNESSETH:  W.A. Shoney  Notary Public.
Must be two witnesses { Richard C Denson
who are citizens  Henry C Stanford

We hereby certify that we are well acquainted with Caledonia Adams a midwife and know her to be reputable and of good standing in the community.

Richard C Denson  _____

Henry C Stanford  _____

## Applications for Enrollment of Choctaw Newborn
## Act of 1905 Volume XIII

BIRTH AFFIDAVIT.

## DEPARTMENT OF THE INTERIOR.
## COMMISSION TO THE FIVE CIVILIZED TRIBES.

IN RE APPLICATION FOR ENROLLMENT, as a citizen of the Choctaw Nation, of Lillian Aline White, born on the 27th day of October, 1904

Name of Father: John R White     a citizen of the Choctaw Nation.
Name of Mother: Lena White     a citizen of the Choctaw Nation.

Postoffice    Idabel, Ind. Ter.

**AFFIDAVIT OF MOTHER.**

UNITED STATES OF AMERICA, Indian Territory,
Central DISTRICT.

I, Lena White, on oath state that I am 29 years of age and a citizen by blood, of the Choctaw Nation; that I am the lawful wife of John R White, who is a citizen, by marriage of the Choctaw Nation; that a female child was born to me on 27th day of October, 1904; that said child has been named Lillian Aline White, and was living March 4, 1905.

                                             Lena White

Witnesses To Mark:

Subscribed and sworn to before me this 11th day of April, 1905

                                             Wirt Franklin
                                             Notary Public.

**AFFIDAVIT OF ATTENDING PHYSICIAN OR MID-WIFE.**

UNITED STATES OF AMERICA, Indian Territory,
Central DISTRICT.

I, Caledonia Adams, a mid-wife, on oath state that I attended on Mrs. Lena White, wife of John R. White on the 27th day of October, 1904; that there was born to her on said date a female child; that said child was living March 4, 1905, and is said to have been named Lillian Aline White

                                             her
                                   Caledonia x Adams
                                         mark

# Applications for Enrollment of Choctaw Newborn
## Act of 1905   Volume XIII

Witnesses To Mark:
{ Vester W Rose
  Robert Anderson

Subscribed and sworn to before me this 11th day of April, 1905

Wirt Franklin
Notary Public.

---

**BIRTH AFFIDAVIT.**

### DEPARTMENT OF THE INTERIOR.
### COMMISSION TO THE FIVE CIVILIZED TRIBES.

---

**IN RE APPLICATION FOR ENROLLMENT,** as a citizen of the Choctaw Nation, of Lillian Aline White, born on the 27 day of October, 1903

Name of Father: John R White     a citizen of the Choctaw Nation.
Name of Mother: Lena White      a citizen of the Choctaw Nation.

Postoffice   Idabel, Ind. Ter.

---

**AFFIDAVIT OF MOTHER.**

UNITED STATES OF AMERICA, Indian Territory, }
Central District   DISTRICT. }

I, Lena White, on oath state that I am 29 years of age and a citizen by blood, of the Choctaw Nation; that I am the lawful wife of John R White, who is a citizen, by blood of the Choctaw Nation; that a female child was born to me on 27 day of October, 1903; that said child has been named Lillian Aline White, and was living March 4, 1905.

Lena White

Witnesses To Mark:
{

Subscribed and sworn to before me this 2$^{nd}$ day of June, 1905

J J Roberts
Notary Public.

# Applications for Enrollment of Choctaw Newborn
## Act of 1905   Volume XIII

**AFFIDAVIT OF ATTENDING PHYSICIAN OR MID-WIFE.**

UNITED STATES OF AMERICA, Indian Territory,  
Central                         DISTRICT.

    I, Call Adams, a Midwife, on oath state that I attended on Mrs. Lena White, wife of John R. White on the 27 day of October, 1903; that there was born to her on said date a female child; that said child was living March 4, 1905, and is said to have been named Lillian Aline White

                              her  
                          Call x Adams  
                             mark

Witnesses To Mark:
- John Marshall
- AM Hoffman

    Subscribed and sworn to before me this 4 day of June, 1905

                        J J Roberts  
                          Notary Public.

---

Choc New Born 899  
    Susan Kaniatobe   b. 8-6-03

              Sily Kanitobe  
              Roll No 2816

              Gibson Kanitobe  
            Roll No 2815

## Applications for Enrollment of Choctaw Newborn
## Act of 1905    Volume XIII

7-NB-899.

Muskogee, Indian Territory, June 1, 1905.

Gibson Kaniatobe,
    Idabel, Indian Territory.

Dear Sir:

    Referring to the application for the enrollment of your infant child, Susan Kaniatobe, born August 3, 1903, it is noted from the affidavits heretofore filed in this office that you attended upon your wife at the time of birth of the applicant.

    If there was no one else in attendance, excepting yourself, it will be necessary that you file in this office the affidavits of two persons, who are disinterested and not related to the applicant, who have actual knowledge of the facts that the child was born, the date of her birth; that she was living on March 4, 1905, and that Sely Kaniatobe is her mother.

    The affidavits of R. A. Taylor, heretofore filed in this office, does not fulfill the requirement, in that it is the affidavit of a person who is related to the applicant.

Respectfully,

Chairman.

---

7 NB 899

Muskogee, Indian Territory, June 30, 1905.

Gibson Kiatobe[sic],
    Idabel, Indian Territory.

Dear Sir:

    Receipt is hereby acknowledged of your letter of June 26, 1905, transmitting affidavits of Elsie Johnson and Lucy Ann Johnson to the birth of Susan Kaniatobe, daughter of Gibson and Sely Kaniatobe, August 3, 1903, and the same have been filed with our records in the matter of the enrollment of said child.

Respectfully,

Chairman.

# Applications for Enrollment of Choctaw Newborn
## Act of 1905  Volume XIII

## AFFIDAVIT OF ATTENDING PHYSICIAN OR MIDWIFE

UNITED STATES OF AMERICA
INDIAN TERRITORY
 Central       DISTRICT

I, Gibson Kaniatobe  a  attendant on oath state that I attended on Mrs. Sely Kaniatobe wife of Gibson Kaniatobe on the 3$^{rd}$ day of August, 190 3, that there was born to her on said date a female child, that said child is now living, and is said to have been named Susan Kaniatobe

Gibson Kaniatobe

Subscribed and sworn to before me this, the 21$^{st}$ day of Jan  190 5

W.A. Shoney  Notary Public.

WITNESSETH:
Must be two witnesses who are citizens
{ Willington Haiskonabbe
  Wilburn Kaniatobe }

We hereby certify that we are well acquainted with Gibson Kaniatobe a attendant and know him to be reputable and of good standing in the community.

Willington Haiskonabbe  _____

Wilburn Kaniatobe  _____

*(The affidavit below typed as given.)*

United States of America
Indian Territory }
Central District

I Elsie Johnson on oath state that I am personaly acquainted with Gibson Kaniatobe and Sely Kaniatobe Choctaw and wife and that I am no relation of thirs and that on August 3$^{rd}$ 1903 there Born to them a female child and said child has been named Susan Kaniatobe and said child was living on March 4, 1905         her
 Witness to mark                     Elsie x Johnson
 GG Merry                                mark
 *(Name Illegible)*
Subscribed and sworn to before me this 26 day of June A.D. 1905

              GG Merry
My commission            Notary Public.
expires April 25, 1908.

## Applications for Enrollment of Choctaw Newborn
## Act of 1905  Volume XIII

United States of America, )
)
Indian Territory,   ) ss.
)
Central District.   )

I, R. A. Taylor, on oath state that I am forty-seven years of age and a citizen by blood of the Choctaw Nation; that my post office address is Garvin, Indian Territory; that Sely Kaniatobe, wife of Gibson Kiniatobe[sic], is my daughter; that I know of my own knowledge that on or about the 3rd day of August, 1903, there was born to the said Sely Kiniatobe[sic] a female child; that said child is now living and has been named Susan Kiniatobe[sic].

R.A. Taylor

Subscribed and sworn to before me this 12th day of April, 1905.

Wirt Franklin
Notary Public.

United States of America
Indian Territory
Central District

I Lucy Ann Johnson on oath state that I am personally acquainted with Gibson Kaniatobe and Sely Kaniatobe Husband and wife and I am no relation of theirs and on August the 3, 1903 there born to them a female child and said child has been named Susan Kaniatobe and said Susan Kaniatobe was living on March 4, 1905

Lucy Ann Johnson

Subscribed and sworn to before me this 26$^{th}$ day of June A.D. 1905

GG Merry
My commission                                         Notary Public.
expires April 25, 1908.

# Applications for Enrollment of Choctaw Newborn
## Act of 1905   Volume XIII

**NEW-BORN AFFIDAVIT.**

Number..................

### ...Choctaw Enrolling Commission...

IN THE MATTER OF THE APPLICATION FOR ENROLLMENT, as a citizen of the Choctaw Nation, of Susan Kaniatobe

born on the $3^{rd}$ day of __August__ 190 3

Name of father   Gibson Kaniatobe   a citizen of   Choctaw Nation final enrollment No.  2815
Name of mother   Sely Kaniatobe   a citizen of   Choctaw Nation final enrollment No.  2816

Postoffice   Idabel, I T

### AFFIDAVIT OF MOTHER.

UNITED STATES OF AMERICA
INDIAN TERRITORY
Central   DISTRICT

I   Sely Kaniatobe   , on oath state that I am 28 years of age and a citizen by   blood   of the   Choctaw   Nation, and as such have been placed upon the final roll of the   Choctaw   Nation, by the Honorable Secretary of the Interior my final enrollment number being   2816 ; that I am the lawful wife of   Gibson Kaniatobe   , who is a citizen of the   Choctaw   Nation, and as such has been placed upon the final roll of said Nation by the Honorable Secretary of the Interior, his final enrollment number being   2815   and that a   female   child was born to me on the $3^{rd}$   day of   August   190 3; that said child has been named   Susan Kaniatobe   , and is now living.

Sely Kaniatobe

Witnesseth.
Must be two Witnesses who are Citizens.   } Willington Haiskonabbe
Wilburn Kaniatobe

Subscribed and sworn to before me this   21   day of   Jan   190 5

W A Shoney
Notary Public.

My commission expires:

# Applications for Enrollment of Choctaw Newborn
## Act of 1905  Volume XIII

BIRTH AFFIDAVIT.

**DEPARTMENT OF THE INTERIOR.**
**COMMISSION TO THE FIVE CIVILIZED TRIBES.**

IN RE APPLICATION FOR ENROLLMENT, as a citizen of the Choctaw Nation, of Susan Kaniatobe, born on the 3rd day of August, 1903

Name of Father: Gibson Kaniatobe   a citizen of the Choctaw Nation.
Name of Mother: Sely Kaniatobe   a citizen of the Choctaw Nation.

Postoffice   Idabel, Ind. Ter.

**AFFIDAVIT OF MOTHER.**

UNITED STATES OF AMERICA, Indian Territory,
Central   DISTRICT.

I, Sely Kaniatobe, on oath state that I am about 28 years of age and a citizen by blood, of the Choctaw Nation; that I am the lawful wife of Gibson Kaniatobe, who is a citizen, by blood of the Choctaw Nation; that a female child was born to me on 3rd day of August, 1903; that said child has been named Susan Kaniatobe, and was living March 4, 1905. *and that no physician or mid-wife attended me at the birth of said child*

Sely Kaniatobe

Witnesses To Mark:

Subscribed and sworn to before me this 12th day of April, 1905

Wirt Franklin
Notary Public.

**AFFIDAVIT OF ATTENDING PHYSICIAN OR MID-WIFE.**

UNITED STATES OF AMERICA, Indian Territory,
Central   DISTRICT.

Sely Kaniatobe, ~~wife of~~ *my wife* on the 3rd day of August, 1903; that there was born to her on said date a female child; that said child was living March 4, 1905, and ~~is said to have~~ *has* been named Susan Kaniatobe *and that no one else was present when said child was born*

Gibson Kaniatobe

# Applications for Enrollment of Choctaw Newborn
## Act of 1905   Volume XIII

Witnesses To Mark:
{

Subscribed and sworn to before me this 12th day of   April   , 1905

Wirt Franklin
Notary Public.

---

Choc New Born 900
Lina Maytobe   b. 5-17-04

**BIRTH AFFIDAVIT.**

## DEPARTMENT OF THE INTERIOR.
## COMMISSION TO THE FIVE CIVILIZED TRIBES.

**IN RE APPLICATION FOR ENROLLMENT**, as a citizen of the   Choctaw   Nation, of Lina Maytobe   , born on the 17th day of May , 1904

Name of Father: Joseph Barney       a citizen of the   Choctaw   Nation.
Name of Mother: Samaie Maytobe      a citizen of the   Choctaw   Nation.

Postoffice   Kullituklo, Ind. Ter.

**AFFIDAVIT OF MOTHER.**

UNITED STATES OF AMERICA, Indian Territory, }
Central            DISTRICT.

I, Samaie Maytobe   , on oath state that I am   20   years of age and a citizen by   blood   , of the   Choctaw   Nation; that I am *not* the lawful wife of   Joseph Barney   , who is a citizen, by blood   of the   Choctaw   Nation; that a female   child was born to me on   17th   day of   May   , 1904; that said child has been named   Lina Maytobe   , and was living March 4, 1905.

                              her
                      Samaie x Maytobe

Witnesses To Mark:                  mark
{ Robert Anderson
  Vester W Rose

# Applications for Enrollment of Choctaw Newborn
## Act of 1905 Volume XIII

Subscribed and sworn to before me this 12th day of April, 1905

Wirt Franklin
Notary Public.

### AFFIDAVIT OF ATTENDING PHYSICIAN OR MID-WIFE.

UNITED STATES OF AMERICA, Indian Territory,
Central DISTRICT.

I, Frances Maytobe, a mid-wife, on oath state that I attended on Mrs. Samaie Maytobe, ~~wife of~~ ................... on the 17th day of May, 1904; that there was born to her on said date a female child; that said child was living March 4, 1905, and is said to have been named Lina Maytobe

her
Frances x Maytobe
mark

Witnesses To Mark:
{ Robert Anderson
{ Vester W Rose

Subscribed and sworn to before me this 12th day of April, 1905

Wirt Franklin
Notary Public.

### AFFIDAVIT OF ATTENDING PHYSICIAN OR MIDWIFE

UNITED STATES OF AMERICA
INDIAN TERRITORY
Central DISTRICT

I, Francis Maytobe a midwife on oath state that I attended on Mrs. Semie Maytobe wife of not married on the 17 day of May, 190 4, that there was born to her on said date a female child, that said child is now living, and is said to have been named Elina[sic] Maytobe

her
Francis x Maytobe
mark

Subscribed and sworn to before me this, the 21$^{st}$ day of Jan 190 5

WA Shoney  Notary Public.

WITNESSETH:
Must be two witnesses { Benson Maytobe
who are citizens { Nicey Allen

## Applications for Enrollment of Choctaw Newborn
## Act of 1905 Volume XIII

We hereby certify that we are well acquainted with Francis Maytobe a midwife and know ................ to be reputable and of good standing in the community.

Benson Maytobe _____

Nicey Allen _____

**NEW-BORN AFFIDAVIT.**

Number................

## ...Choctaw Enrolling Commission...

IN THE MATTER OF THE APPLICATION FOR ENROLLMENT, as a citizen of the Choctaw Nation, of Elina Maytubby[sic]

born on the 17 day of __May__ 190 4

Name of father Joseph Barney     a citizen of    Choctaw
Nation final enrollment No. —
Name of mother Semie Maytobe     a citizen of    Choctaw
Nation final enrollment No. 1379

                         Postoffice    Kullituklo

**AFFIDAVIT OF MOTHER.**

UNITED STATES OF AMERICA
INDIAN TERRITORY
    Central         DISTRICT

        I       Semie Maytobe         , on oath state that I am 21 years of age and a citizen by blood of the Choctaw Nation, and as such have been placed upon the final roll of the Choctaw Nation, by the Honorable Secretary of the Interior my final enrollment number being 1379 ; that I am the lawful wife of not married , who is a citizen of the ———— Nation, and as such has been placed upon the final roll of said Nation by the Honorable Secretary of the Interior, his final enrollment number being............ and that a female child was born to me on the 17 day of May 190 4; that said child has been named Elina Maytobe , and is now living.                                   her
                                            Semie x Maytobe
Witnesseth.                                           mark

   Must be two    }   Benson Maytobe
   Witnesses who
   are Citizens.       Nicey Allen

## Applications for Enrollment of Choctaw Newborn
## Act of 1905 Volume XIII

Subscribed and sworn to before me this  21  day of  Jan  190 5

W A Shoney
Notary Public.

My commission expires:

---

Choc New Born 901
Casey Maytobe  b. 12-9-04

**NEW-BORN AFFIDAVIT.**

Number..............

...Choctaw Enrolling Commission...

IN THE MATTER OF THE APPLICATION FOR ENROLLMENT, as a citizen of the Choctaw  Nation, of  Kizzie[sic] Maytubby[sic]

born on the  $9^{th}$  day of __Dec__ 190 4

Name of father  Raybin Maytubby  a citizen of  Choctaw
Nation final enrollment No.  1376
Name of mother  Nancy Maytubby  a citizen of  Choctaw
Nation final enrollment No.  1377

Postoffice  Kullituklo I T

**AFFIDAVIT OF MOTHER.**

UNITED STATES OF AMERICA
INDIAN TERRITORY
Central  DISTRICT

I  Nancy Maytubby , on oath state that I am 38  years of age and a citizen by  blood  of the  Choctaw  Nation, and as such have been placed upon the final roll of the  Choctaw  Nation, by the Honorable Secretary of the Interior my final enrollment number being  1377 ; that I am the lawful wife of  Raybin Maytubby , who is a citizen of the  Choctaw  Nation, and as such has been placed upon the final roll of said Nation by the Honorable Secretary of the Interior, his final enrollment number being  1376  and that a  female  child was born to me on the  $9^{th}$  day of  December  190 4; that said child has been named  Kizzie Maytubby , and is now living.

109

# Applications for Enrollment of Choctaw Newborn
## Act of 1905 Volume XIII

                                                her
                                       Nancy x Maytubby

Witnesseth.                                         mark
  Must be two        W. S. Ward
  Witnesses who
  are Citizens.        Levi Stewart

      Subscribed and sworn to before me this   21  day of    Jan    190 5

                                          W.A. Shoney
                                                           Notary Public.

My commission expires:

## AFFIDAVIT OF ATTENDING PHYSICIAN OR MIDWIFE

UNITED STATES OF AMERICA
INDIAN TERRITORY
  Central        DISTRICT

     I,  Francis Maytubby      a        midwife
on oath state that I attended on Mrs.  Nancy Maytubby    wife of Raybin Maytubby
on the  9th  day of  Dec  , 190 4 , that there was born to her on said date a    female
child, that said child is now living, and is said to have been named  Kizzie Maytubby
                                                                      her
                                                              Francis x Maytubby
                                                                   mark
                  Subscribed and sworn to before me this, the    21        day of
        Jan      190 5

WITNESSETH:                                W.A. Shoney      Notary Public.
  Must be two witnesses    W.S. Ward
  who are citizens
                              Levi Stewart

      We hereby certify that we are well acquainted with     Francis Maytubby
a    midwife      and know   her      to be reputable and of good standing in the
community.

        W.S. Ward                                   _____

        Levi Stewart                               _____

# Applications for Enrollment of Choctaw Newborn
## Act of 1905 Volume XIII

BIRTH AFFIDAVIT.

## DEPARTMENT OF THE INTERIOR.
## COMMISSION TO THE FIVE CIVILIZED TRIBES.

IN RE APPLICATION FOR ENROLLMENT, as a citizen of the Choctaw Nation, of Casey Maytobe, born on the 9th day of December, 1904

Name of Father: Rayburn[sic] Maytobe    a citizen of the Choctaw Nation.
Name of Mother: Nancy Maytobe    a citizen of the Choctaw Nation.

Postoffice    Kullituklo, Ind. Ter.

### AFFIDAVIT OF MOTHER.

UNITED STATES OF AMERICA, Indian Territory, }
Central    DISTRICT.

I, Nancy Maytobe, on oath state that I am 38 years of age and a citizen by blood, of the Choctaw Nation; that I am the lawful wife of Rayburn Maytobe, who is a citizen, by blood of the Choctaw Nation; that a female child was born to me on 9th day of December, 1904; that said child has been named Casey Maytobe, and was living March 4, 1905.

                                       her
                                 Nancy x Maytobe
Witnesses To Mark:               mark
{ Robert Anderson
  Vester W Rose

Subscribed and sworn to before me this 12th day of April, 1905

                             Wirt Franklin
                                  Notary Public.

### AFFIDAVIT OF ATTENDING PHYSICIAN OR MID-WIFE.

UNITED STATES OF AMERICA, Indian Territory, }
Central    DISTRICT.

I, Francis Maytobe, a mid-wife, on oath state that I attended on Mrs. Nancy Maytobe, wife of Rayburn Maytobe on the 9th day of December, 1904; that there was born to her on said date a female child; that said child was living March 4, 1905, and is said to have been named Casey Maytobe

                                       her
                               Francis x Maytobe
                                     mark

## Applications for Enrollment of Choctaw Newborn
## Act of 1905   Volume XIII

Witnesses To Mark:
   { Robert Anderson
    Vester W Rose

      Subscribed and sworn to before me this   12th day of   April   , 1905

                                    Wirt Franklin
                                      Notary Public.

---

<u>Choc New Born 902</u>
    Mary Lyda Clay   b. 4-29-03

                                                7 N.B. 902.

                    Muskogee, Indian Territory, May 29, 1905.

Mattie Clay,
    Locksburg[sic], Arkansas.

Dear Madam:

    Receipt is hereby acknowledged of your letter of May 21, transmitting bill of divorce between yourself and Abner H. Clay, granting you the custody of your children, which you offer in the matter of the enrollment of your infant child, Mary Lyda Clay, and the same has been filed with the record in this case.

                            Respectfully,

                                            Chairman.

# Applications for Enrollment of Choctaw Newborn
## Act of 1905 Volume XIII

7 NB 902

Muskogee, Indian Territory, June 26, 1905.

Mattie Clay,
    Locksburg[sic], Arkansas.

Dear Madam:

    Receipt is hereby acknowledged of your letter of June 20, 1905, stating that you have been informed the Choctaw and Chickasaw land offices will close by the last of July; that you have not finished filing for your three minor children and you wish to be advised if this is true; also f decision has been rendered in favor of your youngest child Mary Lyda Clay.

    In reply to your letter you are advised that no date has been fixed for the closing of the Choctaw and Chickasaw land offices.

    You are further advised that the name of your daughter Mary Lyda Clay has been placed upon a schedule of citizens by blood of the Choctaw Nation prepared for forwarding to the Secretary of the Interior and you will be notified when her enrollment is approved by the Department.

    Respectfully,

Chairman.

## *Affidavit of Attending Physician or Midwife*

UNITED STATES OF AMERICA,
    INDIAN TERRITORY,
       Central    DISTRICT

    I, Mattie A Denson a Midwife on oath state that I attended on Mrs. Mattie E. Clay wife of Abner H. Clay on the 29$^{th}$ day of April , 190 3, that there was born to her on said date a female child, that said child is now living, and is said to have been named Mary Lyda Clay

Mattie A Denson

Subscribed and sworn to before me this the 16 day of Feb 1905

W.T. Lyon
Notary Public.

## Applications for Enrollment of Choctaw Newborn
## Act of 1905   Volume XIII

WITNESSETH:

Must be two witnesses who are citizens and know the child.
{ Richard C Denson
  Lula Denson

We hereby certify that we are well acquainted with................................................................................
a................................................and know....................to be reputable and of good standing in the community.

Must be two citizen witnesses.
{ Richard C Denson
  Lula Denson

**NEW-BORN AFFIDAVIT.**

Number................

### ...Choctaw Enrolling Commission...

IN THE MATTER OF THE APPLICATION FOR ENROLLMENT, as a citizen of the Choctaw Nation, of   Mary Lyda Clay

born on the   29   day of __April__   190 3

Name of father   Abner H Clay            a citizen of   Choctaw
Nation final enrollment No.   7026
Name of mother   Mattic Clay             a citizen of   Choctaw
Nation final enrollment No.   7507

Postoffice   Garvin Ind Ty

**AFFIDAVIT OF MOTHER.**

UNITED STATES OF AMERICA
INDIAN TERRITORY
   Central   DISTRICT

I   Mattie Clay   , on oath state that I am 34   years of age and a citizen by   Intermarriage   of the   Choctaw Nation, and as such have been placed upon the final roll of the   Choctaw   Nation, by the Honorable Secretary of the Interior my final enrollment number being   7507 ; that I am the lawful wife of   Abner H Clay   , who is a citizen of the   Choctaw   Nation, and as such has been placed upon the final roll of said Nation by the Honorable Secretary of the Interior, his final enrollment number being   7026   and that a   Female   child was born to me on the   29   day of   April   190 3; that said child has been named   Mary Lyda Clay   , and is now living.

Mattie Clay

Applications for Enrollment of Choctaw Newborn
Act of 1905   Volume XIII

Witnesseth.
Must be two ⎫ Lula Denson
Witnesses who ⎬
are Citizens. ⎭  Richard C. Denson

Subscribed and sworn to before me this  23  day of  Jan      190 5

J J Roberts
Notary Public.

My commission expires:  Jan 2 1908

## BILL OF DIVORCE.

### The Choctaw Nation,

In Circuit Court of the Third Judicial District, Regular    July          term 190 3 , a petition of   Mattie E Clay          being presented by   Taylor       Attorney in said Court, for a Bill of Divorce, setting forth the facts, etc., and after the Court hearing the Testimony in regard to the petition do order and decree that a Bill of Divorce be issued to the applicant   Mattie E Clay

THEREFORE I do issue a Bill of Divorce to said applicant   Mattie E Clay
forever releasing   her      from the Banns of Matrimony heretofore existing between   Abner H Clay          and   Mattie E Clay

Given under my hand and seal of office, this the   15$^{th}$   day of   July      A.D. 190 3

C.J. Anderson
Circuit Clerk, 2nd District. C. N.

By ........................................................ Deputy

Choctaw Nation                In Circuit Court
2$^{nd}$ Judicial District          of July Term, 1903

I H.D. Anderson, Judge of the aforesaid District and Nation do hereby order, decree and adjudge that the decree of divorce is granted and that
1. Abner H. Clay Jr
2. Mattie Lurena Clay
3. Myrtle Eugenia Clay
4. Mary Lyda Clay            is hereby granted unto the mother Mrs. Mattie E. Clay in the peaceful possession of the above named children.

Given under my hand and official signature.

# Applications for Enrollment of Choctaw Newborn
## Act of 1905 Volume XIII

This the 15th day of July AD 1903

Attest
CJ Anderson
Circuit Clerk
2nd Judicial District

H D Anderson
Circuit Judge 2nd Jud Dist.

CN

Choctaw Nation

---

**BIRTH AFFIDAVIT.**

### DEPARTMENT OF THE INTERIOR.
### COMMISSION TO THE FIVE CIVILIZED TRIBES.

---

IN RE APPLICATION FOR ENROLLMENT, as a citizen of the Choctaw Nation, of Mary Lyda Clay, born on the 29th day of April, 1903

Name of Father: Abner H Clay     a citizen of the Choctaw Nation.
Name of Mother: Mattie Clay     a citizen of the Choctaw Nation.

Postoffice    Lockesburg, Arkansas

---

**AFFIDAVIT OF MOTHER.**

UNITED STATES OF AMERICA, Indian Territory,
~~Central~~    DISTRICT.

I, Mattie Clay, on oath state that I am 34 years of age and a citizen by Intermarriage, of the Choctaw Nation; that I am the lawful wife of *was the wife at time child was born* Abner H Clay, who is a citizen, by Blood of the Choctaw Nation; that a Female child was born to me on 29th day of April, 1903; that said child has been named Mary Lyda Clay, and was living March 4, 1905.

Mattie Clay

Witnesses To Mark:
{

Subscribed and sworn to before me this 10 day of April, 1905.

W.T. Lyon
Notary Public.

---

116

# Applications for Enrollment of Choctaw Newborn
## Act of 1905   Volume XIII

### AFFIDAVIT OF ATTENDING PHYSICIAN OR MID-WIFE.

UNITED STATES OF AMERICA, Indian Territory, }
~~Central~~           DISTRICT.

    I, Mattie A Denson, a midwife, on oath state that I attended on Mrs. Mattie Clay, wife of Abner H Clay on the 29$^{th}$ day of April 1903, 1........; that there was born to her on said date a Female child; that said child was living March 4, 1905, and is said to have been named Mary Lyda Clay

                                                     Mattie A Denson

Witnesses To Mark:
{

    Subscribed and sworn to before me this 8 day of April, 1905

                                                  W.T. Lyon
                                                  Notary Public.

---

<u>Choc New Born 903</u>
       Frank Victor   b. 11-18-03

United States of America,   )
                                 )
Indian Territory,            )   ss.
                                 )
Central District.            )

    I, Abner Williams, on oath state that I am twenty-four years of age and a citizen by blood of the Choctaw Nation; that my post office address is Garvin, Indian Territory; that I am personally acquainted with Louisa Victor, wife of George Victor; that since their marriage, about two and one half years ago, I have lived within one mile of where they have lived and often stopped at their home; that I know of my own knowledge that on or about the 18th day of November, 1903, there was born to the said Louisa Victor a male child; that said child is now living and is said to have been named Frank Victor.

                                            Abner Williams

Subscribed and sworn to before me this 12th day of April, 1905.

                                            Wirt Franklin
                                            Notary Public.

# Applications for Enrollment of Choctaw Newborn
## Act of 1905 Volume XIII

This the 15th day of July AD 1903

Attest                                   H D Anderson
     CJ Anderson                 Circuit Judge 2nd
       Circuit Clerk                  Jud Dist.
   2nd Judicial District                              CN
                           Choctaw Nation

---

**BIRTH AFFIDAVIT.**

### DEPARTMENT OF THE INTERIOR.
### COMMISSION TO THE FIVE CIVILIZED TRIBES.

---

**IN RE APPLICATION FOR ENROLLMENT**, as a citizen of the Choctaw Nation, of Mary Lyda Clay, born on the 29th day of April, 1903

Name of Father: Abner H Clay      a citizen of the Choctaw Nation.
Name of Mother: Mattie Clay      a citizen of the Choctaw Nation.

         Postoffice     Lockesburg, Arkansas

---

**AFFIDAVIT OF MOTHER.**

UNITED STATES OF AMERICA, Indian Territory, }
     ~~Central~~            DISTRICT.

     I, Mattie Clay, on oath state that I am 34 years of age and a citizen by Intermarriage, of the Choctaw Nation; that I am the lawful wife of *was the wife at time child was born* Abner H Clay, who is a citizen, by Blood of the Choctaw Nation; that a Female child was born to me on 29th day of April, 1903; that said child has been named Mary Lyda Clay, and was living March 4, 1905.

                               Mattie Clay

Witnesses To Mark:
{

     Subscribed and sworn to before me this 10 day of April, 1905

                          W.T. Lyon
                                Notary Public.

# Applications for Enrollment of Choctaw Newborn
## Act of 1905   Volume XIII

### AFFIDAVIT OF ATTENDING PHYSICIAN OR MID-WIFE.

UNITED STATES OF AMERICA, Indian Territory, }
~~Central~~         DISTRICT.

I,  Mattie A Denson  , a  midwife  , on oath state that I attended on Mrs.  Mattie Clay  , wife of  Abner H Clay  on the 29<sup>th</sup> day of  April 1903 , 1........ ; that there was born to her on said date a  Female  child; that said child was living March 4, 1905, and is said to have been named Mary Lyda Clay

                                                Mattie A Denson

Witnesses To Mark:
{

Subscribed and sworn to before me this  8  day of  April  , 1905

                                                W.T. Lyon
                                                Notary Public.

---

<u>Choc New Born 903</u>
       Frank Victor   b.  11-18-03

United States of America,   )
                                  )
Indian Territory,           )   ss.
                                  )
Central District.           )

    I, Abner Williams, on oath state that I am twenty-four years of age and a citizen by blood of the Choctaw Nation; that my post office address is Garvin, Indian Territory; that I am personally acquainted with Louisa Victor, wife of George Victor; that since their marriage, about two and one half years ago, I have lived within one mile of where they have lived and often stopped at their home; that I know of my own knowledge that on or about the 18th day of November, 1903, there was born to the said Louisa Victor a male child; that said child is now living and is said to have been named Frank Victor.

                                                Abner Williams

Subscribed and sworn to before me this 12th day of April, 1905.

                                                Wirt Franklin
                                                Notary Public.

# Applications for Enrollment of Choctaw Newborn
## Act of 1905   Volume XIII

United States of America, )
)
Indian Territory, ) ss.
)
Central District. )

    I, Watt Williams, on oath state that I am twenty-four years of age and a citizen by blood of the Choctaw Nation; that my post office address is Garvin, Indian Territory; that I am personally acquainted with Louisa Victor, wife of George Victor; that since their marriage, about two and one half years ago, I have lived within one mile of where they have lived and often stopped at their home; that I know of my own knowledge that on or about the 18th day of November, 1903, there was born to the said Louisa Victor a male child; that said child is now living and is said to have been named Frank Victor.

                                              Wat[sic] Williams

Subscribed and sworn to before me this 12th day of April, 1905.

                                                Wirt Franklin
                                                   Notary Public.

**BIRTH AFFIDAVIT.**

## DEPARTMENT OF THE INTERIOR.
## COMMISSION TO THE FIVE CIVILIZED TRIBES.

    **IN RE APPLICATION FOR ENROLLMENT,** as a citizen of the     Choctaw    Nation, of Frank Victor    , born on the 18th   day of  November  , 1903

Name of Father: George Victor        a citizen of the   Choctaw   Nation.
Name of Mother: Louisa Victor        a citizen of the   Choctaw   Nation.

                            Postoffice     Lukfatah[sic], Ind. Ter.

### AFFIDAVIT OF MOTHER.

**UNITED STATES OF AMERICA, Indian Territory,** }
    Central                  **DISTRICT.** }

    I, Louisa Victor   , on oath state that I am 24   years of age and a citizen by blood  , of the   Choctaw   Nation; that I am the lawful wife of  George Victor  , who is a citizen, by blood   of the    Choctaw    Nation; that a   male   child was born to me on  18th   day of   November   , 1903; that said child has been named

# Applications for Enrollment of Choctaw Newborn
## Act of 1905 Volume XIII

Frank Victor, and was living March 4, 1905. *and that no physician or mid-wife attended me at the birth of said child.*

                                her
Witnesses To Mark:         Louisa x Victor
  { Robert Anderson           mark
    Vester W Rose

    Subscribed and sworn to before me this 11th day of April, 1905

                               Wirt Franklin
                               Notary Public.

---

### AFFIDAVIT OF ATTENDING PHYSICIAN OR MID-WIFE.

UNITED STATES OF AMERICA, Indian Territory,
   Central               DISTRICT.

    I, George Victor, ~~a~~ ................., on oath state that I attended on Mrs. Louisa Victor, ~~wife of~~ *my wife* on the 18th day of November, 1903; that there was born to her on said date a male child; that said child was living March 4, 1905, and ~~is said to have~~ *has* been named Frank Victor *and that no one else was present when said child was born*

                              George Victor
Witnesses To Mark:
  {

    Subscribed and sworn to before me this 11th day of April, 1905

                               Wirt Franklin
                               Notary Public.

---

Choc New Born 904
    Wilsie Williams b. 8-16-03

## Applications for Enrollment of Choctaw Newborn
## Act of 1905   Volume XIII

7 NB 904

Muskogee, Indian Territory, June 17, 1905.

Abner Williams,
   Idabel, Indian Territory.

Dear Sir:

   Receipt is hereby acknowledged of your letter of June 14, 1905, asking if you can file for your child Wilcey Williams when you enrolled April 13, 1905.

   In reply to your letter you are advised that the name of your child Wilcey Williams is being placed upon a schedule of citizens by blood of the Choctaw Nation prepared for forwarding to the Secretary of the Interior, but pending the approval of her enrollment no selection of allotment can be made in her behalf.

Respectfully,

Chairman.

# NEW BORN AFFIDAVIT

No ...........

## CHOCTAW ENROLLING COMMISSION

IN THE MATTER OF THE APPLICATION FOR ENROLLMENT as a citizen of the Choctaw Nation, of    Wilsie Williams    born on the 16$^{th}$ day of August   190 3

Name of father   Abner Williams   a citizen of   Choctaw   Nation,
final enrollment No.  1137
Name of mother   Lucy Ann Johnson   a citizen of   Choctaw   Nation,
final enrollment No.  1676

Idabel, I.T.                Postoffice.

# Applications for Enrollment of Choctaw Newborn
## Act of 1905   Volume XIII

**AFFIDAVIT OF MOTHER**

UNITED STATES OF AMERICA  
INDIAN TERRITORY  
DISTRICT   Central

I   Lucy Ann Johnson   , on oath state that I am   27   years of age and a citizen by   blood   of the   Choctaw   Nation, and as such have been placed upon the final roll of the   Choctaw   Nation, by the Honorable Secretary of the Interior my final enrollment number being   1676   ; that I am the lawful wife of   Abner Williams , who is a citizen of the   Choctaw   Nation, and as such has been placed upon the final roll of said Nation by the Honorable Secretary of the Interior, his final enrollment number being   1137   and that a   female   child was born to me on the   $16^{th}$   day of   August   190 3; that said child has been named   Wilsie Williams   , and is now living.

WITNESSETH:                                       Lucy Ann Johnson  
Must be two witnesses { Byington Williams  
who are citizens          Moses Williams

Subscribed and sworn to before me this, the   13   day of   Feb   , 190 5

                                                W.A. Shoney  
                                                Notary Public.

My Commission Expires:  
            Jan 10, 1909

## AFFIDAVIT OF ATTENDING PHYSICIAN OR MIDWIFE

UNITED STATES OF AMERICA  
INDIAN TERRITORY  
   Central         DISTRICT

I,   Wacie Williams   a   midwife on oath state that I attended on Mrs.   Lucy Ann Johnson   wife of   Abner Williams on the   $16^{th}$   day of   August   , 190 3 , that there was born to her on said date a   female child, that said child is now living, and is said to have been named   Wilsie Williams

                                                Wacie Williams  
         Subscribed and sworn to before me this, the   15   day of   Feb   190 5

WITNESSETH:                                W.A. Shoney      Notary Public.  
Must be two witnesses { Byington Williams  
who are citizens          Moses Williams

# Applications for Enrollment of Choctaw Newborn
## Act of 1905   Volume XIII

We hereby certify that we are well acquainted with     Wacie Williams    a    midwife    and know    her    to be reputable and of good standing in the community.

Byington Williams                                 _____

Moses Williams                                    _____

_____

**BIRTH AFFIDAVIT.**

### DEPARTMENT OF THE INTERIOR.
### COMMISSION TO THE FIVE CIVILIZED TRIBES.

_____

**IN RE APPLICATION FOR ENROLLMENT,** as a citizen of the    Choctaw    Nation, of Wilsie Williams    , born on the 16th   day of August   , 1903

Name of Father: Abner Williams           a citizen of the   Choctaw   Nation.
Name of Mother: Lucy Ann Williams        a citizen of the   Choctaw   Nation.

Postoffice    Garvin, Ind. Ter.

_____

**AFFIDAVIT OF MOTHER.**

**UNITED STATES OF AMERICA, Indian Territory,** ⎱
    Central             **DISTRICT.** ⎰

I, Lucy Ann Williams    , on oath state that I am   28   years of age and a citizen by    blood    , of the    Choctaw    Nation; that I am the lawful wife of Abner Williams    , who is a citizen, by blood    of the    Choctaw    Nation; that a    female    child was born to me on    16th   day of   August   , 1903; that said child has been named   Wilsie Williams    , and was living March 4, 1905.

Lucy Ann Williams

Witnesses To Mark:
{

Subscribed and sworn to before me this 12th   day of    April    , 1905

Wirt Franklin
Notary Public.

_____

# Applications for Enrollment of Choctaw Newborn
## Act of 1905 Volume XIII

**AFFIDAVIT OF ATTENDING PHYSICIAN OR MID-WIFE.**

UNITED STATES OF AMERICA, Indian Territory, }
Central                DISTRICT.

I, Wacie Thompson[sic]  , a  mid-wife  , on oath state that I attended on Mrs. Lucy Ann Williams  , wife of  Abner Williams  on the  16th  day of August  , 1903; that there was born to her on said date a  female  child; that said child was living March 4, 1905, and is said to have been named  Wilsie Williams

                                            Wacie Thompson
Witnesses To Mark:
{

Subscribed and sworn to before me this  12th  day of  April  , 1905

                                            Wirt Franklin
                                            Notary Public.

---

Choc New Born 905
   Hattie Juzan   b. 3-1-04

$W^m O.B.$

| COMMISSIONERS:<br>TAMS BIXBY,<br>THOMAS B. NEEDLES,<br>C.R. BRECKINBRIDGE.<br>—<br>WM. O. BEALL<br>Secretary | **DEPARTMENT OF THE INTERIOR,**<br>**COMMISSIONER TO THE FIVE CIVILIZED TRIBES.** | REFER IN REPLY TO THE FOLLOWING:<br>———————<br>7-NB-905. |

ADDRESS ONLY THE
COMMISSION TO THE FIVE CIVILIZED TRIBES.

                                   Muskogee, Indian Territory, May 29, 1905.

Philliston Juzan,
    Goodwater, Indian Territory.

Dear Sir:

    There is enclosed you herewith for execution application for the enrollment of your infant child.

    In the affidavits of January 21, 1905, heretofore filed in this office, the name of the applicant is given as Hattie Juzan and the date of her birth as February 28, 1904,

# Applications for Enrollment of Choctaw Newborn
## Act of 1905   Volume XIII

while in the affidavits of April 12, 1905, her name appears as Eddie Juzan and the date of birth as March 1, 1904. In the enclosed application the name of the applicant and the date of birth is left blank. Please insert the correct name and date of birth and, when the affidavits are properly executed, return them to this office.

If you were the only one in attendance upon your wife at the time of birth of the applicant, it will also be necessary that you file in this office the affidavits of two persons, who have actual knowledge of the facts that the child was born, the date of her birth; that she was living on March 4, 1905, and the Sattie Juzan is her mother.

In having these affidavits executed care should be exercised to see that all names are written in full, as they appear in the body of the affidavit, and in the event that either of the persons signing the affidavit are unable to write, signatures by mark must be attested by two witnesses. Each affidavit must be executed before a Notary Public and the notarial seal and signature of the officer must be attached to each separate affidavit.

Respectfully,<br>Tams Bixby<br>Chairman.

VR 29-2.

---

7 NB-905

Muskogee, Indian Territory, June 23, 1905.

Philliston Juzan,
    Goodwater, Indian Territory.

Dear Sir:

Receipt is hereby acknowledged of the affidavits of Sattie Juzan and Jackaway Juzan to the birth of Hattie Juzan, daughter of Philliston and Sattie Juzan, March 1, 1904, and the same have been filed with our records in the matter of the enrollment of said child.

Respectfully,

Chairman.

## Applications for Enrollment of Choctaw Newborn
## Act of 1905  Volume XIII

**BIRTH AFFIDAVIT.**

### DEPARTMENT OF THE INTERIOR.
### COMMISSION TO THE FIVE CIVILIZED TRIBES.

**IN RE APPLICATION FOR ENROLLMENT,** as a citizen of the   Choctaw   Nation, of Eddie Juzan   , born on the 1st   day of March  , 1904

Name of Father: Philliston Juzan         a citizen of the   Choctaw   Nation.
Name of Mother: Sattie Juzan             a citizen of the , Choctaw   Nation.

Postoffice   Goodwater, Ind. Ter.

**AFFIDAVIT OF MOTHER.**

UNITED STATES OF AMERICA, Indian Territory, }
Central           DISTRICT.

I, Sattie Juzan   , on oath state that I am   30   years of age and a citizen by blood   , of the   Choctaw   Nation; that I am the lawful wife of   Philliston Juzan   , who is a citizen, by blood   of the   Choctaw   Nation; that a   female   child was born to me on   1st   day of   March   , 1904; that said child has been named Eddie Juzan   , and was living March 4, 1905. *and that no one but my husband was present when said child was born*

                                         her
                              Sattie x Juzan
Witnesses To Mark:              mark
 { Robert Anderson
 { Vester W Rose

Subscribed and sworn to before me this  12th  day of  April   , 1905

Wirt Franklin
Notary Public.

**AFFIDAVIT OF ATTENDING PHYSICIAN OR MID-WIFE.**

UNITED STATES OF AMERICA, Indian Territory, }
Central           DISTRICT.

I,  Philliston Juzan         , ~~a~~ ................., on oath state that I attended on Mrs.  Sattie Juzan       , ~~wife of~~ *my wife*   on the  1st  day of  March  , 1904; that there was born to her on said date a   female   child; that said child was living March 4, 1905, and is said to have been named Eddie Juzan  *and that no one else was present when said child was born.*

# Applications for Enrollment of Choctaw Newborn
## Act of 1905   Volume XIII

                                his
                       Philliston x Juzan

Witnesses To Mark:           mark
{ Robert Anderson
{ Vester W Rose

Subscribed and sworn to before me this 12th day of April, 1905

                        Wirt Franklin
                        Notary Public.

---

## AFFIDAVIT OF ATTENDING PHYSICIAN OR MIDWIFE

UNITED STATES OF AMERICA
INDIAN TERRITORY
  Central   DISTRICT

I, Philiston[sic] Juzan a attendant on oath state that I attended on Mrs. Sudie[sic] Juzan wife of Philiston Juzan on the 28 day of February, 190 4, that there was born to her on said date a female child, that said child is now living, and is said to have been named Hattie Juzan

                        his
                 Philiston x Juzan
                     mark

Subscribed and sworn to before me this, the 20 day of Jan 190 5

WITNESSETH:               W A Shoney    Notary Public.
Must be two witnesses { W S Ward
who are citizens       { S.C. Williston

We hereby certify that we are well acquainted with Philiston Juzan a attendant and know him to be reputable and of good standing in the community.

    W.S. Ward                                _____

    S. C. Williston                         _____

Applications for Enrollment of Choctaw Newborn
Act of 1905 Volume XIII

**NEW-BORN AFFIDAVIT.**

Number..................

**...Choctaw Enrolling Commission...**

IN THE MATTER OF THE APPLICATION FOR ENROLLMENT, as a citizen of the Choctaw Nation, of Hattie Juzan

born on the 28 day of ___February___ 190 4

Name of father  Philiston Juzan            a citizen of   Choctaw
Nation final enrollment No.  2575
Name of mother  Suttie Juzan               a citizen of   Choctaw
Nation final enrollment No.  3657

Postoffice   Goodwater I.T.

**AFFIDAVIT OF MOTHER.**

UNITED STATES OF AMERICA
INDIAN TERRITORY
  Central     DISTRICT

I   Suttie Juzan                , on oath state that I am 30 years of age and a citizen by blood of the Choctaw Nation, and as such have been placed upon the final roll of the Choctaw Nation, by the Honorable Secretary of the Interior my final enrollment number being 3657 ; that I am the lawful wife of Philiston Juzan , who is a citizen of the Choctaw Nation, and as such has been placed upon the final roll of said Nation by the Honorable Secretary of the Interior, his final enrollment number being 2575 and that a female child was born to me on the 28 day of February 190 4; that said child has been named Hattie Juzan , and is now living.

                                          her
                                Sudie[sic]  x  Juzan
Witnesseth.                              mark
  Must be two  } W.S. Ward
  Witnesses who
  are Citizens.    S.C. Williston

Subscribed and sworn to before me this  21  day of  Jan  190 5

                         W A Shoney
                                Notary Public.
My commission expires: Jan 10, 1909

## Applications for Enrollment of Choctaw Newborn
## Act of 1905   Volume XIII

**BIRTH AFFIDAVIT.**

### DEPARTMENT OF THE INTERIOR.
### COMMISSION TO THE FIVE CIVILIZED TRIBES.

IN RE APPLICATION FOR ENROLLMENT, as a citizen of the   Choctaw   Nation, of Hattie Juzan   , born on the 1st   day of March   , 1904

Name of Father: Philliston Juzan        a citizen of the   Choctaw   Nation.
Name of Mother: Sattie Juzan            a citizen of the   Choctaw   Nation.

Postoffice   Goodwater, Ind. Ter.

**AFFIDAVIT OF MOTHER.**

UNITED STATES OF AMERICA, Indian Territory, }
Central   DISTRICT.

I, Sattie Juzan   , on oath state that I am   30   years of age and a citizen by blood   , of the   Choctaw   Nation; that I am the lawful wife of   Philliston Juzan   , who is a citizen, by blood   of the   Choctaw   Nation; that a   female   child was born to me on 1st   day of   March   , 1904; that said child has been named Hattie Juzan   , and was living March 4, 1905.

her
Sattie x Juzan
mark

Witnesses To Mark:
{ *(Name Illegible)*
{ WJ Whiteman

Subscribed and sworn to before me this 17th   day of   June   , 1905

WJ Whiteman
Notary Public.

**AFFIDAVIT OF ATTENDING PHYSICIAN OR MID-WIFE.**

UNITED STATES OF AMERICA, Indian Territory, }
Central   DISTRICT.

*was present when*

I, Jackaway Juzan   , a ................., on oath state that I ~~attended on~~ Mrs. Sattie Juzan   , wife of   Philliston Juzan   on the 1st   day of   March   , 1904; that there was born to her on said date a   female   child; that said child was living March 4, 1905, and is said to have been named Hattie Juzan

her
Jackaway x Juzan
mark

# Applications for Enrollment of Choctaw Newborn
## Act of 1905 Volume XIII

Witnesses To Mark:
{ (Name Illegible)
{ WJ Whiteman

Subscribed and sworn to before me this 17th day of June, 1905

WJ Whiteman
Notary Public.

---

Choc New Born 906
Washington Watson b. 2-20-04

**BIRTH AFFIDAVIT.**
**DEPARTMENT OF THE INTERIOR.**
**COMMISSION TO THE FIVE CIVILIZED TRIBES.**

**IN RE APPLICATION FOR ENROLLMENT,** as a citizen of the Choctaw Nation, of Washington Watson, born on the 20th day of February, 1904

Name of Father: Sam Watson    a citizen of the Choctaw Nation.
Name of Mother: Emma Watson   a citizen of the Choctaw Nation.

Postoffice   Smithville, Ind. Ter.

**AFFIDAVIT OF MOTHER.**

UNITED STATES OF AMERICA, Indian Territory, }
Central         DISTRICT.                    }

I, Emma Watson, on oath state that I am 18 years of age and a citizen by blood, of the Choctaw Nation; that I am the lawful wife of Sam Watson, who is a citizen, by blood of the Choctaw Nation; that a male child was born to me on 20th day of February, 1904; that said child has been named Washington Watson, and was living March 4, 1905.

Emma Watson

Witnesses To Mark:
{
{

# Applications for Enrollment of Choctaw Newborn
## Act of 1905   Volume XIII

Subscribed and sworn to before me this 5th   day of   April   , 1905

Wirt Franklin<br>
Notary Public.

---

**AFFIDAVIT OF ATTENDING PHYSICIAN OR MID-WIFE.**

UNITED STATES OF AMERICA, Indian Territory, }
   Central                 DISTRICT. }

    I, Margaret Watson   , a   midwife   , on oath state that I attended on Mrs.   Emma Watson   , wife of   Sam Watson   on the 20th   day of   February , 1904; that there was born to her on said date a   male   child; that said child was living March 4, 1905, and is said to have been named   Washington Watson

Margaret Watson

Witnesses To Mark:
{

    Subscribed and sworn to before me this 5th   day of   April   , 1905

Wirt Franklin<br>
Notary Public.

---

Choc New Born 907
        Mary Hicks   b. 12-8-04
        Adam Hicks   b. 4-6-03

7-NB-907.

Muskogee, Indian Territory, May 29, 1905.

Cephus Hicks,
     Bethel, Indian Territory.

Dear Sir:

    Referring to the application for the enrollment of your infant children, Adam Hicks and Mary Hicks, born April 6, 1903 and December 8, 1904, respectively, it is noted from the affidavits heretofore filed in this office that you were the only one in attendance upon your wife at the time of birth of the applicant.

## Applications for Enrollment of Choctaw Newborn
## Act of 1905  Volume XIII

Before these cases can be finally determined it will be necessary for you to file in this office, in each case, the affidavits of two parties, who are disinterested and not related to the applicants, who have actual knowledge of the facts that the child was born, the date of its birth; that it was living on March 4, 1905, and that Lincey Hicks is its mother.

The affidavit of Byington Bond, in support of these facts, has been filed with this office in each of the above mentioned cases. It will, therefore, be necessary for you to secure a similar affidavit from another person to be filed with each case.

Respectfully,

Chairman.

---

7-N.B. 907.

Muskogee, Indian Territory, June 20, 1905.

Cephus Hicks,
Bethel, Indian Territory.

Dear Sir:

Receipt is hereby acknowledged of the affidavit of John Noah to the birth of your infant children, Adam Hicks and Mary Hicks.

In his affidavit in support of the application of Adam Hicks, he states that the applicant was born on April 8, 1903, while all the other affidavits heretofore filed in this office give the date of the applicant's birth as April 6, 1903. If this latter date is the correct one you will please have John Noah re-execute his affidavit.

This affidavit should show the date of the applicant's birth, his name, that he was living on March 4, 1905, and that Lincey Hicks is his mother.

This matter should receive your immediate attention as no further action can be taken until this affidavit is filed with the Commission.

Respectfully,

Chairman.

# Applications for Enrollment of Choctaw Newborn
## Act of 1905   Volume XIII

7-NB-907

Muskogee, Indian Territory July 5, 1905.

Cephus Hicks,
    Bethel, Indian Territory.

Dear Sir:

    Receipt is hereby acknowledged of the affidavit of John Noah to the birth of Adam Hicks child of Lincey Hicks April 6, 1903, and the same has been filed with the records of this office in the matter of the enrollment of this child.

        Respectfully,

            Commissioner.

---

$W^m O.B.$

**COMMISSIONERS:**
TAMS BIXBY,
THOMAS B. NEEDLES,
C.R. BRECKINBRIDGE.

WM. O. BEALL
Secretary

**DEPARTMENT OF THE INTERIOR,**
**COMMISSIONER TO THE FIVE CIVILIZED TRIBES.**

REFER IN REPLY TO THE FOLLOWING:

7-N.B. 907.

ADDRESS ONLY THE
COMMISSION TO THE FIVE CIVILIZED TRIBES.

Muskogee, Indian Territory, June 20, 1905.

Cephus Hicks,
    Bethel, Indian Territory.

Dear Sir:

    Receipt is hereby acknowledged of the affidavit of John Noah to the birth of your infant children, Adam Hicks and Mary Hicks.

    In his affidavit in support of the application of Adam Hicks, he states that the applicant was born on April 8, 1903, while all the other affidavits heretofore filed in this office give the date of the applicant's birth as April 6, 1903. If this latter date is the correct one you will please have John Noah re-execute his affidavit.

    This affidavit should show the date of the applicant's birth, his name, that he was living on March 4, 1905, and that Lincey Hicks is his mother.

    This matter should receive your immediate attention as no further action can be taken until this affidavit is filed with the Commission.

## Applications for Enrollment of Choctaw Newborn
## Act of 1905 Volume XIII

Respectfully,
Tams Bixby
Chairman.

*(Affidavit below typed as given.)*

Cane before me a Notary Public this 26 day of June 1905 John Noah *(illegible)* known to me and stats on oath that Adam Hicks was born on April 6 day 1903, and was living March 4-1905 and is living at this time John Noah and Lincey Hicks is his mother

Subscribed and sworn to before me this 26 day of June 1905

J H Matthews
Notary Public

My commission
expires Feb 13=1909

United States of America, )
                                )
Indian Territory,            )   ss.
                                )
Central District.              )

     I, Byington Bond, on oath state that I am forty-four years of age and a citizen by blood of the Choctaw Nation; that I am personally acquainted with Lincey Hicks, wife of Cephus Hicks; that I have known said parties for about twenty year; that during the time I have known said parties they have lived within four miles of where I have lived near Bethel, Indian Territory; that there was born to the said Lincey Hicks on or about the 8th day of December 1904, a female child; that said child is now living and is said to have been named Mary Hicks.

                                                                                       his
                                                         Byington x Bond
                                                                   mark

Subscribed and sworn to before me this 5th day of April, 1905.

                                                           Wirt Franklin
                                                           Notary Public.

Witnesses to mark.
   Robert Anderson
   Vester W Rose

# Applications for Enrollment of Choctaw Newborn
## Act of 1905   Volume XIII

*(The affidavit below typed as given.)*

United States of America,
    Indian Territory
Central District.
    Affidavit of Acquaintance.

I John Noah on oath state that I am 21 years of age and a citizen by blood of the Choctaw Nation, that my post office address is Noah, Ind. Ter. that I am not related to the applicant; who is a citizen by blood of the Choctaw Nation, that I am personally acquainted with Lincey Hicks, wife of Cephus Hicks, who is a citizen by blood of the Choctaw Nation, and that a female child was born to Lincey Hicks on the 8th day of December 1904 and that said female child has been named Mary Hicks, and the said Mary Hicks was living on the 4th day of March 1905, and is now living, and that I have personal knowledge that Lincey Hicks is the mother of the said Mary Hicks

                                            John Noah

Subscribed and sworn to before me this 12th day of June 1905.

                                      W.H. McKinney
                                      Notary Public.

My Commission
    expires on the 30th day of
    March 1909

                    DEPARTMENT OF THE INTERIOR,
                Commission to the Five Civilized Tribes.
## FILED
JUN 21 1905

*Tams Bixby* CHAIRMAN

---

**BIRTH AFFIDAVIT.**
## DEPARTMENT OF THE INTERIOR.
## COMMISSION TO THE FIVE CIVILIZED TRIBES.

---

       IN RE APPLICATION FOR ENROLLMENT, as a citizen of the     Choctaw     Nation, of Mary Hicks     , born on the 8th   day of  December  , 1904

Name of Father: Cephus Hicks           a citizen of the   Choctaw   Nation.
Name of Mother: Lincey Hicks           a citizen of the   Choctaw   Nation.

                          Postoffice    Bethel, Ind. Ter.

# Applications for Enrollment of Choctaw Newborn
## Act of 1905 Volume XIII

### AFFIDAVIT OF MOTHER.

UNITED STATES OF AMERICA, Indian Territory,　}
Central　　　　　　　　　　　DISTRICT.

I, Lincey Hicks, on oath state that I am 27 years of age and a citizen by blood, of the Choctaw Nation; that I am the lawful wife of Cephus Hicks, who is a citizen, by blood of the Choctaw Nation; that a female child was born to me on 8th day of December, 1904; that said child has been named Mary Hicks, and was living March 4, 1905. *and that no physician or mid-wife attended me at the birth of said child*

　　　　　　　　　　　　　　　her
　　　　　　　　　　　Lincey x Hicks
Witnesses To Mark:　　　mark
{ Robert Anderson
{ Vester W Rose

Subscribed and sworn to before me this 5th day of April, 1905

　　　　　　　　Wirt Franklin
　　　　　　　　Notary Public.

---

### AFFIDAVIT OF ATTENDING PHYSICIAN OR MID-WIFE.

UNITED STATES OF AMERICA, Indian Territory,　}
Central　　　　　　　　　　　DISTRICT.

I, Cephus Hicks, a ~~~~~~~~~~, on oath state that I attended on Mrs. Lincey Hicks my, wife ~~of~~ ~~~~~~~~~~ on the 8th day of December, 1904; that there was born to her on said date a female child; that said child was living March 4, 1905, and is said to have been named Mary Hicks *and that no one else was present when said child was born*

　　　　　　　　　　　　　　　his
　　　　　　　　　　　Cephus x Hicks
Witnesses To Mark:　　　mark
{ Robert Anderson
{ Vester W Rose

Subscribed and sworn to before me this 5th day of April, 1905

　　　　　　　　Wirt Franklin
　　　　　　　　Notary Public.

# Applications for Enrollment of Choctaw Newborn
## Act of 1905   Volume XIII

United States of America, )
)
Indian Territory, )  ss.
)
Central District. )

    I, Byington Bond, on oath state that I am forty-four years of age and a citizen by blood of the Choctaw Nation; that I am personally acquainted with Lincey Hicks, wife of Cephus Hicks; that I have known said parties for about twenty year; that during the time I have known said parties they have lived within four miles of where I have lived near Bethel, Indian Territory; that there was born to the said Lincey Hicks on or about the 6th day of April, 1903, a male child; that said child is now living and is said to have been named Adam Hicks.

                                                                                   his
                                                  Byington x Bond
                                                        mark

Subscribed and sworn to before me this 5th day of April, 1905.

                                                          Wirt Franklin
                                                              Notary Public.

Witnesses to mark.
  Robert Anderson
  Vester W Rose

---

*(The affidavit below typed as given.)*

United States of America,
Indian Territory
Central District.
        Affidavit of Acquaintance.

    I John Noah on oath state that I am 21 years of age and a citizen by blood of the Choctaw Nation, that my post office address is Noah, Ind. Ter. that I am not related to the applicant who is citizen by blood of the Choctaw Nation, that I am personally acquainted with Lincey Hicks, wife of Cephus Hicks, who is a citizen by blood of the Choctaw Nation, and that a male child was born to Lincey Hicks on the April 8[sic], 1903 and that said male child has been named Adam Hicks, and the said Adam Hicks was living on the 4$^{th}$ day of March 1905, and is now living, and that I have personal knowledge that Lincey Hicks the mother of said Adam Hicks

                                       John Noah

Subscribed and sworn to before me this 12$^{th}$ day of June 1905.

                                              W.H. McKinney
                                              Notary Public.

# Applications for Enrollment of Choctaw Newborn
## Act of 1905 Volume XIII

My Commission
expires March 30- 1909

DEPARTMENT OF THE INTERIOR,
Commission to the Five Civilized Tribes.

**FILED**
JUN 21 1905

Tams Bixby CHAIRMAN

---

**BIRTH AFFIDAVIT.**

### DEPARTMENT OF THE INTERIOR.
### COMMISSION TO THE FIVE CIVILIZED TRIBES.

---

IN RE APPLICATION FOR ENROLLMENT, as a citizen of the Choctaw Nation, of Adam Hicks, born on the 6th day of April, 1903

Name of Father: Cephus Hicks     a citizen of the Choctaw Nation.
Name of Mother: Lincey Hicks     a citizen of the Choctaw Nation.

Postoffice    Bethel, Ind. Ter.

---

**AFFIDAVIT OF MOTHER.**

UNITED STATES OF AMERICA, Indian Territory,
Central DISTRICT.

I, Lincey Hicks, on oath state that I am 27 years of age and a citizen by blood, of the Choctaw Nation; that I am the lawful wife of Cephus Hicks, who is a citizen, by blood of the Choctaw Nation; that a male child was born to me on 6th day of April, 1903; that said child has been named Adam Hicks, and was living March 4, 1905. *and that no physician or mid-wife attended me at the birth of said child*

                                       her
                              Lincey x Hicks
Witnesses To Mark:            mark
    { Robert Anderson
      Vester W Rose

Subscribed and sworn to before me this 5th day of April, 1905

                         Wirt Franklin
                           Notary Public.

## Applications for Enrollment of Choctaw Newborn
## Act of 1905   Volume XIII

### AFFIDAVIT OF ATTENDING PHYSICIAN OR MID-WIFE.

UNITED STATES OF AMERICA, Indian Territory, }
Central       DISTRICT.

I,   Cephus Hicks   , a ......................., on oath state that I attended on Mrs. Lincey Hicks   my   , wife ~~of~~ ....................... on the 6th day of April, 1903; that there was born to her on said date a   male   child; that said child was living March 4, 1905, and is said to have been named Adam Hicks *and that no one else was present at the birth of said child*

his
Cephus x Hicks
Witnesses To Mark:             mark
  { Robert Anderson
  { Vester W Rose

Subscribed and sworn to before me this  5th  day of  April  , 1905

Wirt Franklin
Notary Public.

---

Choc New Born 908
  William Leo Ellis  b. 10-23-04

### AFFIDAVIT OF ATTENDING PHYSICIAN OR MIDWIFE

UNITED STATES OF AMERICA
INDIAN TERRITORY
  Central    DISTRICT
             *Caroline*
I,   ~~Mary~~ Davis    a       midwife
on oath state that I attended on Mrs. Ada B. Ellis    wife of  Thomas J Ellis
on the  23  day of  October  , 190 4 , that there was born to her on said date a   male child, that said child is now living, and is said to have been named William Leo Ellis

Caroline Davis     *M.D.*
Subscribed and sworn to before me this, the   22    day of
  February     190 5

WITNESSETH:                James Bower    Notary Public.
Must be two witnesses  { E A Moore
who are citizens       { *(Name Illegible)*

138

## Applications for Enrollment of Choctaw Newborn
## Act of 1905 Volume XIII

We hereby certify that we are well acquainted with Caroline Davis a midwife and know her to be reputable and of good standing in the community.

_____   E A Moore

_____   *(Name Illegible)*

BIRTH AFFIDAVIT.

### DEPARTMENT OF THE INTERIOR.
### COMMISSION TO THE FIVE CIVILIZED TRIBES.

**IN RE APPLICATION FOR ENROLLMENT**, as a citizen of the Choctaw Nation, of William Leo Ellis , born on the 23rd day of October , 1904

Name of Father: John Thomas Ellis    a citizen of the United States ~~Nation~~.
Name of Mother: Ada Byron Ellis    a citizen of the Choctaw Nation.

Postoffice   Oaklodge, Ind. Ter.

**AFFIDAVIT OF MOTHER.**

UNITED STATES OF AMERICA, Indian Territory,  }
    Central           DISTRICT.

I, Ada Byron Ellis , on oath state that I am 20 years of age and a citizen by blood , of the Choctaw Nation; that I am the lawful wife of John Thomas Ellis , who is a citizen, ~~by~~ ................. of the United States ~~Nation~~; that a male child was born to me on 23rd day of October , 1904; that said child has been named William Leo Ellis , and was living March 4, 1905.

Ada Byron Ellis

Witnesses To Mark:
{

Subscribed and sworn to before me this 31st day of March , 1905

Wirt Franklin
Notary Public.

## Applications for Enrollment of Choctaw Newborn
## Act of 1905   Volume XIII

**AFFIDAVIT OF ATTENDING PHYSICIAN OR MID-WIFE.**

UNITED STATES OF AMERICA, Indian Territory,  
　Central　　　　　　　　DISTRICT.

   I, Caroline Davis, a mid wife, on oath state that I attended on Mrs. Ada Byron Ellis, wife of John Thomas Ellis on the 23rd day of October, 1904; that there was born to her on said date a male child; that said child was living March 4, 1905, and is said to have been named William Leo Ellis

　　　　　　　　　　　　　　　　Caroline Davis

Witnesses To Mark:
{

   Subscribed and sworn to before me this 31st day of March, 1905

　　　　　　　　　　　　　　　Wirt Franklin
　　　　　　　　　　　　　　　　Notary Public.

---

**NEW-BORN AFFIDAVIT.**

　　　　　Number..............

### ...Choctaw Enrolling Commission...

---

   IN THE MATTER OF THE APPLICATION FOR ENROLLMENT, as a citizen of the Choctaw Nation, of Willia Leo Ellis

born on the 23 day of ___October___ 190 4

Name of father  Thomas[sic] J[sic] Ellis　　　　a citizen of　white  
Nation final enrollment No. —  
Name of mother  Ada B Ellis　　　　　　　　a citizen of　Choctaw  
Nation final enrollment No. 7530

　　　　　　　　　　　　　　Postoffice　Oak Lodge I.T.

**AFFIDAVIT OF MOTHER.**

UNITED STATES OF AMERICA  
INDIAN TERRITORY  
　Central　　DISTRICT

   I   Ada B Ellis　　　　　　, on oath state that I am 19 years of age and a citizen by blood of the Choctaw Nation, and as such have been placed upon the final roll of the Choctaw Nation, by the Honorable Secretary of the Interior my final enrollment number being 7530 ; that I am the lawful wife

# Applications for Enrollment of Choctaw Newborn
## Act of 1905   Volume XIII

of  Thomas J Ellis  , who is a citizen of the  ——  Nation, and as such has been placed upon the final roll of said Nation by the Honorable Secretary of the Interior, his final enrollment number being  ——  and that a  Male  child was born to me on the  23 day of  October  190 4; that said child has been named  William Leo Ellis , and is now living.

Ada B Ellis

Witnesseth.

Must be two Witnesses who are Citizens.   } E A Moore

(Name Illegible)

Subscribed and sworn to before me this  22  day of  Feb  190 5

James Bower<br>Notary Public.

My commission expires:
Sept 23-1907

---

Choc New Born 909
   Clayton Wade  b. 12-9-03

7 NB 909

Muskogee, Indian Territory, May 5, 1905.

Barnett Wade,
   Eagletown, Indian Territory.

Dear Sir:

Receipt is hereby acknowledged of the joint affidavit of Abbott Elliott and Lamus Stpehen[sic] to the birth of Clayton Wade son of Barnett and Emeline Wade, December 9, 1903, and the same have been filed with our records as an application for the enrollment of said child.

Respectfully,<br><br>Commissioner in Charge.

# Applications for Enrollment of Choctaw Newborn
## Act of 1905   Volume XIII

7-NB-909

Muskogee, Indian Territory, July 14, 1905.

Barnett Wade,
    Eagletown, Indian Territory.

Dear Sir:

    Receipt is hereby acknowledged of the affidavits of Roar Hydson[sic] and Dixon Tonehka to the birth of Clayton Wade son of Barnett and Emeline Wade, December 9, 1903, and the same have been filed with the records of this office in the matter of the enrollment of said child.

Respectfully,

Commissioner.

---

$W^m O.B.$

| COMMISSIONERS:<br>TAMS BIXBY,<br>THOMAS B. NEEDLES,<br>C.R. BRECKINBRIDGE.<br><br>WM. O. BEALL<br>Secretary | **DEPARTMENT OF THE INTERIOR,**<br>**COMMISSIONER TO THE FIVE CIVILIZED TRIBES.** | REFER IN REPLY TO THE FOLLOWING:<br><br>7-NB-909. |

ADDRESS ONLY THE
COMMISSION TO THE FIVE CIVILIZED TRIBES.

Muskogee, Indian Territory, May 31, 1905.

Barnett Wade,
    Eagletown, Indian Territory.

Dear Sir:

    Referring to the application for the enrollment of your infant child, Clayton Wade, born December 9, 1903, it is noted that you were the only one in attendance upon your wife at the time of birth of the applicant.

    In this event it will be necessary that you file in this office the affidavits of two persons, who are disinterested and not related to the applicant, who have actual knowledge of the facts that the child was born, the date of his birth; that he was living on March 4, 1905, and that Emeline Wade is his mother. The affidavits of Abbott Elliott and Lamus Stephen, heretofore filed in this office, show the child was living on March 3, 1905, and are, therefore, insufficient.

Respectfully,
Tams Bixby
Chairman.

# Applications for Enrollment of Choctaw Newborn
## Act of 1905 Volume XIII

Indian Territory
  Eagletown, Choctaw Nation
  Central District

    Be it remembered that on this the 29$^{th}$ day of April 1905, personally appeared before me the undersigned, a notary public within and for the Central Judicial District of the United States Court for Indian Territory at Eagletown I.T, duly commissioned and acting. Abbott Elliott 28 years of age and Lamus Stephen 35 years of age, both of them to me personally well known, on oath states as follows: That I am personally well acquainted with Barnett Wade and his wife Emeline Wade and that on the 9$^{th}$ day of December 1903 a male child was born to them, named Claton Wade and was living on March 3$^{rd}$ 1905.

                                                                        his
                                                                     Abbott x Elliott
Witness Scott Gardner                      mark
  (Name Illegible)                            his
                                                                   Lamus x Stephen
                                                                    mark

Subscribed and sworn to before me this the 29$^{th}$ day of April 1905

My Commission                                      Jeff Gardner
    Expires 23$^{rd}$ Dec 1905                      Notary Public

---

*(The affidavit below typed as given.)*

United States of America,
    Indian Territory,
    Central District.

    I    Roar Hudson    on oath states that I am    22    years of age, that my post office address is    Eagletown I.T.    that I am personally acquainted with    Emeline Wade    and know that there was born to her on the    9$^{th}$    day of    December 1903    a male child, said child was named    Clayton Wade    and was living on march 4, 1905.

                                                        Roar Hudson

Sworh to and subscribed before me this    8$^{th}$    day of    July    1905.

                                                    Jeff Gardner
                                                    Notary public.
My commission expires 23 December 1905.

# Applications for Enrollment of Choctaw Newborn
## Act of 1905   Volume XIII

*(The affidavit below typed as given.)*

United States of America,
    Indian Territory,
    Central District.

    I   Dixon Tonehka   on oath states that I am   36   years of age, that my post office address is   Eagletown I.T.   that I am personally acquainted with   Emeline Wade   and know that there was born to her on the   9$^{th}$   day of   December 1903   a male   child, said child was named   Clayton Wade   and was living on march 4, 1905.

                                  Dixon Tonehka

Sworh to and subscribed before me this   8$^{th}$   day of   July   1905.

                                  Jeff Gardner
                                  Notary public.
My commission expires 23 December 1905.

---

**BIRTH AFFIDAVIT.**

## DEPARTMENT OF THE INTERIOR.
## COMMISSION TO THE FIVE CIVILIZED TRIBES.

---

    **IN RE APPLICATION FOR ENROLLMENT,** as a citizen of the   Choctaw   Nation, of   Clayton Wade   , born on the 9th   day of   December   , 1903

Name of Father: Barnett Wade       a citizen of the   Choctaw   Nation.
Name of Mother: Emeline Wade       a citizen of the   Choctaw   Nation.

                      Postoffice   Eagletown, Ind Ter.

---

**AFFIDAVIT OF MOTHER.**

UNITED STATES OF AMERICA, Indian Territory, }
    Central                DISTRICT.

    I,   Emeline Wade   , on oath state that I am   25   years of age and a citizen by   blood   , of the   Choctaw   Nation; that I am the lawful wife of   Barnett Wade   , who is a citizen, by blood   of the   Choctaw   Nation; that a male   child was born to me on   9th   day of   December   , 1903; that said child has been named   Clayton Wade   , and was living March 4, 1905. *and that no physician or midwife attended me*       her

                                Emeline x Wade
                                  mark

# Applications for Enrollment of Choctaw Newborn
## Act of 1905 Volume XIII

Witnesses To Mark:
- Robert Anderson
- Vester W Rose

Subscribed and sworn to before me this 12th day of April, 1905

Wirt Franklin
Notary Public.

---

**AFFIDAVIT OF ATTENDING PHYSICIAN OR MID-WIFE.**

UNITED STATES OF AMERICA, Indian Territory,
Central DISTRICT.

I, Barnett Wade, ~~a~~ , on oath state that I attended on Mrs. Emeline Wade, ~~wife of~~ *my wife* on the 9th day of December, 1903; that there was born to her on said date a male child; that said child was living March 4, 1905, and is said to have been named Clayton Wade *and that no one else was present when said child was born*

Barnett Wade

Witnesses To Mark:

Subscribed and sworn to before me this 12th day of April, 1905

Wirt Franklin
Notary Public.

---

Choc New Born 910
Acy Fobb b. 11-1-04

BIRTH AFFIDAVIT.

**DEPARTMENT OF THE INTERIOR.**
**COMMISSION TO THE FIVE CIVILIZED TRIBES.**

IN RE APPLICATION FOR ENROLLMENT, as a citizen of the Choctaw Nation, of Acy Fobb, born on the 1st day of November, 1904

Name of Father: Simeon Fobb    a citizen of the Choctaw Nation.
Name of Mother: Eliza Fobb    a citizen of the Choctaw Nation.

# Applications for Enrollment of Choctaw Newborn
## Act of 1905   Volume XIII

Postoffice   Eagletown, Ind. Ter.

**AFFIDAVIT OF MOTHER.**

UNITED STATES OF AMERICA, Indian Territory,  
Central   DISTRICT.

I, Eliza Fobb, on oath state that I am 40 years of age and a citizen by blood, of the Choctaw Nation; that I am the lawful wife of Simeon Fobb, who is a citizen, by blood of the Choctaw Nation; that a female child was born to me on 1st day of November, 1904; that said child has been named Acy Fobb, and was living March 4, 1905.

                      her  
                    Eliza x Fobb  
Witnesses To Mark:      mark  
{ Robert Anderson  
  Simeon Jacob

Subscribed and sworn to before me this 10th day of April, 1905

                  Wirt Franklin  
                  Notary Public.

**AFFIDAVIT OF ATTENDING PHYSICIAN OR MID-WIFE.**

UNITED STATES OF AMERICA, Indian Territory,  
Central   DISTRICT

I, Selina Hotubbee, a mid-wife, on oath state that I attended on Mrs. Eliza Fobb, wife of Simeon Fobb on the 1st day of November, 1904; that there was born to her on said date a female child; that said child was living March 4, 1905, and is said to have been named Acy Fobb

                    her  
                Selina x Hotubbee  
Witnesses To Mark:    mark  
{ Robert Anderson  
  Simeon Jacob

Subscribed and sworn to before me this 10th day of April, 1905

                  Wirt Franklin  
                Notary Public.

## Applications for Enrollment of Choctaw Newborn
## Act of 1905 Volume XIII

Choc New Born 911
Sallie James   b. 11-24-03

Choctaw 2153.

Muskogee, Indian Territory, April 14, 1905.

Patterson James,
Muse, Indian Territory.

Dear Sir:

Receipt is hereby acknowledged of the affidavit of Sallie Ann Williams, Crawford J. Anderson, Sarah James and Patterson James to the birth of Sallie James, daughter of Patterson and Sarah James, November 24, 1903, and the same have been filed with our records as an application for the enrollment of said child.

Respectfully,

Commissioner in Charge.

I Sallie Ann Williams do solemnly swear that I am personally acquainted with Sarah James wife of Patterson James and that their child born November 24 1903 has been named Sallie James and was liveing[sic] March 4 1905 my age is 55 years my Post Office Talihina I T

                                        her
                                  Sallie x Ann Williams
Witness to mark                    mark
Crawford J Anderson  Interpreter
Markus L Thomas

Subscribed and sworn to before me this 10 day of April 1905

Sam T. Roberts Jr

My commission expires Feb. 4, 1908
Commission from U.S. Court at So. McAlester I.T.
MY OFFICE TALIHINA, I. T.

## Applications for Enrollment of Choctaw Newborn
## Act of 1905   Volume XIII

I C J Anderson do solemnly swear that I am personally acquainted with Sarah James wife of Patterson James and that her child born November 24 1903 has been named Sallie James and was liveing[sic] March 4 1905, my age is 37 my Post Office Talihina I T

Crawford J Anderson

Subscribed and sworn to before me this 10 day of April 1905

My commission expires Feb. 4, 1908
Commission from U.S. Court at So. McAlester I.T.
MY OFFICE TALIHINA, I. T.

Sam T. Roberts Jr

**BIRTH AFFIDAVIT.**

### DEPARTMENT OF THE INTERIOR.
### COMMISSION TO THE FIVE CIVILIZED TRIBES.

**IN RE APPLICATION FOR ENROLLMENT,** as a citizen of the Choctaw Nation, of Sallie James, born on the 24 day of November, 1903

Name of Father: Patterson James    a citizen of the Choctaw Nation.
Name of Mother: Sarah James    a citizen of the Choctaw Nation.

Postoffice    Muse, I T

*CJ Anderson Interpreter*

### AFFIDAVIT OF MOTHER.

UNITED STATES OF AMERICA, Indian Territory,
Central    DISTRICT.

I, Sarah James, on oath state that I am about 28 years of age and a citizen by Blood, of the Choctaw Nation; that I am the lawful wife of Patterson James, who is a citizen, by Blood of the Choctaw Nation; that a female child was born to me on 24 day of November, 1903; that said child has been named Sallie James, and was living March 4, 1905.

Sarah James

Witnesses To Mark:
{

Subscribed and sworn to before me this 10 day of April, 1905

Sam T. Roberts Jr
Notary Public.

## Applications for Enrollment of Choctaw Newborn
## Act of 1905   Volume XIII

### AFFIDAVIT OF ATTENDING PHYSICIAN OR MID-WIFE.

UNITED STATES OF AMERICA, Indian Territory,
Central        DISTRICT.

I, Patterson James  , a  ————  , on oath state that I attended on Mrs. Sarah James  , wife of  *my wife*  on the 24 day of November  , 1903; that there was born to her on said date a  female  child; that said child was living March 4, 1905, and is said to have been named Sallie James

              Patterson James

Witnesses To Mark:
{

Subscribed and sworn to before me this  10  day of  April  , 1905

            Sam T. Roberts Jr
            Notary Public.

---

Choc New Born 912
  Mary A. Plummer   b. 2-4-03

---

                Choctaw 4046.

          Muskogee, Indian Territory, April 14, 1905.

Raymond Plummer,
  Nixon, Indian Territory.

Dear Sir:

  Receipt is hereby acknowledged of the affidavits of Laura B. Plummer and Mary S. Plummer to the birth of Mary A. Plummer, daughter of Raymond and Laura B. Plummer, February 4, 1903, and the same have been filed with our records as an application for the enrollment of said child.

          Respectfully,

              Commissioner in Charge.

## Applications for Enrollment of Choctaw Newborn
## Act of 1905 Volume XIII

**BIRTH AFFIDAVIT.**

### DEPARTMENT OF THE INTERIOR.
### COMMISSION TO THE FIVE CIVILIZED TRIBES.

IN RE APPLICATION FOR ENROLLMENT, as a citizen of the Choctaw Nation, of Mary A Plummer, born on the 4$^{th}$ day of February, 1903

Name of Father: Raymond Plummer  a citizen of the Choctaw Nation.
Name of Mother: Laura B Plummer  a citizen of the Choctaw Nation.

Postoffice  Nixon IT

**AFFIDAVIT OF MOTHER.**

UNITED STATES OF AMERICA, Indian Territory, }
Central  DISTRICT. }

I, Laura B Plummer, on oath state that I am 30 years of age and a citizen by marriage, of the Choctaw Nation; that I am the lawful wife of Raymond Plummer, who is a citizen, by Blood of the Choctaw Nation; that a Female child was born to me on 4$^{th}$ day of February, 1903; that said child has been named Mary A Plummer, and was living March 4, 1905.

Laura B Plummer

Witnesses To Mark:
 { Jno R Warren
 { J.A. Strong

Subscribed and sworn to before me this 11$^{th}$ day of April, 1905

Commission expires  Jno D Baldwin
4/6/08  Notary Public.

**AFFIDAVIT OF ATTENDING PHYSICIAN OR MID-WIFE.**

UNITED STATES OF AMERICA, Indian Territory, }
Central  DISTRICT. }

I, Mary S Plummer, a midwife, on oath state that I attended on Mrs. Mary A Plummer, wife of Raymond Plummer on the 4$^{th}$ day of February, 1903; that there was born to her on said date a Female child; that said child was living March 4, 1905, and is said to have been named Mary A Plummer

Mary S Plummer

# Applications for Enrollment of Choctaw Newborn
# Act of 1905   Volume XIII

Witnesses To Mark:
{ Jno R Warren
{ J.A. Strong

Subscribed and sworn to before me this  11$^{th}$  day of April  , 1905

Jno D Baldwin
Notary Public.

## AFFIDAVIT OF ATTENDING PHYSICIAN OR MIDWIFE

UNITED STATES OF AMERICA }
INDIAN TERRITORY
   Central       DISTRICT

I,  Mrs M S Plummer       a       midwife on oath state that I attended on Mrs.  Laura B Plummer   wife of  Raymond Plummer on the   Fourth    day of  February  , 190 3 , that there was born to her on said date a Female  child, that said child is now living, and is said to have been named Mary A Plummer

M.S. Plummer   ~~M.D.~~ *midwife*

Subscribed and sworn to before me this, the  20$^{th}$  day of  January       190 5

William K Morgan
Notary Public.

WITNESSETH:
Must be two witnesses  { Lewis Benton
who are citizens and   {
know the child.        { Ellen Benton

We hereby certify that we are well acquainted with   M.S. Plummer a   Midwife      and know    her     to be reputable and of good standing in the community.

{ Lewis Benton
{ Ellen Benton

## Applications for Enrollment of Choctaw Newborn
## Act of 1905 Volume XIII

**NEW-BORN AFFIDAVIT.**

Number..................

## Choctaw Enrolling Commission.

IN THE MATTER OF THE APPLICATION FOR ENROLLMENT, as a citizen of the Choctaw Nation, of Mary A Plummer

born on the Fourth day of February 1903

Name of father Raymond Plummer a citizen of Choctaw Nation final enrollment No 11381
Name of mother Laura B Plummer a citizen of Choctaw Nation final enrollment No 381

Postoffice Nixon IT

**AFFIDAVIT OF MOTHER.**

UNITED STATES OF AMERICA, }
  INDIAN TERRITORY, }
  Central DISTRICT }

I Laura B Plummer on oath state that I am Thirty years of age and a citizen by Intermarriage of the Choctaw Nation, and as such have been placed upon the final roll of the Choctaw Nation, by the Honorable Secretary of the Interior my final enrollment number being 381 ; that I am the lawful wife of Raymond Plummer , who is a citizen of the Choctaw Nation, and as such has been placed upon the final roll of said Nation by the Honorable Secretary of the Interior, his final enrollment number being 11318 and that a Female child was born to me on the Fourth day of February 1903 ; that said child has been named Mary A Plummer , and is now living.

WITNESSETH: Laura B Plummer

Must be two Witnesses who are Citizens. } Lewis Benton
Ellen Benton

Subscribed and sworn to before me this 20th day of January 1905

William K Morgan
Notary Public.

My commission expires Feb 13th 1907

# Applications for Enrollment of Choctaw Newborn
## Act of 1905 Volume XIII

Choc New Born 913
Oscar Lee Bacon b. 4-1-04

Choctaw 2123.

Muskogee, Indian Territory, April 14, 1906.

Jefferson Bacon,
Talihina, Indian Territory.

Dear Sir:

Receipt is hereby acknowledged of the affidavits of Melvinie Bacon and Leviney Anderson to the birth of Oscar Lee Bacon, son of Jefferson and Melvinie Bacon, April 1, 1904, and the same have been filed with our records as an application for the enrollment of said child.

Respectfully,

Commissioner in Charge.

**BIRTH AFFIDAVIT.**
### DEPARTMENT OF THE INTERIOR.
### COMMISSION TO THE FIVE CIVILIZED TRIBES.

**IN RE APPLICATION FOR ENROLLMENT,** as a citizen of the Choctaw Nation, of Oscar Lee Bacon, born on the 1 day of April, 1904

Name of Father: Jefferson Bacon          a citizen of the Choctaw Nation.
Name of Mother: Melviney[sic] Bacon      a citizen of the Choctaw Nation.

Postoffice   Talihina I.T.

**AFFIDAVIT OF MOTHER.**

UNITED STATES OF AMERICA, Indian Territory,
Central           DISTRICT.

I, Melvinie Bacon, on oath state that I am about 25 years of age and a citizen by Blood, of the Choctaw Nation; that I am the lawful wife of Jefferson Bacon, who is a citizen, by Blood of the Choctaw Nation; that a male child was born to me on 1st day of April, 1904, that said child has been named Oscar Lee Bacon, and is now living.

# Applications for Enrollment of Choctaw Newborn
## Act of 1905   Volume XIII

Melvinie Bacon

Witnesses To Mark:
{

Subscribed and sworn to before me this   10   day of   April   , 1905.

Sam T. Roberts, Jr.
Notary Public.

---

**AFFIDAVIT OF ATTENDING PHYSICIAN OR MID-WIFE.**

UNITED STATES OF AMERICA, Indian Territory, }
  Central           DISTRICT.

I,   Leviney Anderson   , a   Midwife   , on oath state that I attended on Mrs.   Melvinie Bacon   , wife of   Jefferson Bacon   on the   1st   day of April   , 1904; that there was born to her on said date a   male   child; that said child is now living and is said to have been named   Oscar Lee Bacon

                          her
                 Leviney  x  Anderson

Witnesses To Mark:           mark
{ Solomon Daney
  D. Thomas

Subscribed and sworn to before me this   10   day of   April   , 1905.

Sam T. Roberts, Jr.
Notary Public.

---

Choc New Born 914
    Don W. Cochnauer  b. 7-5-03

## Applications for Enrollment of Choctaw Newborn
## Act of 1905  Volume XIII

BIRTH AFFIDAVIT.

### DEPARTMENT OF THE INTERIOR.
### COMMISSION TO THE FIVE CIVILIZED TRIBES.

**IN RE APPLICATION FOR ENROLLMENT,** as a citizen of the Choctaw Nation, of Don W. Cochnauer, born on the 5 day of July, 1903

Name of Father: David W. Cochnauer    a citizen of the Choctaw Nation.
Name of Mother: Rhoda Cochnauer    a citizen of the Choctaw Nation.

Postoffice    Bokchito Ind. Ter.

### AFFIDAVIT OF MOTHER.

UNITED STATES OF AMERICA, Indian Territory, } 
Central    DISTRICT.

I, Mrs. Rhoda Cochnauer, on oath state that I am 29 years of age and a citizen by Blood, of the Choctaw Nation; that I am the lawful wife of David W. Cochnauer, who is a citizen, by Blood of the Choctaw Nation; that a male child was born to me on 5 day of July, 1903; that said child has been named Don W. Cochnauer, and was living March 4, 1905.

Rhoda Cochnauer

Witnesses To Mark:
{

Subscribed and sworn to before me this 11$^{th}$ day of April, 1905

E.W. Frey
Notary Public.

### AFFIDAVIT OF ATTENDING PHYSICIAN OR MID-WIFE.

UNITED STATES OF AMERICA, Indian Territory, }
Central    DISTRICT.

I, J J Breaker, a Physician, on oath state that I attended on Mrs. Rhoda Cochnauer, wife of David W Cochnauer on the 5 day of July, 1903; that there was born to her on said date a male child; that said child was living March 4, 1905, and is said to have been named Don W Cochnauer

J J Breaker

Witnesses To Mark:
{

## Applications for Enrollment of Choctaw Newborn
## Act of 1905   Volume XIII

Subscribed and sworn to before me this 11<sup>th</sup> day of April, 1905

                E.W. Frey
                      Notary Public.

---

                              Choctaw 3576.

            Muskogee, Indian Territory, April 14, 1905.

David W. Cochnauer,
    Bokchito, Indian Territory.

Dear Sir:

    Receipt is hereby acknowledged of the affidavits of Rhoda Cochnauer and J. J. Breaker to the birth of Don W. Cochnauer, son of David W. and Rhoda Cochnauer, July 5, 1903, and the same have been filed with our records as an application for the enrollment of said child.

                Respectfully,

                              Commissioner in Charge.

---

**NEW-BORN AFFIDAVIT.**

        Number...............

## Choctaw Enrolling Commission.

    IN THE MATTER OF THE APPLICATION FOR ENROLLMENT, as a citizen of the Choctaw   Nation, of   Don W. Cochnauer

born on the  5   day of   July   190 3

Name of father   David W. Cochnauer   a citizen of   Choctaw Nation
Nation final enrollment No   10113
Name of mother   Rhoda Cochnauer   a citizen of   Choctaw
Nation final enrollment No   10114

                Postoffice   Bokchito I.T.

# Applications for Enrollment of Choctaw Newborn
## Act of 1905   Volume XIII

### AFFIDAVIT OF MOTHER.

UNITED STATES OF AMERICA,  
INDIAN TERRITORY,  
Cent Jud        DISTRICT

I     Rhoda Cochnauer     on oath state that I am 28 years of age and a citizen by  blood  of the Choctaw Nation, and as such have been placed upon the final roll of the Choctaw Nation, by the Honorable Secretary of the Interior my final enrollment number being  10114 ; that I am the lawful wife of  David W Cochnauer , who is a citizen of the Choctaw Nation, and as such has been placed upon the final roll of said Nation by the Honorable Secretary of the Interior, his final enrollment number being  10113  and that a  male child was born to me on the  5  day of  July  190 3 ; that said child has been named  Don W Cochnauer , and is now living.

Rhoda Cochnauer

WITNESSETH:  
Must be two Witnesses who are Citizens.     Daniel H Gardner  
*(Name Illegible)*

Subscribed and sworn to before me this   23ᵈ   day of   Jany    190 5

E.W. Frey  
Notary Public.

My commission expires _____

---

## AFFIDAVIT OF ATTENDING PHYSICIAN OR MIDWIFE

*State of Missouri*  
*City of St. Louis*

I,   J. J. Breaker   a   physician   on oath state that I attended on Mrs. Rhoda Cochnauer   wife of  David W. Cochnauer  on the  5ᵗʰ  day of  July , 190 3 , that there was born to her on said date a  Male child, that said child is now living, and is said to have been named   Don W. Cochnauer

J.J. Breaker                                M.D.

Subscribed and sworn to before me this, the  27ᵗʰ  day of  January   190 5  
*My com expires April 10-1908*

*(Name Illegible)*  
Notary Public.

WITNESSETH:  
Must be two witnesses who are citizens and know the child.     D H Gardner  
*(Name Illegible)*

# Applications for Enrollment of Choctaw Newborn
## Act of 1905   Volume XIII

      We hereby certify that we are well acquainted with   J.J. Breaker a physician   and know   him   to be reputable and of good standing in the community.

$\left\{\begin{array}{l}\text{James Boland} \\ \text{T.J. Impson}\end{array}\right.$

---

Choc New Born 915
    Elisebeth[sic] Compton   b. 12-22-04

---

                                              Choctaw 3368.

                Muskogee, Indian Territory, April 14, 1905.

E. W. Compton,
    Amos, Indian Territory.

Dear Sir:

      Receipt is hereby acknowledged of the affidavits of Sarah Compton and Betty Compton to the birth of Elizabeth Compton, daughter of E. W. and Sarah Compton, December 22, 1904, and the same have been filed with our records as an application for the enrollment of said child.

                              Respectfully,

                                              Commissioner in Charge.

---

                                                  7-NB-915
                                                  7-3368

                Muskogee, Indian Territory, July 14, 1905.

E. W. Compton,
    Amos, Indian Territory.

Dear Sir:

      Receipt is hereby acknowledged of your letter of July 3, 1905, addresses to the United States Indian Agent which has been by him referred to this office for appropriate action. Therein you ask why your child Elizabeth Compton has not yet been approved;

## Applications for Enrollment of Choctaw Newborn
## Act of 1905   Volume XIII

and request to be advised if you can be approved as an intermarried citizen as you married Sarah H. Compton in 1894 under United States law.

In reply to your letter you are advised that the name of your daughter Elisebeth[sic] has been placed upon a schedule of citizens by blood of the Choctaw Nation which has been forwarded the Secretary of the Interior and you will be notified when her enrollment is approved by the Department.

You are further advised that it does not appear that application was made to the Commission to the Five Civilized Tribes prior to December 25, 1902, for your enrollment as an intermarried citizen of the Choctaw Nation and under the provisions of the act of Congress approved July 1, 1902, no authority now exists for the reception of original applications for enrollment in the Choctaw and Chickasaw Nations.

Respectfully,

Commissioner.

---

7-NB-915

Muskogee, Indian Territory, February 11, 1907.

Sarah Compton,
Amos, Indian Territory.

Dear Madam:

Receipt is hereby acknowledged of your letter of February 2, 1907, asking the status of the enrollment of your child.

In reply to your letter you are advised that on July 22, 1905, the Secretary of the Interior approved the enrollment of Elisabeth Compton, child of E. W. and Sarah Compton, as a new born citizen of the Choctaw Nation under the Act of Congress approved March 3, 1905.

Respectfully,

Commissioner.

## Applications for Enrollment of Choctaw Newborn
## Act of 1905   Volume XIII

BIRTH AFFIDAVIT.

### DEPARTMENT OF THE INTERIOR.
### COMMISSION TO THE FIVE CIVILIZED TRIBES.

IN RE APPLICATION FOR ENROLLMENT, as a citizen of the Choctaw Nation, of Elisebeth Compton, born on the 22 day of Dec, 1904

Name of Father: E. W. Compton      a citizen of the Choctaw Nation.
Name of Mother: Sarah Compton      a citizen of the Choctaw Nation.

Postoffice   Amos I.T.

### AFFIDAVIT OF MOTHER.

UNITED STATES OF AMERICA, Indian Territory,
Southern           DISTRICT.

I, Sarah Compton, on oath state that I am 27 years of age and a citizen by Birth, of the Choctaw Nation; that I am the lawful wife of E.W. Compton, who is a citizen, by Intermarriage of the Choctaw Nation; that a Female child was born to me on 22 day of December, 1904; that said child has been named Elisebeth Compton, and was living March 4, 1905.

                her
           Sarah x Compton
Witnesses To Mark:    mark
  Emma Compton
  Amanda Compton

Subscribed and sworn to before me this 4 day of April, 1905

        M.D. Bell
          Notary Public.

### AFFIDAVIT OF ATTENDING PHYSICIAN OR MID-WIFE.

UNITED STATES OF AMERICA, Indian Territory,
................................................... DISTRICT.

I, Betty Compton, a midwife, on oath state that I attended on Mrs. Sarah Compton, wife of E. W. Compton on the 22 day of Dec, 1904; that there was born to her on said date a Female child; that said child was living March 4, 1905, and is said to have been named Elisebeth Compton

           her
      Betty x Compton
        mark

## Applications for Enrollment of Choctaw Newborn
## Act of 1905 Volume XIII

Witnesses To Mark:
{ Emma Compton
{ Amanda Compton

Subscribed and sworn to before me this 4 day of   April   , 1905

M.D. Bell
Notary Public.

---

Choc New Born 916
Sarah N. C. Strickland  b. 4-25-04

Choctaw 3496.

Muskogee, Indian Territory, April 14, 1904[sic].

C. E. Strickland,
Utica, Indian Territory.

Dear Sir:

Receipt is hereby acknowledged of the affidavits of Arcola Strickland and A. J. Wells to the birth of Sarah N.C. Strickland, daughter of C. E. and Arcola Strickland, April 25, 1904, and the same have been filed with our records as an application for the enrollment of said child.

Respectfully,

Commissioner in Charge.

**NEW-BORN AFFIDAVIT.**

Number..............

## Choctaw Enrolling Commission.

IN THE MATTER OF THE APPLICATION FOR ENROLLMENT, as a citizen of the Choctaw   Nation, of   Sarah N. C. Strickland

born on the 25   day of   April   190 4

## Applications for Enrollment of Choctaw Newborn
## Act of 1905 Volume XIII

Name of father  Charles E. Strickland         a citizen of   white
Nation final enrollment No  —
Name of mother  Arcola Strickland             a citizen of   Choctaw
Nation final enrollment No  9951

Postoffice   Utica I.T.

### AFFIDAVIT OF MOTHER.

UNITED STATES OF AMERICA,  
INDIAN TERRITORY,  
Central       DISTRICT

I          Arcola Strickland                          on oath state that I am 30 years of age and a citizen by blood of the Choctaw Nation, and as such have been placed upon the final roll of the Choctaw Nation, by the Honorable Secretary of the Interior my final enrollment number being 9951 ; that I am the lawful wife of Charles E. Strickland, who is a citizen of the Choctaw Nation, and as such has been placed upon the final roll of said Nation by the Honorable Secretary of the Interior, his final enrollment number being —— and that a female child was born to me on the 25 day of April 190 4 ; that said child has been named Sarah N. C. Strickland, and is now living.

WITNESSETH:                        Arcola Strickland
Must be two   } Mary A Gardner
Witnesses who }
are Citizens.   Basil L Gardner

Subscribed and sworn to before me this  16  day of  January  190 5

James Bower
Notary Public.

My commission expires  Sept 23 1907

### AFFIDAVIT OF ATTENDING PHYSICIAN OR MIDWIFE

UNITED STATES OF AMERICA  
INDIAN TERRITORY  
Central      DISTRICT

I,  A. J. Wells       a     Practicing Physician on oath state that I attended on Mrs. Arcola Strickland wife of Charles E. Strickland on the 25 day of April , 190 4 , that there was born to her on said date a Female child, that said child is now living, and is said to have been named Sarah N.C. Strickland

A.J. Wells               M.D.

# Applications for Enrollment of Choctaw Newborn
## Act of 1905 Volume XIII

Subscribed and sworn to before me this, the 25 day of Jan 190 5

W.J. O'Donby
Notary Public.

WITNESSETH:
Must be two witnesses who are citizens and know the child.
{ Mary A Gardner
Basil L. Gardner

We hereby certify that we are well acquainted with Dr A. J. Wells a Physician and know him to be reputable and of good standing in the community.

{ Mary A Gardner
Basil L. Gardner

---

BIRTH AFFIDAVIT.

## DEPARTMENT OF THE INTERIOR.
## COMMISSION TO THE FIVE CIVILIZED TRIBES.

---

IN RE APPLICATION FOR ENROLLMENT, as a citizen of the Choctaw Nation, of Sarah N.C. Strickland, born on the 25$^{th}$ day of April, 1904

Name of Father: C.E. Strickland        a citizen of the ———— Nation.
Name of Mother: Arcola Strickland      a citizen of the Choctaw Nation.

Postoffice    Utica I.T.

---

**AFFIDAVIT OF MOTHER.**

UNITED STATES OF AMERICA, Indian Territory, }
Central            DISTRICT.

I, Arcola Strickland, on oath state that I am 30 years of age and a citizen by Blood, of the Choctaw Nation; that I am the lawful wife of C. E. Strickland, who is a citizen, by———of the ———— Nation; that a Female child was born to me on 25$^{th}$ day of April, 1904; that said child has been named Sarah N.C. Strickland, and was living March 4, 1905.

Arcola Strickland

Witnesses To Mark:
{

## Applications for Enrollment of Choctaw Newborn
## Act of 1905   Volume XIII

Subscribed and sworn to before me this   10<sup>th</sup>   day of    April    , 1905

                                      W.J. O'Donby
                                      Notary Public.

**AFFIDAVIT OF ATTENDING PHYSICIAN OR MID-WIFE.**

UNITED STATES OF AMERICA, Indian Territory, }
   Central                     DISTRICT. }

    I,   A.J. Wells   , a   Physician   , on oath state that I attended on Mrs.   Arcola Strickland  , wife of   C.E. Strickland   on the 25<sup>th</sup>   day of   April  , 190; that there was born to her on said date a     Female     child; that said child was living March 4, 1905, and is said to have been named   Sarah N.C. Strickland

                                      A.J. Wells, MD

Witnesses To Mark:
{

    Subscribed and sworn to before me this   10<sup>th</sup>   day of    April    , 1905

                                      W.J. O'Donby
                                      Notary Public.

---

Choc New Born 917
       Forrest C. Allen   b. 6-13-03

       roll # N.B. 1386

                                                  Choctaw 3935.

                        Muskogee, Indian Territory, April 14, 1905.

Charley Allen,
     Caddo, Indian Territory.

Dear Sir:

    Receipt is hereby acknowledged of the affidavits of Cora E. Allen and LeRoy Long to the birth of Forrest C. Allen, son of Charley and Cora E. Allen, June 13, 1903,

## Applications for Enrollment of Choctaw Newborn
## Act of 1905   Volume XIII

and the same have been filed with our records as an application for the enrollment of said child.

                Respectfully,

                                Commissioner in Charge.

7-NB-917.

Muskogee, Indian Territory, June 1, 1905.

Charley Allen,
    Caddo, Indian Territory.

Dear Sir:

    There is enclosed your[sic] herewith for execution application for the enrollment of your infant child, Forrest C. Allen.

    In the affidavits filed in this office on April 17, 1905, the date of the applicant's birth is given by the mother as June 15, 1903, while the midwife gives it as June 13, 1903. The affidavits filed on April 25, 1905, gives it as June 13, 1903. In the enclosed application the date of birth is left blank. Please insert the correct date and, when the affidavits are properly executed, return them to this office.

    In having these affidavits executed care should be exercised to see that all names are written in full, as they appear in the body of the affidavit, and in the event that either of the persons signing the affidavit are unable to write, signatures by mark must be attested by two witnesses. Each affidavit must be executed before a Notary Public and the notarial seal and signature of the officer must be attached to each separate affidavit.

                Respectfully,

VR 1-1.                                                                         Chairman.

## Applications for Enrollment of Choctaw Newborn
## Act of 1905   Volume XIII

7 NB 917

Muskogee, Indian Territory, June 16, 1905.

Leroy Long,
    South McAlester, Indian Territory.

Dear Sir:

    Receipt is hereby acknowledged of your letter of June 10, 1905, transmitting affidavits of Cora E. Allen and Leroy Long to the birth of Forrest C. Allen, son of Charley and Cora E. Allen, June 13, 1903, and the same have been filed with our records in the matter of the enrollment of said child.

Respectfully,

Chairman.

---

**BIRTH AFFIDAVIT.**

### DEPARTMENT OF THE INTERIOR.
### COMMISSION TO THE FIVE CIVILIZED TRIBES.

**IN RE APPLICATION FOR ENROLLMENT,** as a citizen of the Choctaw Nation, of Forrest C. Allen, born on the 13$^{th}$ day of June, 1903

Name of Father: Charley Allen     a citizen of the Choctaw Nation.
Name of Mother: Cora E. Allen     a citizen of the Choctaw Nation.

Postoffice    Caddo, I.T.

---

**AFFIDAVIT OF MOTHER.**

UNITED STATES OF AMERICA, Indian Territory,
    Central      DISTRICT.

    I, Cora E. Allen, on oath state that I am 20 years of age and a citizen by blood, of the Choctaw Nation; that I am the lawful wife of Charley Allen, who is a citizen, by intermarriage of the Choctaw Nation; that a male child was born to me on 15$^{th}$ [sic] day of June, 1903; that said child has been named Forrest E. Allen, and was living March 4, 1905.

Cora E Allen

Witnesses To Mark:

## Applications for Enrollment of Choctaw Newborn
## Act of 1905   Volume XIII

Subscribed and sworn to before me this 30$^{th}$ day of March, 1905

W.H. Angell
Notary Public.

---

**AFFIDAVIT OF ATTENDING PHYSICIAN OR MID-WIFE.**

UNITED STATES OF AMERICA, Indian Territory,
Central   DISTRICT.

I, LeRoy Long, a physician, on oath state that I attended on Mrs. Cora E. Allen, wife of Charley Allen on the 13$^{th}$ day of June, 1903; that there was born to her on said date a male child; that said child was living March 4, 1905, and is said to have been named Forrest C. Allen

LeRoy Long

Witnesses To Mark:
{

Subscribed and sworn to before me this 11$^{th}$ day of April, 1905

Brooks Fort
Notary Public.

Com Ex 3/6/07

---

**BIRTH AFFIDAVIT.**

### DEPARTMENT OF THE INTERIOR.
### COMMISSION TO THE FIVE CIVILIZED TRIBES.

IN RE APPLICATION FOR ENROLLMENT, as a citizen of the Choctaw Nation, of Forrest C. Allen, born on the 13th day of June, 1903

Name of Father: Charley Allen     a citizen of the Choctaw Nation.
Name of Mother: Cora E. Allen     a citizen of the Choctaw Nation.

Postoffice   Caddo, Indian Territory.

---

**AFFIDAVIT OF MOTHER.**

UNITED STATES OF AMERICA, Indian Territory,
Central   DISTRICT.

I, Cora E. Allen, on oath state that I am 20 years of age and a citizen by blood, of the Choctaw Nation; that I am the lawful wife of Charley Allen,

## Applications for Enrollment of Choctaw Newborn
## Act of 1905   Volume XIII

who is a citizen, by  Inter-Marriage    of the    Choctaw Nation    Nation; that a male    child was born to me on   Thirteenth   day of   June   , 1903; that said child has been named   Forrest E. Allen   , and was living March 4, 1905.

Cora E Allen

Witnesses To Mark:

{

Subscribed and sworn to before me this  Seventh   day of   June   , 1905

Sol. J. Homer<br>Notary Public.

---

**AFFIDAVIT OF ATTENDING PHYSICIAN OR MID-WIFE.**

UNITED STATES OF AMERICA, Indian Territory, }
   Central            DISTRICT.

I,   LeRoy Long   , a   Physician   , on oath state that I attended on Mrs.   Cora E. Allen   , wife of   Charley Allen   on the 13th   day of  June 1903 , 1......; that there was born to her on said date a   male   child; that said child was living March 4, 1905, and is said to have been named   Forrest C. Allen

LeRoy Long

Witnesses To Mark:

{

Subscribed and sworn to before me this  10$^{th}$   day of   June   , 1905

(Name Illegible)<br>Notary Public.<br>NOTARY PUBLIC<br>My Commission expires Apr. 24, 1907

Applications for Enrollment of Choctaw Newborn
Act of 1905  Volume XIII

# NEW BORN AFFIDAVIT

No ............

## CHOCTAW ENROLLING COMMISSION

IN THE MATTER OF THE APPLICATION FOR ENROLLMENT as a citizen of the Choctaw Nation, of       Forest[sic] Claud Allen       born on the 13$^{th}$ day of   June    190 3

Name of father  Charley Allen     a citizen of  Choctaw  Nation, final enrollment No .................
Name of mother  Cora E Allen     a citizen of  Choctaw  Nation, final enrollment No.  15057

Caddo I.T.         Postoffice.

### AFFIDAVIT OF MOTHER

UNITED STATES OF AMERICA  
INDIAN TERRITORY  
DISTRICT    Central

I    Cora E. Allen       , on oath state that I am  21   years of age and a citizen by  blood   of the   Choctaw   Nation, and as such have been placed upon the final roll of the  Choctaw    Nation, by the Honorable Secretary of the Interior my final enrollment number being   15057   ; that I am the lawful wife of    Charley Allen   , who is a citizen of the   Choctaw     Nation, and as such has been placed upon the final roll of said Nation by the Honorable Secretary of the Interior, his final enrollment number being ................ and that a  male  child was born to me on the   13$^{th}$   day of  June    190 3; that said child has been named   Forest Claud Allen  , and is now living.

WITNESSETH:                                                Cora E Allen  
 Must be two witnesses  { W.F. Ward  
 who are citizens     { (Name Illegible)

Subscribed and sworn to before me this, the  22$^{d}$ day of  February   , 190 5

A.E. Folsom  
Notary Public.

My Commission Expires:  
Jan 9-1909

# Applications for Enrollment of Choctaw Newborn
## Act of 1905 Volume XIII

### *Affidavit of Attending Physician or Midwife*

UNITED STATES OF AMERICA,  
INDIAN TERRITORY,  
Central DISTRICT

I, Le Roy Long a Practicing Physician on oath state that I attended on Mrs. Cora E. Allen wife of Charley Allen on the 13$^{th}$ day of June, 190 3, that there was born to her on said date a male child, that said child is now living, and is said to have been named Forest[sic] Claud Allen

LeRoy Long M. D.

Subscribed and sworn to before me this the 23$^{d}$ day of February 1905

Brooks Fort

Com Ex 3/6/07 Notary Public.

WITNESSETH:

Must be two witnesses who are citizens and know the child. { W.F. Ward
*(Name Illegible)*

We hereby certify that we are well acquainted with D$^{r}$ LeRoy Long a Physician and know him to be reputable and of good standing in the community.

Must be two citizen witnesses. { *(Name Illegible)*
W.F. Ward

Choc New Born 918
Lora Goodman b. 7-19-04

## Applications for Enrollment of Choctaw Newborn
## Act of 1905   Volume XIII

Choctaw 5614.

Muskogee, Indian Territory, April 14, 1905.

Joe W. Goodman,
Muldrow, Indian Territory.

Dear Sir:

Receipt is hereby acknowledged of the affidavits of Ida I. Goodman and Julia Davis to the birth of Lora Goodman, daughter of Joe W. and Ida Goodman, July 19, 1904, and the same have been filed with our records as an application for the enrollment of said child.

Respectfully,

Commissioner in Charge.

---

**BIRTH AFFIDAVIT.**

**DEPARTMENT OF THE INTERIOR.**
**COMMISSION TO THE FIVE CIVILIZED TRIBES.**

---

**IN RE APPLICATION FOR ENROLLMENT**, as a citizen of the   Choctaw   Nation, of Lora Goodman   , born on the 19   day of   July   , 1904

Name of Father: Joe W Goodman         a citizen of the   Choctaw   Nation.
Name of Mother: Ida Goodman           a citizen of the   Choctaw   Nation.

Postoffice   Muldrow IT

---

**AFFIDAVIT OF MOTHER.**

**UNITED STATES OF AMERICA, Indian Territory,**
Northern     **DISTRICT.**

I,   Ida Goodman   , on oath state that I am   35   years of age and a citizen by Blood   , of the   Choctaw   Nation; that I am the lawful wife of   Joe W Goodman, who is a citizen, by Adaption   of the   Cherokee   Nation; that a   Female child was born to me on   19$^{th}$   day of   July   , 1904; that said child has been named Lora Goodman   , and was living March 4, 1905.

Ida I Goodman

Witnesses To Mark:

# Applications for Enrollment of Choctaw Newborn
## Act of 1905  Volume XIII

Subscribed and sworn to before me this 10 day of     April    , 1905

My com expires Nov 6$^{th}$ 1906         W.H. Norriel
                                          Notary Public.

---

**AFFIDAVIT OF ATTENDING PHYSICIAN OR MID-WIFE.**

UNITED STATES OF AMERICA, Indian Territory, }
  Northern          DISTRICT.

I,  Julia Davis  , a  Midwife  , on oath state that I attended on Mrs.  Ida Goodman  , wife of  Joe W Goodman  on the  19 day of  July , 1904; that there was born to her on said date a  Female  child; that said child was living March 4, 1905, and is said to have been named  Lora Goodman

                 her
          Julia x Davis
Witnesses To Mark:     mark
 { W.A. Davis
   Joe W Goodman

Subscribed and sworn to before me this  10 day of  April    , 1905

          W H Norriel
          Notary Public.

---

Choc New Born 919
     Timothy Carney  b. 4-15-04

7-NB-919.

Muskogee, Indian Territory, June 1, 1905.

Payson Carney,
     Smithville, Indian Territory.

Dear Sir:

     Referring to the application for the enrollment of your infant child, Timothy Carney, born April 15, 1904, it is noted from the affidavits heretofore filed in this office that you attended upon your wife at the time of birth of the applicant.

## Applications for Enrollment of Choctaw Newborn
## Act of 1905   Volume XIII

In this event it will be necessary that you file in this office the affidavits of two persons, who are disinterested and not related to the applicant, who have actual knowledge of the facts that the child was born, the date of his birth; that he was living on March 4, 1905, and that Mary Carney is his mother.

The affidavit of Louina Plumbbi to these facts has been filed. It will, therefore be necessary that you secure a similar affidavit from another person.

Respectfully,

Chairman.

---

7 NB 919

Muskogee, Indian Territory, July 1, 1905.

Payson Carney,
   Smithville, Indian Territory.

Dear Sir:

Receipt is hereby acknowledged of the affidavits of Wilmon Johnson to the birth of Timothy Carney, son of Payson and Mary Carney, April 15, 1904, and the same has been filed with our records in the matter of the enrollment of said child.

Respectfully,

Commissioner.

---

United States of America
   Indian Territory
Central District
Affidavit of Acquaintance

I, Wilmon Johnson on oath state that I am 28 years of age and a citizen by blood of the Choctaw Nation, that my post office address is Smithville Ind Terr; that I am not related to the applicant, that I am personally acquainted with Mary Carney, wife of Payson Carney who is a citizen by blood of the Choctaw Nation, and that a male child was born to Mary Carney on the 15$^{th}$ day of April 1904 and that said male child has been named Timothy Carney, and was living on the 4$^{th}$ day of March 1905, and that Mary Carney is the mother of the said Timothy Carney of which I have perfect knowledge.

Wilmon Jonson

## Applications for Enrollment of Choctaw Newborn
## Act of 1905  Volume XIII

Subscribed and sworn to before me this the 26<sup>th</sup> day of June 1905

My Com expires
March 30-1909

W.H. McKinney
Notary Public

DEPARTMENT OF THE INTERIOR,
Commission to the Five Civilized Tribes.

**FILED**
JUN 30 1905

Tams Bixby  CHAIRMAN

---

United States of America, )
) 
Indian Territory, ) ss.
)
Central District. )

I, Louina Plumbbi, on oath state that I am forty-three years of age and a citizen by blood of the Choctaw Nation; that my post office address is Smithville, Indian Territory; that I am personally acquainted with Mary Carney, wife of Payson Carney; that there was born to the said Mary Carney on the 15th day of April, 1904, a male child; that said child is now living and has been named Timothy Carney; that the way I know of the birth of said child is that I came to the home of said Payson and Mary Carney about an hour after the birth of said child, and then and there learned of the circumstanced attending the birth of said child.

                                                          her
                                        Louina  x  Plumbbi
                                                   mark

Subscribed and sworn to before me this 5th day of April, 1905.

                                             Wirt Franklin
                                             Notary Public.

Witnesses to mark.
        Vester W Rose
        Robert Anderson

# Applications for Enrollment of Choctaw Newborn
## Act of 1905  Volume XIII

BIRTH AFFIDAVIT.

### DEPARTMENT OF THE INTERIOR.
### COMMISSION TO THE FIVE CIVILIZED TRIBES.

IN RE APPLICATION FOR ENROLLMENT, as a citizen of the Choctaw Nation, of Timothy Carney, born on the 15th day of April, 1904

Name of Father: Payson Carney    a citizen of the Choctaw Nation.
Name of Mother: Mary Carney    a citizen of the Choctaw Nation.

Postoffice    Smithville, Ind. Ter.

### AFFIDAVIT OF MOTHER.

UNITED STATES OF AMERICA, Indian Territory, }
Central    DISTRICT. }

I, Mary Carney, on oath state that I am 35 years of age and a citizen by blood, of the Choctaw Nation; that I am the lawful wife of Payson Carney, who is a citizen, by blood of the Choctaw Nation; that a male child was born to me on 15th day of April, 1904; that said child has been named Timothy Carney, and was living March 4, 1905.

 her
Mary x Carney
 mark

Witnesses To Mark:
{ Robert Anderson
{ Vester W Rose

Subscribed and sworn to before me this 5th day of April, 1905

Wirt Franklin
Notary Public.

### AFFIDAVIT OF ATTENDING PHYSICIAN OR MID-WIFE.

UNITED STATES OF AMERICA, Indian Territory, }
Central    DISTRICT. }

I, Payson Carney, ~~a~~, on oath state that I attended on Mrs. Mary Carney, ~~wife of~~ my wife on the 15th day of April, 1904; that there was born to her on said date a male child; that said child was living March 4, 1905, and is said to have been named Timothy Carney

 his
Payson x Carney
 mark

175

## Applications for Enrollment of Choctaw Newborn
## Act of 1905 Volume XIII

Witnesses To Mark:
   { Robert Anderson
    Vester W Rose

      Subscribed and sworn to before me this 5th day of     April  , 1905

                               Wirt Franklin
                               Notary Public.

---

Choc New Born 920
    Sam Bond   b. 3-21-04

                                           7-NB-920.

                      Muskogee, Indian Territory, June 1, 1905.

Byington Bond,
    Bethel, Indian Territory.

Dear Sir:

      Referring to the application for the enrollment of your infant child, Sam Bond, born March 21, 1904, it is noted from the affidavits heretofore filed in this office that you were the only one in attendance upon your wife at the time of birth of the applicant.

      In this event it will be necessary that you file in this office the affidavits of two persons, who are disinterested and not related to the applicant, who have actual knowledge of the facts that the child was born, the date of his birth; that he was living on March 4, 1905, and that Dixie[sic] Bond is his mother. The affidavit of Ananias Watson to these facts has been filed. It will, therefore, be necessary that you secure a similar affidavit from another person.
                                Respectfully,

                                                 Chairman.

## Applications for Enrollment of Choctaw Newborn
## Act of 1905   Volume XIII

7 NB 920

Muskogee, Indian Territory, June 16, 1905.

Byington Bond,
Bethel, Indian Territory.

Dear Sir:

Receipt is hereby acknowledged of the affidavits of Liksi Noahobi and Almon Carterby to the birth of Sam Bond, son of Byington Bond and Liksi Noahobi, March 11[sic], 1904, and the same have been filed with our records in the matter of the enrollment of said child.

Respectfully,

Chairman.

---

7-NB-920

Muskogee, Indian Territory, August 3, 1905.

Byington Bond,
Bethel, Indian Territory.

Dear Sir:

There is inclosed you herewith for execution application for the enrollment of your infant child, Sam Bond, born March 21, 1904.

In the affidavits of April 5, 1905, heretofore filed in this office, the name of the mother appears as Lixie Bond; in the affidavits of June 10, 1905, the name of mother appears as Lixie Noahabi.

It appears from the records of this office that Lixie Noahabi is the maiden name of the mother of the child, and the name under which she was enrolled as a citizen by blood of the Choctaw Nation.

In the inclosed affidavits the name of the mother is given as Lixie Bond, and she should so sign her affidavit.

You are requested to have the affidavits of the mother and two witnesses, Almon Carterby and Hephus[sic] Hicks properly executed and return to this office immediate[sic], as no further action can be taken relative to the enrollment of your said child until the evidence requested is supplied.

# Applications for Enrollment of Choctaw Newborn
## Act of 1905   Volume XIII

*LM 1/3*

Respectfully,

Commissioner.

7-NB-920

Muskogee, Indian Territory, August 22, 1905.

Byington Bond,
    Bethel, Indian Territory.

Dear Sir:

    Receipt is hereby acknowledged of the affidavit of Liksi Bond and the joint affidavit of Almon Carterby and Cephus Hicks to the birth of Sam Bond, son of Byington Bond and Liksi Bond, March 21, 1905[sic], and the same are returned you herewith for the reason that the Notaries Public before whom the affidavits of the mother and the acquaintances were executed failed to attach their seals to the affidavits; it will also be necessary that you secure another witness to the signature by mark must be attested by two witnesses of Liksi Bond.

Respectfully,

Commissioner.

LM 103

7-NB-920

Muskogee, Indian Territory, March 19, 1906.

W. H. McKinney,
    Smithville, Indian Territory.

Dear Madam:

    Receipt is hereby acknowledged of your letter of March 12, 1906, inclosing affidavits of Colbert Battiest to the birth of Sam Bond, child of Byington Bond and Liksi Noahobi, March 11[sic], 1904, and the same has been filed with the record in this case.

    You are advised that the name of Sam Bond has been placed upon a schedule of new born citizens of the Choctaw Nation which has been forwarded the Secretary of the Interior, but this office has not yet been notified of Departmental action thereon.

Respectfully,

Acting Commissioner.

# Applications for Enrollment of Choctaw Newborn
## Act of 1905 Volume XIII

BIRTH AFFIDAVIT.

### DEPARTMENT OF THE INTERIOR.
### COMMISSION TO THE FIVE CIVILIZED TRIBES.

IN RE APPLICATION FOR ENROLLMENT, as a citizen of the Choctaw Nation, of Sam , born on the 11 day of March , 1904.

Name of Father: Byington Bond     a citizen of the Choctaw Nation.
Name of Mother: Liksi Noahobi     a citizen of the Choctaw Nation.

Postoffice    Bethel, I.T.

**AFFIDAVIT OF ATTENDING PHYSICIAN OR MID-WIFE.**

UNITED STATES OF AMERICA, Indian Territory,
Central DISTRICT.

*am well acquainted with*

I, Colbert Battiest , a~~n~~ acquaintance , on oath state that I ~~attended on~~ Mrs. Liksi Noahobi , wife of Byington Bond on the 11 day of March, 1904; that there was born to her on said date a male child; that said child is now living and is said to have been named Sam

                 Colbert Battiest

Witnesses To Mark:
{

Subscribed and sworn to before me this 13 day of March , 1906.

         W.H. M$^{c}$Kinney
             Notary Public.

My Com expires March 30$^{th}$ 1909

# Applications for Enrollment of Choctaw Newborn
## Act of 1905 Volume XIII

United States of America, )
)
Indian Territory, ) ss.
)
Central District. )

I, Ananias Watson, on oath state that I am about twenty-eight years of age and a citizen by blood of the Choctaw Nation; that I am personally acquainted with Dixie[sic] Bond, wife of Byington Bond; that I have known said parties for about twenty years; that there was born to the said Dixie Bond on or about March 21, 1904, a male child; that said child has been named Sam Bond it is now living.

                        his
                 Ananias x Watson
                      mark

Subscribed and sworn to before me this 5th day of April, 1905.

                  Wirt Franklin
                  Notary Public.

Witnesses to mark.
    Vester W Rose
    Robert Anderson

---

**BIRTH AFFIDAVIT.**

## DEPARTMENT OF THE INTERIOR.
## COMMISSION TO THE FIVE CIVILIZED TRIBES.

IN RE APPLICATION FOR ENROLLMENT, as a citizen of the Choctaw Nation, of Sam Bond, born on the 21st day of March, 1904

Name of Father: Byington Bond    a citizen of the Choctaw Nation.
Name of Mother: Dixie Bond      a citizen of the Choctaw Nation.

                Postoffice    Bethel, Ind. Ter.

---

**AFFIDAVIT OF MOTHER.**

UNITED STATES OF AMERICA, Indian Territory, }
    Central            DISTRICT.

I, Dixie Bond, on oath state that I am 28 years of age and a citizen by blood, of the Choctaw Nation; that I am the lawful wife of Byington Bond, who is a citizen, by blood of the Choctaw Nation; that a male child was born to me on 21st day of March, 1904; that said child has been named

# Applications for Enrollment of Choctaw Newborn
## Act of 1905  Volume XIII

Sam Bond, and was living March 4, 1905. *and that no physician or mid-wife attended me at the birth of said child.*

Witnesses To Mark:
{ Vester W Rose
  Robert Anderson

her
Dixie x Bond
mark

Subscribed and sworn to before me this 5th day of April, 1905

Wirt Franklin
Notary Public.

---

### AFFIDAVIT OF ATTENDING PHYSICIAN OR MID-WIFE.

UNITED STATES OF AMERICA, Indian Territory, }
Central           DISTRICT.             }

I, Byington Bond, ~~a~~ ................, on oath state that I attended on Mrs. Dixie Bond, ~~wife of~~ *my wife* on the 21st day of March, 1904; that there was born to her on said date a male child; that said child was living March 4, 1905, and ~~is said to have~~ *has* been named Sam Bond; *and that no one else was present when said child was born*

his
Byington x Bond
mark

Witnesses To Mark:
{ Vester W Rose
  Robert Anderson

Subscribed and sworn to before me this 5th day of April, 1905

Wirt Franklin
Notary Public.

---

BIRTH AFFIDAVIT.

## Department of the Interior,
COMMISSION TO THE FIVE CIVILIZED TRIBES.

---

IN RE APPLICATION FOR ENROLLMENT, as a citizen of the Choctaw Nation, of Sam Bond, born on the 21 day of March, 1904

Name of Father: Byington Bond    a citizen of the Choctaw Nation.
Name of Mother: Liksi Noahobi    a citizen of the Choctaw Nation.

Post-Office:  Bethel Ind Teritoy[sic]

## Applications for Enrollment of Choctaw Newborn
## Act of 1905   Volume XIII

### AFFIDAVIT OF MOTHER.

UNITED STATES OF AMERICA, }
    INDIAN TERRITORY,
    Central    District.

I, Liksi Noahobi , on oath state that I am 23 years of age and a citizen by Blood , of the Choctaw Nation; that I am the lawful wife of Byington Bond , who is a citizen, by Blood of the Choctaw Nation; that a Male child was born to me on 21 day of March , 190 4, that said child has been named Sam Bond , and is now living. *was living on 4 day of March 1905*

                                                         her
                                              Liksi x Noahobi

WITNESSES TO MARK:                              mark
{ *(Name Illegible)* Bethel I.T.
  Almon Carterby Bethel I.T.

Subscribed and sworn to before me this 10 day of June , 190 .

                                              Joseph H Matthews
                                                     *Notary Public.*

---

### AFFIDAVIT OF ATTENDING PHYSICIAN OR MID-WIFE.

UNITED STATES OF AMERICA, }
    INDIAN TERRITORY,
    Central    District.

I, Almon Carterby and Cephus Hicks , on oath state that I attended on Mrs. *we have actual knowledge* , wife of *that the said Sam Bond was borned*[sic] *to Liksi Noahobi on March 21 1904 and was living March 4=1904* on the 21 day of March , 1904 ; that there was born to her on said date a male child; that said child is now living and is said to have been named Sam Bond *was living on 4 day of March 1905*

WITNESSES TO MARK:                       Almon Carterby Bethel I.T.
{ *to the fact that Sam bond*
  *was born to Liksi Noahobi*              Cephus Hicks Bethel I T
  *on March 21 1904*

Subscribed and sworn to before me this 10 day of June , 190 5
My commission expires
Feb 13=1907                                    J H Matthews
                                                   *Notary Public.*

Applications for Enrollment of Choctaw Newborn
Act of 1905   Volume XIII

BIRTH AFFIDAVIT.   7 NB 920

DEPARTMENT OF THE INTERIOR.
## COMMISSION TO THE FIVE CIVILIZED TRIBES.

IN RE APPLICATION FOR ENROLLMENT, as a citizen of the   Choctaw   Nation, of Sam Bond  , born on the 21  day of March  , 1904

Name of Father: Byington Bond  Roll 1029   a citizen of the Choctaw  Nation.
Name of Mother: Liksi Bond  Roll 1567   a citizen of the Choctaw  Nation.

Postoffice   Bethel Ind Ter

### AFFIDAVIT OF MOTHER.

UNITED STATES OF AMERICA, Indian Territory, }
Central   DISTRICT.

I,  Liksi Bond  , on oath state that I am  28  years of age and a citizen by blood , of the  Choctaw  Nation; that I am the lawful wife of  Byington Bond , who is a citizen, by blood  of the  Choctaw  Nation; that a  male  child was born to me on  21$^{st}$  day of  March  , 1904; that said child has been named Sam Bond , and was living March 4, 1905.

                              her
                        Liksi x Bond
Witnesses To Mark:          mark
 { Colbert Battiest
   Williamson Washuby

Subscribed and sworn to before me this  12  day of  Aug  , 1905

(Name Illegible)
Notary Public.

### AFFIDAVIT OF ATTENDING PHYSICIAN OR MID-WIFE.

UNITED STATES OF AMERICA, Indian Territory, }
Central   DISTRICT.

*we are acquainted with*
*We*,  Almon Carterby and Cephus Hicks  , on oath state that ~~I attended on~~ Mrs.  Liksi Bond  , wife of  Byington Bond  *and that* on *or about* the 21$^{st}$  day of  March  , 1904; that there was born to her on said date a  male  child; that said child was living March 4, 1905, and is said to have been named Sam Bond; *that we are not related to the applicant, nor interested in said case.*

183

## Applications for Enrollment of Choctaw Newborn
## Act of 1905   Volume XIII

Witnesses To Mark:
{

Cephus Hicks
Almon F. Carterby

Subscribed and sworn to before me this  15   day of     Aug       , 1905

J.H. Matthews
Notary Public.

---

Choc New Born 921
    Sampson Colbert   b.  3-4-03

7-NB-921.

Muskogee, Indian Territory, June 7, 1905.

Levi Colbert,
    Cove, Arkansas.

Dear Sir:

    There is enclosed herewith for execution application for the enrollment of your infant child, Sampson Colbert.

    In the mother's affidavit of January 28, 1905, heretofore filed in this office, the date of the applicant's birth is given as March 3, 1904, while in the affidavits of April 6, 1905, this date is given as March 4, 1903.

    In the enclosed application the date of the birth is left blank.  Please insert the correct date, and when the affidavits are properly executed return them to this office.

    In having these affidavits executed care should be exercised to see that all names are written in full, as they appear in the body of the affidavit, and in the event that either of the persons signing the affidavit are unable to write, signatures by mark must be attested by two witnesses.  Each affidavit must be executed before a Notary Public and the notarial seal and signature of the officer must be attached to each separate affidavit.

    It appears from your affidavit of April 6, 1905, that you attended upon your wife at the time of the birth of the applicant.  If there was a physician, or midwife, also in attendance, it will be necessary that you secure his, or her, affidavit, but if you are the only one who was in attendance it will be necessary that you file in this office the affidavits of two persons who are disinterested and not related to the applicant, who have

## Applications for Enrollment of Choctaw Newborn
## Act of 1905   Volume XIII

actual knowledge of the facts; that the child was born, the date of his birth, that he was living on March 4, 1905, and that Louina Colbert is his mother.

You wife states in her affidavit that she is a citizen by blood of the Choctaw Nation. If this is correct you will please state when, where and under what name she was listed for enrollment, the name of her parents and other members of her family for whom application was made at the same time, and if she has selected an allotment, give her roll number as it appears upon her allotment certificate.

Respectfully,

Commissioner in Charge.

DeB-1/7

---

7-NB-921

Muskogee, Indian Territory, July 3, 1905.

Levi Colbert,
    Cove, Arkansas.

Dear Sir:

Receipt is hereby acknowledged of the affidavits of Winnie Colbert, Euson[sic] Jefferson, Easton McCoy and Levi Colbert to the birth of Sampson Colbert, son of Levi and Winnie[sic] Colbert, March 4, 1904, and the same have been filed with the records of this office in the matter of the enrollment of said child.

Respectfully,

Commissioner.

---

**NEW-BORN AFFIDAVIT.**

Number..............

## ...Choctaw Enrolling Commission...

---

IN THE MATTER OF THE APPLICATION FOR ENROLLMENT, as a citizen of the Choctaw Nation, of Sampson Colbert

born on the 3 day of __March__ 190 4

# Applications for Enrollment of Choctaw Newborn
## Act of 1905 Volume XIII

Name of father   Levi Colbert              a citizen of   Choctaw
Nation final enrollment No. ..................
Name of mother   Luena[sic] Colbert        a citizen of   Choctaw
Nation final enrollment No. ..................

                                           Postoffice   Cove Arkansas

### AFFIDAVIT OF MOTHER.

UNITED STATES OF AMERICA
INDIAN TERRITORY
.................... DISTRICT

I   Luena Colbert   , on oath state that I am 34   years of age and a citizen by   birth   of the   Choctaw   Nation, and as such have been placed upon the final roll of the   Choctaw   Nation, by the Honorable Secretary of the Interior my final enrollment number being.................. ; that I am the lawful wife of   Levi Colbert   , who is a citizen of the   Choctaw   Nation, and as such has been placed upon the final roll of said Nation by the Honorable Secretary of the Interior, his final enrollment number being .................. and that a   Male   child was born to me on the   3$^{rd}$ day of   March   190 4; that said child has been named   Sampson Colbert   , and is now living.

                                              her
                              Luena x Colbert
Witnesseth.                       mark

Must be two   ⎫  (Name Illegible)
Witnesses who ⎬
are Citizens. ⎭   William J Colbert

Subscribed and sworn to before me this   28   day of   January   190 5

                              B. H. Barton
                                        Notary Public.
My commission expires:
Aug 12 1908

---

**BIRTH AFFIDAVIT.**

### DEPARTMENT OF THE INTERIOR.
### COMMISSION TO THE FIVE CIVILIZED TRIBES.

---

IN RE APPLICATION FOR ENROLLMENT, as a citizen of the   Choctaw   Nation, of   Sampson Colbert   , born on the   4th   day of March   , 1903

Name of Father: Levi Colbert         a citizen of the   Choctaw   Nation.
Name of Mother: Louina Colbert       a citizen of the   Choctaw   Nation.

                    Postoffice   Cove, Arkansas

---

# Applications for Enrollment of Choctaw Newborn
# Act of 1905   Volume XIII

**AFFIDAVIT OF MOTHER.**

UNITED STATES OF AMERICA, Indian Territory, }
Central                DISTRICT.

I, Louina Colbert, on oath state that I am 30 years of age and a citizen by blood, of the Choctaw Nation; that I am the lawful wife of Levi Colbert, who is a citizen, by blood of the Choctaw Nation; that a male child was born to me on 4th day of March, 1903; that said child has been named Sampson Colbert, and was living March 4, 1905.

                                                her
                                    Louina  x  Colbert
Witnesses To Mark:               mark
{ Robert Anderson
  Vester Rose

Subscribed and sworn to before me this 6th day of April, 1905

                                     Wirt Franklin
                                     Notary Public.

---

**AFFIDAVIT OF ATTENDING PHYSICIAN OR MID-WIFE.**

UNITED STATES OF AMERICA, Indian Territory, }
Central                DISTRICT.

I, Levi Colbert, ~~a~~ ............, on oath state that I attended on Mrs. Louina Colbert, ~~wife of~~ *my wife* on the 4th day of March, 1903; that there was born to her on said date a male child; that said child was living March 4, 1905, and ~~is said to have~~ *has* been named Sampson Colbert

                                      his
                                  Levi  x  Colbert
Witnesses To Mark:              mark
{ Robert Anderson
  Vester Rose

Subscribed and sworn to before me this 6th day of April, 1905

                                     Wirt Franklin
                                     Notary Public.

## Applications for Enrollment of Choctaw Newborn
## Act of 1905   Volume XIII

United States of America
Indian Territory
Central District
          Affidavit of Acquaintance

I, Edson Jefferson on oath state that I am 35 years of age and a citizen by blood of the Choctaw Nation, that my post office address is Smithville, I.T. that I am not related to the applicant, who is a citizen by blood of the Choctaw Nation, that I am personally acquainted with Winnie Colbert, wife of Levi Colbert who is a citizen by blood of the Choctaw Nation and that a male child was born to Winnie Colbert on $4^{th}$ day of March 1904 and that said male child has been named Sampson Colbert and the said Sampson Colbert was living on the $4^{th}$ day of March 1905, and I have personal knowledge that Winnie Colbert is the mother of said Sampson Colbert.

                                      Edson Jefferson

Subscribed and sworn to before me this $6^{th}$ day of June 1905

                                        W.H. McKinney
My commission expires                       Notary Public
March 30-1909

---

United States of America
Indian Territory
Central District
          Affidavit of Acquaintance

I Easton M$^{c}$Coy on oath state that I am 30 years of age and a citizen by blood of the Choctaw Nation, that my post office address is Smithville, Ind Ter that I am not related to the applicant who is a citizen by blood of the Choctaw Nation, that I am personally acquainted with Winnie Colbert, wife of Levi Colbert who is a citizen by blood of the Choctaw Nation, and that a male child was born to Winnie Colbert on the 4 day of March 1904, and that said male child has been named Sampson Colbert, and the said Sampson Colbert was living on the $4^{th}$ day of March 1905, and that I have personal knowledge that Winnie Colbert is the mother of said Sampson Colbert.

                                      Easton M$^{c}$Coy

Subscribed and sworn to before me this $26^{th}$ day of June 1905

                                        W.H. M$^{c}$Kinney
My commission expires                       Notary Public
March 30-1909

# Applications for Enrollment of Choctaw Newborn
## Act of 1905   Volume XIII

United States of America
Indian Territory
Central District

I Levi Colbert on oath state that I attended on my wife Winnie Colbert on the $4^{th}$ day of March 1904 as there was born to her on said date a male child & that child was living March 4, 1905 and has been named Sampson Colbert

Witness to mark
Wilmon Johnson
Byington Horner

Levi x Colbert (his mark)

Subscribed and sworn to before me this $26^{th}$ day of June 1905

W.H. M$^c$Kinney
Notary Public

My Com expires
March 30-1909

Cove, Arkansas

Commission to the Five Civilized Tribes
Muskogee, I.T.

Gentlemen:-

   Receipt is hereby acknowledged of your letter of June 7 1905 enclosing blank application of enrollment of new born child and in which I'm asked to be informed of the number of Choctaw Roll of Louina Colbert, her parent's name and her sister's name and when and where she was registered
In reply will say that my wife's name is not Louina but Winnie Colbert and her father's name was Tushka Billy and that she was registered by the Honorable Dawes Commission at Tuslika Homa, Indian Territory.  She has filed on her land for her allotment and her number of roll is 13339
my number is 13338
   When I appeared before the enrolling Commission at Smithville, Ind. terr. and stated that my wife's name is Winnie Colbert, but some how her name has been changed from Winnie to Louina.  Winnie is the proper name for my wife and I hope this explanation is sufficient

Yours very truly
Levi x Colbert (his mark)

Witness to mark
 Wilmon Johnson
 Jamison Lewis

Dictated

# Applications for Enrollment of Choctaw Newborn
## Act of 1905   Volume XIII

United States of America
Indian Territory
Central District

This is to certify that Winnie Colbert is the lawful wife of Levi Colbert both being citizens by blood of the Choctaw Nation. I have known Winnie and Levi Colbert for several years.

WH M$^c$Kinney
Notary Public

My com expires March 30-1909.

---

United States of America
Indian Territory
Central District

In Re application for enrollment as a citizen of the Choctaw Nation of Sampson Colbert, born on the 4$^{th}$ day of March 1904

Name of Father  Levi Colbert a citizen of the Choctaw Nation
Name of Mother  Winnie Colbert a citizen of the Choctaw Nation

Post Office  Cove, Arkansas.
"Roll 13339"

I Winnie Colbert on oath state that I am 30 years of age and a citizen by blood of the Choctaw Nation that I am the lawful wife of Levi Colbert Roll "13338" who is a citizen by blood of the Choctaw Nation, that a male child was born to me on 4$^{th}$ day of March 1904; that said child has been named Sampson Colbert and was living March 4, 1905

|  |  |
|---|---|
| Witness to mark | her |
| Chas A Wilson | Winnie x Colbert |
| Thomas Nolen Jr. | mark |

Subscribed and sworn to before me this 26$^{th}$ day of June 1905

W.H. M$^c$Kinney
Notary Public.

My com expires March 30-1909

# Applications for Enrollment of Choctaw Newborn
# Act of 1905 Volume XIII

Choc New Born 922
  Green Wilson b. 6-24-04

---

Kitsy Wilson's father's name Eastman Brown. Her mother's name is Louisa Brown (Llod)

===

Jerry Wilson's father's name is Reuben Wilson (Dead). His mother's name is Ishtemus Wilson (Dead)

---

7-N.B. 922.

Muskogee, Indian Territory, June 7, 1905.

Jerry Wilson,
  America, Indian Territory.

Dear Sir:

Referring to the application for the enrollment of your infant child, Green Wilson, born June 24, 1904, it is noted from the affidavits heretofore filed in this office that you claim to be a citizen by blood of the Choctaw Nation. If this is correct, you are requested to state when, where and under what name you were listed for enrollment, the names of your parents and other members of your family for whom application was made at the same time, and if you have selected an allotment give your roll number as it appears upon your allotment certificate.

This matter should receive your immediate attention, as no further action can be taken until this information is furnished the Commission.

Respectfully,

Commissioner in Charge.

Charley Wilson
  Roll # 14640
    (Card #1143)

# Applications for Enrollment of Choctaw Newborn
## Act of 1905   Volume XIII

BIRTH AFFIDAVIT.

## DEPARTMENT OF THE INTERIOR.
## COMMISSION TO THE FIVE CIVILIZED TRIBES.

IN RE APPLICATION FOR ENROLLMENT, as a citizen of the Choctaw Nation, of Green Wilson, born on the 24th day of June, 1904

Name of Father: Jerry Wilson    a citizen of the Choctaw Nation.
Name of Mother: Kitsy Wilson    a citizen of the Choctaw Nation.

Postoffice   America, Ind. Ter.

### AFFIDAVIT OF MOTHER.

UNITED STATES OF AMERICA, Indian Territory,
Central   DISTRICT.

I, Kitsy Wilson, on oath state that I am about 18 years of age and a citizen by blood, of the Choctaw Nation; that I am the lawful wife of Jerry Wilson, who is a citizen, by blood of the Choctaw Nation; that a male child was born to me on 24th day of June, 1904; that said child has been named Green Wilson, and was living March 4, 1905.

                                          her
                                  Kitsy x Wilson
Witnesses To Mark:              mark
   { Robert Anderson
    Vester Rose

Subscribed and sworn to before me this 10th day of April, 1905

Wirt Franklin
Notary Public.

### AFFIDAVIT OF ATTENDING PHYSICIAN OR MID-WIFE.

UNITED STATES OF AMERICA, Indian Territory,
Central   DISTRICT.

I, Wincey Thompson, a mid-wife, on oath state that I attended on Mrs. Kitsy Wilson, wife of Jerry Wilson on the 24th day of June, 1904; that there was born to her on said date a male child; that said child was living March 4, 1905, and is said to have been named Green Wilson

Wincey Thompson

# Applications for Enrollment of Choctaw Newborn
## Act of 1905   Volume XIII

Witnesses To Mark:

{

Subscribed and sworn to before me this 10th day of April, 1905

Wirt Franklin
Notary Public.

---

Choc New Born 923
    Allie Wilson   b. 2-3-03
    Bryant Wilson   b. 10-2-04

7-NB-923

Muskogee, Indian Territory, July 18, 1905.

Charles Wilson,
    Hatfield, Indian Territory.

Dear Sir:

    Receipt is hereby acknowledged of your letter of July 10, 1905, asking if your children Allie and Bryant Wilson are enrolled.

    In reply to your letter you are advised that the names of your children Allie and Bryant Wilson have been placed upon a schedule of citizens by blood of the Choctaw Nation which has been forwarded the Secretary of the Interior and you will be notified when their enrollment is approved by him.

Respectfully,

Commissioner.

## Applications for Enrollment of Choctaw Newborn
## Act of 1905   Volume XIII

United States of America, )
)
Indian Territory, ) ss.
)
Central District. )

    I, Singlin Forbit, on oath state that I am about forty years of age and a citizen by blood of the Choctaw Nation; that my post office address is Smithville, Indian Territory; that I was personally acquainted with Lucinda Wilson, wife of Charles Wilson, during her life time; that I have known said parties for many years; that on or about the 3rd day of February, 1903, there was born to the said Lucinda Wilson, deceased, a female child; that said child is now living and is said to have been named Allie Wilson; and that the said Lucinda Wilson died the 23rd day of January, 1905.

                                                   his
                                         Singlin x Forbit
                                               mark

Subscribed and sworn to before me this 7th day of April, 1905.

                                          Wirt Franklin
                                              Notary Public.

Witnesses to mark.
        Robert Anderson
        Vester Rose

-----------------

United States of America, )
)
Indian Territory, ) ss.
)
Central District. )

    I, Sallie Wilson, on oath state that I am about forty years of age and a citizen by blood of the Choctaw Nation; that my post office address is Smithville, Indian Territory; that I was personally acquainted with Lucinda Wilson, wife of Charles Wilson, during her life time; that I have known said parties for many years; that on or about the 3rd day of February, 1903, there was born to the said Lucinda Wilson, deceased, a female child; that said child is now living and is said to have been named Allie Wilson.

                                                   her
                                         Sallie x Wilson
                                             mark

Subscribed and sworn to before me this 7th day of April, 1905.

                                          Wirt Franklin
Witnesses to mark.                              Notary Public
Robert Anderson, Vester Rose

# Applications for Enrollment of Choctaw Newborn
## Act of 1905   Volume XIII

BIRTH AFFIDAVIT.

### DEPARTMENT OF THE INTERIOR.
### COMMISSION TO THE FIVE CIVILIZED TRIBES.

IN RE APPLICATION FOR ENROLLMENT, as a citizen of the    Choctaw    Nation, of Allie Wilson    , born on the 3rd    day of    February    , 1903

Name of Father: Charles Wilson          a citizen of the    Choctaw    Nation.
Name of Mother: Lucinda Wilson          a citizen of the    Choctaw    Nation.

Postoffice    Hatfield, Arkansas.

### AFFIDAVIT OF MOTHER.

UNITED STATES OF AMERICA, Indian Territory,
Central          DISTRICT.

I,    Charles Wilson    , on oath state that I am   26   years of age and a citizen by    blood    , of the    Choctaw    Nation; that I ~~am~~ was the lawful ~~wife~~ husband of Lucinda Wilson, deceased  , who ~~is~~ was a citizen, by    blood    of the    Choctaw    Nation; that a    female    child was born to me on   3rd   day of    February    , 1903; that said child has been named    Allie Wilson    , and was living March 4, 1905. and that the mother of said child and the attending mid-wife at its birth are both dead.

Charles Wilson

Witnesses To Mark:
{

Subscribed and sworn to before me this  7th   day of   April    , 1905

Wirt Franklin
Notary Public.

United States of America,   )
                            )
Indian Territory,           )  ss.
                            )
Central District.           )

I, Singlin Forbit, on oath state that I am about forty years of age and a citizen by blood of the Choctaw Nation; that my post office address is Smithville, Indian Territory; that I was personally acquainted with Lucinda Wilson, wife of Charles Wilson, during

## Applications for Enrollment of Choctaw Newborn
## Act of 1905 Volume XIII

her life time; that I have known said parties for many years; that on or about the 2nd day of October, 1904, there was born to the said Lucinda Wilson, deceased, a male child; that said child is now living and is said to have been named Bryant Wilson.

                                          his
                                  Singlin x Forbit
                                        mark

Subscribed and sworn to before me this 7th day of April, 1905.

                                        Wirt Franklin
                                        Notary Public.

Witnesses to mark.
       Robert Anderson
       Vester Rose

-----------------

United States of America, )
                            )
Indian Territory,          )   ss.
                            )
Central District.          )

     I, Sallie Wilson, on oath state that I am about forty years of age and a citizen by blood of the Choctaw Nation; that my post office address is Smithville, Indian Territory; that I was personally acquainted with Lucinda Wilson, wife of Charles Wilson, during her life time; that I have known said parties for many years; that on or about the 2nd day of October, 1904, there was born to the said Lucinda Wilson, deceased, a male child; that said child is now living and is said to have been named Bryant Wilson; and that the said Lucinda Wilson died on the 23rd day of January, 1905.

                                        her
                                  Sallie x Wilson
                                      mark

Subscribed and sworn to before me this 7th day of April, 1905.

                                    Wirt Franklin
Witnesses to mark.                           Notary Public
       Robert Anderson
       Vester Rose

## Applications for Enrollment of Choctaw Newborn
## Act of 1905   Volume XIII

BIRTH AFFIDAVIT.

### DEPARTMENT OF THE INTERIOR.
### COMMISSION TO THE FIVE CIVILIZED TRIBES.

IN RE APPLICATION FOR ENROLLMENT, as a citizen of the Choctaw Nation, of Bryant Wilson, born on the 2nd day of October, 1904

Name of Father: Charles Wilson  a citizen of the Choctaw Nation.
Name of Mother: Lucinda Wilson  a citizen of the Choctaw Nation.

Postoffice  Hatfield, Arkansas.

### AFFIDAVIT OF MOTHER.

UNITED STATES OF AMERICA, Indian Territory,
Central  DISTRICT.

I, Charles Wilson, on oath state that I am 26 years of age and a citizen by blood, of the Choctaw Nation; that I ~~am~~ was the lawful ~~wife~~ husband of Lucinda Wilson, deceased, who ~~is~~ was a citizen, by blood of the Choctaw Nation; that a male child was born to me on 2nd day of October, 1904; that said child has been named Bryant Wilson, and was living March 4, 1905. and that the mother of said child and the attending mid-wife at its birth are both dead.

Charles Wilson

Witnesses To Mark:

Subscribed and sworn to before me this 7th day of April, 1905

Wirt Franklin
Notary Public.

Choc New Born 924
  Perry Jefferson  b. 12-6-03

## Applications for Enrollment of Choctaw Newborn
## Act of 1905   Volume XIII

$W^m O.B.$

**COMMISSIONERS:**
TAMS BIXBY,
THOMAS B. NEEDLES,
C.R. BRECKINBRIDGE.

WM. O. BEALL
Secretary

**DEPARTMENT OF THE INTERIOR,**
**COMMISSIONER TO THE FIVE CIVILIZED TRIBES.**

REFER IN REPLY TO THE FOLLOWING:

7-NB-852.

ADDRESS ONLY THE
COMMISSION TO THE FIVE CIVILIZED TRIBES.

Muskogee, Indian Territory, June 1, 1905.

Austin Jefferson,
    Bethel, Indian Territory.

Dear Sir:

    Referring to the application for the enrollment of your infant child, Berry Jefferson, born December 6, 1903, it is noted from the affidavits heretofore filed in this office that you attended upon your wife at the time of birth of the applicant.

    In this event it will be necessary that you file in this office the affidavits of two persons, who are disinterested and not related to the applicant, who have knowledge of the facts that the child was born, the date of his birth; that he was living on March 4, 1905, and that Agnes Jefferson is his mother.

    The affidavit of Nicholas Columbus to these facts has been filed.  It will, therefore, be necessary that you secure a similar affidavit from another person.

               Respectfully,
               T.B. Needles
                      Commissioner in Charge.

---

*(The letter above given again.)*

---

*(The affidavit below typed as given.)*

I Stephen Gipson on oath state that I am acquanted with Agnes Jefferson and Allson ~~Berry~~ Perry Jefferson and I further state that Agnes Jefferson is the mother of Perry Jefferson the child Perry Jefferson was borned to Agnes Jefferson on 6 day of December 1903 and was living March 4, 1905.                             Post Office

                    Stephen Gipson      Bethel IT

Witness

# Applications for Enrollment of Choctaw Newborn
# Act of 1905  Volume XIII

Subscribed and sworn to before me this 4 day of July = 1905

                                       J H Matthews
                                       Notary Public

My commission expires
Feb 13=1909

                                       7 NB-924

                Muskogee, Indian Territory, July 10, 1905.

Austin Jefferson,
        Bethel, Indian Territory.

Dear Sir:

        Receipt is hereby acknowledged of the affidavit of Stephen Gipson to the birth of Perry Jefferson, December 6, 1903, and the same has been filed with the records of this office in the matter of the enrollment of said child.

                             Respectfully,

                                               Commissioner.

7-NB-924

                Muskogee, Indian Territory, July 28, 1905.

Austin Jefferson,
        Bethel, Indian Territory.

Dear Sir:

        Referring to the application for the enrollment of your infant child, born December 6, 1903, it is noted that in the affidavits of the mother, Agnes Jefferson and Nicholas Columbus, a witness, executed April 6, 1905, the name of the child is given as Berry Jefferson, while in the affidavit of Stephen Gibson, also a witness executed July 4, 1905, the name is given as Perry Jefferson.

        There is inclosed you herewith for execution by the mother, Agnes Jefferson, affidavit in which the name of the child is left blank. Please insert the correct name, and when properly executed, return to this office.

        This matter should receive your immediate attention as no further action can be taken relative to the enrollment of this child until the evidence requested is supplied.

# Applications for Enrollment of Choctaw Newborn
## Act of 1905   Volume XIII

Respectfully,

LM 6/28

Commissioner.

---

7-NB-924

Muskogee, Indian Territory, August 12, 1905.

Austin Jefferson,
   Bethel, Indian Territory.

Dear Sir:

   Receipt is hereby acknowledged of the affidavit of Agnes Jefferson to the birth of Perry Jefferson, December 6, 1903, and the same is returned you herewith for the reason that the Notary Public failed to affix his seal to said affidavit. Please have correction made and the affidavit returned as early as practicable.

Respectfully,

Acting Commissioner.

LM 6-28

---

7-NB-924

Muskogee, Indian Territory, August 25, 1905.

Austin Jefferson,
   Bethel, Indian Territory.

Dear Sir:

   Receipt is hereby acknowledged of the affidavits of Agnes Jefferson to the birth of Perry Jefferson, December 6, 1903, and the same has been filed in the matter of the enrollment of said child.

Respectfully,

Commissioner.

---

Agnes Jefferson on final roll as Agnes Brewer. Her first husband's name Ellis Brewer. Her father's name is Istiatubbee. Her mother's name is Mary.

---

# Applications for Enrollment of Choctaw Newborn
## Act of 1905 Volume XIII

United States of America, )
)
Indian Territory, ) ss.
)
Central District. )

    I, Nicholas Columbus, on oath state that I am twenty years of age and a citizen by blood of the Choctaw Nation; that I am personally acquainted with Agnes Jefferson, wife of Austin Jefferson, and have known said parties for about fifteen years; that during the time I have known them I have lived withing[sic] four miles of where they have lived, near Bethel, Indian Territory; that on or about the 6th day of December, 1903, there was born to the said Agnes Jefferson a male child; that said child is now living and is said to have been named Berry[sic] Jefferson.

                                                                             Nicholas Columbus

Subscribed and sworn to before me this 6th day of April, 1905.

                                                           Wirt Franklin
                                                           Notary Public.

BIRTH AFFIDAVIT.    7 - nB 924

## DEPARTMENT OF THE INTERIOR.
## COMMISSION TO THE FIVE CIVILIZED TRIBES.

    IN RE APPLICATION FOR ENROLLMENT, as a citizen of the    Choctaw    Nation, of _____, born on the 6th   day of  December  , 1903

Name of Father: Austin Jefferson         a citizen of the   Choctaw    Nation.
Name of Mother: Agnes Jefferson        a citizen of the   Choctaw    Nation.

                                Postoffice     Bethel Ind Ter

### AFFIDAVIT OF MOTHER.

UNITED STATES OF AMERICA, Indian Territory, }
      Central              DISTRICT. }

    I, Agnes Jefferson   , on oath state that I am 35   years of age and a citizen by   blood   , of the   Choctaw   Nation; that I am the lawful wife of   Austin Jefferson   , who is a citizen, by blood   of the   Choctaw   Nation; that a male   child was born to me on 6th   day of   December   , 1903; that said child has been named   Perry Jefferson   , and was living March 4, 1905.

                                                          Agnes Jefferson

## Applications for Enrollment of Choctaw Newborn
## Act of 1905   Volume XIII

Witnesses To Mark:
{

Subscribed and sworn to before me this 5 day of Aug , 1905

J.H. Matthews
Notary Public.

---

**BIRTH AFFIDAVIT.**

### DEPARTMENT OF THE INTERIOR.
### COMMISSION TO THE FIVE CIVILIZED TRIBES.

---

IN RE APPLICATION FOR ENROLLMENT, as a citizen of the Choctaw Nation, of Berry[sic] Jefferson , born on the 6th day of December , 1903

Name of Father: Austin Jefferson         a citizen of the Choctaw Nation.
Name of Mother: Agnes Jefferson       a citizen of the Choctaw Nation.

Postoffice   Bethel, Indian Territory.

---

**AFFIDAVIT OF MOTHER.**

UNITED STATES OF AMERICA, Indian Territory, }
Central                   DISTRICT.

I, Agnes Jefferson , on oath state that I am 35 years of age and a citizen by blood , of the Choctaw Nation; that I am the lawful wife of Austin Jefferson , who is a citizen, by blood of the Choctaw Nation; that a male child was born to me on 6th day of December , 1903; that said child has been named Berry Jefferson , and was living March 4, 1905.

          her
       Agnes x Jefferson
Witnesses To Mark:    mark
{ Robert Anderson
{ Vester W Rose

Subscribed and sworn to before me this 6th day of April , 1905

Wirt Franklin
Notary Public.

# Applications for Enrollment of Choctaw Newborn
# Act of 1905  Volume XIII

### AFFIDAVIT OF ATTENDING PHYSICIAN OR MID-WIFE.

UNITED STATES OF AMERICA, Indian Territory, }
  Central                    DISTRICT.

I, Austin Jefferson, ~~a~~ ............................., on oath state that I attended on Mrs. Agnes Jefferson, ~~wife of~~ *my wife* on the 6th day of December, 1903; that there was born to her on said date a male child; that said child was living March 4, 1905, and ~~is said to have~~ *has* been named Berry Jefferson

Austin Jefferson

Witnesses To Mark:
{

Subscribed and sworn to before me this 6th day of April, 1905

Wirt Franklin
Notary Public.

---

Choc New Born 925
  Lincoln Winship  b. 10-24-02
  Anderson Winship  b. 12-25-04

BIRTH AFFIDAVIT.

### DEPARTMENT OF THE INTERIOR.
### COMMISSION TO THE FIVE CIVILIZED TRIBES.

IN RE APPLICATION FOR ENROLLMENT, as a citizen of the Choctaw Nation, of Lincoln Winship, born on the 24th day of October, 1902

Name of Father: Isaac Winship          a citizen of the Choctaw Nation.
Name of Mother: Eunittie Winship    a citizen of the Choctaw Nation.

Postoffice   Bethel, Ind. Ter.

## Applications for Enrollment of Choctaw Newborn
## Act of 1905   Volume XIII

### AFFIDAVIT OF MOTHER.

UNITED STATES OF AMERICA, Indian Territory, }
Central    DISTRICT.

I, Eunittie Winship, on oath state that I am 20 years of age and a citizen by blood, of the Choctaw Nation; that I am the lawful wife of Isaac Winship, who is a citizen, by blood of the Choctaw Nation; that a male child was born to me on 24th day of October, 1902; that said child has been named Lincoln Winship, and was living March 4, 1905.

                    her
             Eunittie x Winship

Witnesses To Mark:      mark
{ Vester W Rose
  Robert Anderson

Subscribed and sworn to before me this 5th day of April, 1905

             Wirt Franklin
             Notary Public.

---

### AFFIDAVIT OF ATTENDING PHYSICIAN OR MID-WIFE.

UNITED STATES OF AMERICA, Indian Territory, }
Central    DISTRICT.

I, Mary Miashintubbee, a mid-wife, on oath state that I attended on Mrs. Eunittie Winship, wife of Isaac Winship on the 24th day of October, 1902; that there was born to her on said date a male child; that said child was living March 4, 1905, and is said to have been named Lincoln Winship

             her
           Mary x Miashintubbee

Witnesses To Mark:      mark
{ Vester W Rose
  Robert Anderson

Subscribed and sworn to before me this 5th day of April, 1905

             Wirt Franklin
             Notary Public.

## Applications for Enrollment of Choctaw Newborn
## Act of 1905   Volume XIII

BIRTH AFFIDAVIT.

### DEPARTMENT OF THE INTERIOR.
### COMMISSION TO THE FIVE CIVILIZED TRIBES.

IN RE APPLICATION FOR ENROLLMENT, as a citizen of the Choctaw Nation, of Anderson Winship, born on the 25th day of December, 1904

Name of Father: Isaac Winship    a citizen of the Choctaw Nation.
Name of Mother: Eunittie Winship    a citizen of the Choctaw Nation.

Postoffice    Bethel, Ind. Ter.

**AFFIDAVIT OF MOTHER.**

UNITED STATES OF AMERICA, Indian Territory,　}
Central      DISTRICT.

I, Eunittie Winship, on oath state that I am 20 years of age and a citizen by blood, of the Choctaw Nation; that I am the lawful wife of Isaac Winship, who is a citizen, by blood of the Choctaw Nation; that a male child was born to me on 25th day of December, 1904; that said child has been named Anderson Winship, and was living March 4, 1905.

                       her
               Eunittie x Winship
Witnesses To Mark:        mark
{ Robert Anderson
   Vester W Rose

Subscribed and sworn to before me this 5th day of April, 1905

               Wirt Franklin
                   Notary Public.

**AFFIDAVIT OF ATTENDING PHYSICIAN OR MID-WIFE.**

UNITED STATES OF AMERICA, Indian Territory,　}
Central      DISTRICT.

I, Nancy Baker, a mid-wife, on oath state that I attended on Mrs. Eunittie Winship, wife of Isaac Winship on the 25th day of December, 1904; that there was born to her on said date a male child; that said child was living March 4, 1905, and is said to have been named Anderson Winship

                       her
               Nancy x Baker
                  mark

## Applications for Enrollment of Choctaw Newborn
## Act of 1905   Volume XIII

Witnesses To Mark:
- Robert Anderson
- Vester W Rose

Subscribed and sworn to before me this  5th  day of   April     , 1905

Wirt Franklin
Notary Public.

---

Choc New Born 926
Robinson Going  b. 12-7-04

**NEW-BORN AFFIDAVIT.**

Number..................

...Choctaw Enrolling Commission...

IN THE MATTER OF THE APPLICATION FOR ENROLLMENT, as a citizen of the Choctaw Nation, of Robnson[sic] Going

born on the  7  day of __Dec__  190 4

Name of father   Vinson Going            a citizen of   Choctaw
Nation final enrollment No. ..................
Name of mother  Silsainey Going          a citizen of   Choctaw
Nation final enrollment No.  6000

Postoffice   Smithville I.T.

**AFFIDAVIT OF MOTHER.**

UNITED STATES OF AMERICA
INDIAN TERRITORY
   Central      DISTRICT

I   Silsainey Going                  , on oath state that I am 18 years of age and a citizen by  Blood   of the  Choctaw         Nation, and as such have been placed upon the final roll of the    Choctaw  Nation, by the Honorable Secretary of the Interior my final enrollment number being   6000 ; that I am the lawful wife of   Vinson Going     , who is a citizen of the   Choctaw        Nation, and as such has been placed upon the final roll of said Nation by the Honorable Secretary of the Interior, his

206

## Applications for Enrollment of Choctaw Newborn
## Act of 1905   Volume XIII

final enrollment number being ............... and that a    mail[sic]    child was born to me on the 7    day of    December    190 4; that said child has been named    Robinson Going , and is now living.

                                                    her
                                      Silsainey  x  Going

Witnesseth.                                                                           mark

Must be two Witnesses who are Citizens.  }  Peter Going
                            Osborne Going

Subscribed and sworn to before me this    21    day of    Jan    190 5

                                        C L Lester
                                                Notary Public.

My commission expires:  Oct 15-1905

---

## AFFIDAVIT OF ATTENDING PHYSICIAN OR MIDWIFE

UNITED STATES OF AMERICA
INDIAN TERRITORY
   Central    DISTRICT

    I,    Annie McCoy    a    midwife on oath state that I attended on Mrs.  Silsainey Going    wife of  Vinson Going on the   7    day of    Dec  , 190 4 , that there was born to her on said date a    mail    child, that said child is now living, and is said to have been named    Robinson Going

                Subscribed and sworn to before me this, the    21    day of    Jan    190 5

WITNESSETH:                                              C L Lester    Notary Public.

Must be two witnesses who are citizens  {  Peter Going
                                  Osborne Going

We hereby certify that we are well acquainted with  a    and know    to be reputable and of good standing in the community.
                                                            her
            Osborne Going                                      Annie  x  McCoy
                                                            mark

            Peter Going                                  _____

## Applications for Enrollment of Choctaw Newborn
## Act of 1905   Volume XIII

Selseniey[sic] Going's father's name is Logan Jones (Dead) Her mother's name is Nancy Harris formerly Jones

---

Vinson Going's father's Gibson Going. Mother's name is Elyara Going

---

**BIRTH AFFIDAVIT.**

### DEPARTMENT OF THE INTERIOR.
### COMMISSION TO THE FIVE CIVILIZED TRIBES.

---

**IN RE APPLICATION FOR ENROLLMENT**, as a citizen of the Choctaw Nation, of Robinson Going, born on the 7th day of December, 1904

Name of Father: Vinson Going          a citizen of the Choctaw Nation.
Name of Mother: Silseiney Going       a citizen of the Choctaw Nation.

Postoffice

---

**AFFIDAVIT OF MOTHER.**

UNITED STATES OF AMERICA, Indian Territory,
Central   DISTRICT.

I, Silseiney Going, on oath state that I am 19 years of age and a citizen by blood, of the Choctaw Nation; that I am the lawful wife of Vinson Going, who is a citizen, by blood of the Choctaw Nation; that a male child was born to me on 7th day of December, 1904; that said child has been named Robinson Going, and was living March 4, 1905.

                         her
                   Silseiney x Going
Witnesses To Mark:            mark
  Robert Anderson
  Vester W Rose

Subscribed and sworn to before me this 6th day of April, 1905

                       Wirt Franklin
                           Notary Public.

# Applications for Enrollment of Choctaw Newborn
## Act of 1905 Volume XIII

### AFFIDAVIT OF ATTENDING PHYSICIAN OR MID-WIFE.

UNITED STATES OF AMERICA, Indian Territory, }
   Central                    DISTRICT.

I, Annie McCoy, a mid-wife, on oath state that I attended on Mrs. Silseiney Going, wife of Vinson Going on the 7th day of December, 1904; that there was born to her on said date a male child; that said child was living March 4, 1905, and is said to have been named Robinson Going

                                                        her
Witnesses To Mark:            Annie x McCoy
   { Robert Anderson             mark
   { Vester W Rose

Subscribed and sworn to before me this 6th day of April, 1905

                                 Wirt Franklin
                                 Notary Public.

---

Choc New Born 927
    Joseph Tushka   b. 6-18-03

BIRTH AFFIDAVIT.
### DEPARTMENT OF THE INTERIOR.
### COMMISSION TO THE FIVE CIVILIZED TRIBES.

IN RE APPLICATION FOR ENROLLMENT, as a citizen of the Choctaw Nation, of Joseph Tushka, born on the 18th day of June, 1903

Name of Father: Impson W. Tushka       a citizen of the Choctaw Nation.
Name of Mother: Nellie Tushka          a citizen of the Choctaw Nation.

                         Postoffice    Idabel, Ind. Ter.

# Applications for Enrollment of Choctaw Newborn
## Act of 1905  Volume XIII

**AFFIDAVIT OF MOTHER.**

UNITED STATES OF AMERICA, Indian Territory, }
Central        DISTRICT.

I, Nellie Tushka, on oath state that I am 43 years of age and a citizen by blood, of the Choctaw Nation; that I am the lawful wife of Impson W Tushka, who is a citizen, by blood of the Choctaw Nation; that a male child was born to me on 18th day of June, 1903; that said child has been named Joseph Tushka, and was living March 4, 1905.

                              her
                      Nellie x Tushka

Witnesses To Mark:          mark
{ Robert Anderson
  Vester W Rose

Subscribed and sworn to before me this 11th day of April, 1905

                    Wirt Franklin
                    Notary Public.

---

**AFFIDAVIT OF ATTENDING PHYSICIAN OR MID-WIFE.**

UNITED STATES OF AMERICA, Indian Territory, }
Central        DISTRICT.

I, Lizzie Tushka, a mid-wife, on oath state that I attended on Mrs. Nellie Tushka, wife of Impson W Tushka on the 18th day of June, 1903; that there was born to her on said date a male child; that said child was living March 4, 1905, and is said to have been named Joseph Tushka

                              her
                      Lizzie x Tushka

Witnesses To Mark:          mark
{ Robert Anderson
  Vester W Rose

Subscribed and sworn to before me this 11th day of April, 1905

                    Wirt Franklin
                    Notary Public.

Applications for Enrollment of Choctaw Newborn
Act of 1905  Volume XIII

**NEW-BORN AFFIDAVIT.**

Number..............

## Choctaw Enrolling Commission.

IN THE MATTER OF THE APPLICATION FOR ENROLLMENT, as a citizen of the Choctaw Nation, of  Josie Tushka

born on the $18^{th}$ day of June 190 3

Name of father  Impson W Tushka   a citizen of   Choctaw Nation final enrollment No   3011
Name of mother  Nellie Tushka   a citizen of   Choctaw Nation final enrollment No   3012

Postoffice   Idabel I.T.

**AFFIDAVIT OF MOTHER.**

UNITED STATES OF AMERICA,
   INDIAN TERRITORY,
Central     DISTRICT

I   Nellie Tushka   on oath state that I am  43  years of age and a citizen by  blood  of the  Choctaw  Nation, and as such have been placed upon the final roll of the  Choctaw  Nation, by the Honorable Secretary of the Interior my final enrollment number being  3012  ; that I am the lawful wife of  Impson W Tushka  , who is a citizen of the  Choctaw  Nation, and as such has been placed upon the final roll of said Nation by the Honorable Secretary of the Interior, his final enrollment number being  3011  and that a  male  child was born to me on the $18^{th}$ day of  June   190 3 ; that said child has been named  Josie Tushka , and is now living.

                                                    her
                                        Nellie x Tushka
                                           mark

WITNESSETH:
  Must be two    Dixon Parker
  Witnesses who
  are Citizens.    Robert S Harrison

Subscribed and sworn to before me this   24   day of   Jan   190 5

                                        W. A. Shoney
                                                  Notary Public.

My commission expires   Jan 10 1909

# Applications for Enrollment of Choctaw Newborn
## Act of 1905   Volume XIII

## AFFIDAVIT OF ATTENDING PHYSICIAN OR MIDWIFE

UNITED STATES OF AMERICA
INDIAN TERRITORY
   Central   DISTRICT

I, Lizzie Tushka   a   midwife on oath state that I attended on Mrs. Nellie Tushka   wife of Impson W Tushka on the 18th day of June, 190 3, that there was born to her on said date a   male child, that said child is now living, and is said to have been named Josie Tushka

                      her
              Lizzie x Tushka
                 mark

Subscribed and sworn to before me this, the   24   day of Jan   190 5

WITNESSETH:   W.A. Shoney   Notary Public.

Must be two witnesses who are citizens { Dixon Parker
Robert S. Harrison

We hereby certify that we are well acquainted with   Lizzie Tushka a   midwife   and know   her   to be reputable and of good standing in the community.

Richard C. Denson   _____

Ruth Shaw   _____

Choc New Born 928
   Minnie Dyer   b. 2-13-04

## Applications for Enrollment of Choctaw Newborn
## Act of 1905   Volume XIII

7-NB-928.

Muskogee, Indian Territory, June 1, 1905.

Joel Dyer,
    Eagletown, Indian Territory.

Dear Sir:

    Referring to the application for the enrollment of your infant child, Minnie Dyer, born February 13, 1904, it is noted from the affidavits heretofore filed in this office that you were the only one in attendance upon your wife at the time of birth of the applicant.

    In this event it will be necessary that you file in this office the affidavits of two persons, who are disinterested and not related to the applicant, who have actual knowledge of the facts that the child was born, the date of her birth; that she was living on March 4, 1905, and that Mary Dyer is her mother.

    The affidavit of John Tenihka to these facts has been filed. It will, therefore, be necessary that you secure a similar affidavit from another person.

    Respectfully,

    Chairman.

---

7 NB 928

Muskogee, Indian Territory, June 30, 1905.

Joel Dyer,
    Eagletown, Indian Territory.

Dear Sir:

    Receipt is hereby acknowledged of the affidavits of Albert Gable and Lemon Butler to the birth of Minnie Dyer, daughter of Joel and Mary Dyer, February 18, 1904, and the same have been filed with our record in the matter of the enrollment of said child.

    Respectfully,

    Chairman.

## Applications for Enrollment of Choctaw Newborn
## Act of 1905   Volume XIII

**BIRTH AFFIDAVIT.**

## DEPARTMENT OF THE INTERIOR.
## COMMISSION TO THE FIVE CIVILIZED TRIBES.

IN RE APPLICATION FOR ENROLLMENT, as a citizen of the Choctaw Nation, of Minnie Dyer, born on the 18th day of February, 1904

Name of Father: Joel Dyer　　　　　a citizen of the Choctaw Nation.
Name of Mother: Mary Dyer　　　　a citizen of the Choctaw Nation.

　　　　　　　　　Postoffice　　Eagletown, Ind. Ter.

**AFFIDAVIT OF MOTHER.**

UNITED STATES OF AMERICA, Indian Territory, }
　Central　　　　　　DISTRICT.

I, Mary Dyer, on oath state that I am about 30 years of age and a citizen by blood, of the Choctaw Nation; that I am the lawful wife of Joel Dyer, who is a citizen, by blood of the Choctaw Nation; that a female child was born to me on 18th day of February, 1904; that said child has been named Minnie Dyer, and was living March 4, 1905. *and that no physician or midwife attended me at the birth of said child*

　　　　　　　　　　　　　　　　her
　　　　　　　　　　　　　　Mary x Dyer
Witnesses To Mark:　　　　　　mark
　{ Robert Anderson
　　Vester W Rose

Subscribed and sworn to before me this 11th day of April, 1905

　　　　　　　　　　Wirt Franklin
　　　　　　　　　　　Notary Public.

**AFFIDAVIT OF ATTENDING PHYSICIAN OR MID-WIFE.**

UNITED STATES OF AMERICA, Indian Territory, }
　Central　　　　　　DISTRICT.

I, Joel Dyer, a................., on oath state that I attended on Mrs. Mary Dyer, wife of Joel Dyer on the 18th day of February, 1904; that there was born to her on said date a female child; that said child was living March 4, 1905, and is said to have been named Minnie Dyer *and that no one else was present when said child was born*

　　　　　　　　　　Joel Dyer

## Applications for Enrollment of Choctaw Newborn
## Act of 1905 Volume XIII

Witnesses To Mark:
{

Subscribed and sworn to before me this 11th day of April , 1905

Wirt Franklin
Notary Public.

---

**BIRTH AFFIDAVIT.**

## DEPARTMENT OF THE INTERIOR,
### COMMISSION TO THE FIVE CIVILIZED TRIBES.

---

IN RE *Application for Enrollment,* as a citizen of the Choctaw Nation, of Minnie Dyer , born on the 18$^{th}$ day of February , 1904

Name of Father: Joel Dyer a citizen of the Choctaw Nation.
Name of Mother: Mary Dyer a citizen of the Choctaw Nation.

Post-Office: Eagletown

---

**AFFIDAVIT OF MOTHER.**

---

UNITED STATES OF AMERICA, }
    INDIAN TERRITORY.
Central District.

I, Albert Gable , on oath state that I am 47 years of age and a citizen by Freedman , of the Choctaw Nation; that I *have the actual knowledge of the fact that Minnie Dyer, was born on the 18$^{th}$ day of Feb 1904 and that Mary Dyer is the mother of the said Minnie Dyer and that she said child was living on March 4$^{th}$ 1905*

          his
Albert x Gable
**WITNESSES TO MARK:**      mark
{ W.H. Seale
  C H Bowers

*Subscribed and sworn to before me this* 24 *day of* June , 1905.
My Commission
expires 23$^{rd}$ Dec 1905          Jeff Gardner
                                    **NOTARY PUBLIC.**

# Applications for Enrollment of Choctaw Newborn
## Act of 1905   Volume XIII

**AFFIDAVIT OF ATTENDING PHYSICIAN OR MID-WIFE.**

UNITED STATES OF AMERICA,  
   INDIAN TERRITORY.  
Central      District.

*Freedman*

I, Lemon Butler ^ *That I am 40 years of age*, on oath state that I *have the actual knowledge of the fact that Minnie Dyer was born on the 18th day of Feb 1904, and that Mary Dyer is the mother of the said Minnie Dyer and that the said child was living on March 4th 1905*

                                                  Lemon Butler

**WITNESSES TO MARK:**

{

    Subscribed and sworn to before me this   24   day of   June   , 1905.  
My Commission  
expires 23rd Dec 1905                      Jeff Gardner  
                                                    *NOTARY PUBLIC.*

United States of America,    )  
                                  )  
Indian Territory,              )   ss.  
                                  )  
Central District.              )

    I, John Tonihka, on oath state that I am twenty-seven years of age and a citizen by blood of the Choctaw Nation; that my post office address is Eagletown, Indian Territory; that I am personally acquainted with Mary Dyer, wife of Joel Dyer; that I have known said parties for about eight years, and during this time I have lived within one mile of where they have lived, near Eagletown, Indian Territory, and have been at their home often; that I know of my own knowledge that on or about the 18th day of February, 1904, there was born to the said Mary Dyer a female child; that said child is now living and is said to have been names Minnie Dyer.

                                                    John Tonihka

Subscribed and sworn to before me this 11th day of April, 1905.

                                                   Wirt Franklin  
                                                 Notary Public.

# Applications for Enrollment of Choctaw Newborn
## Act of 1905 Volume XIII

Choc New Born 929
Rhoda Kaniatobe  b. 3-11-03

**NEW-BORN AFFIDAVIT.**

Number............

...Choctaw Enrolling Commission...

IN THE MATTER OF THE APPLICATION FOR ENROLLMENT, as a citizen of the Choctaw Nation, of Rhoda Kaniatobe born on the 11$^{th}$ day of __March__ 190 3

Name of father  Wilburn Kaniatobe    a citizen of   Choctaw
Nation final enrollment No.  2827
Name of mother  Rosa Kaniatobe    a citizen of   Choctaw
Nation final enrollment No.  1060

Postoffice   Idabel I.T.

**AFFIDAVIT OF MOTHER.**

UNITED STATES OF AMERICA
INDIAN TERRITORY
Central   DISTRICT

I   Rosa Kaniatobe   , on oath state that I am 28   years of age and a citizen by   blood   of the   Choctaw   Nation, and as such have been placed upon the final roll of the   Choctaw   Nation, by the Honorable Secretary of the Interior my final enrollment number being   1060 ; that I am the lawful wife of  Wilburn Kaniatobe   , who is a citizen of the   Choctaw   Nation, and as such has been placed upon the final roll of said Nation by the Honorable Secretary of the Interior, his final enrollment number being   2827   and that a   female   child was born to me on the  11$^{th}$ day of   March   190 3; that said child has been named   Rhoda Kaniatobe   , and is now living.

Rosa Kaniatobe

Witnesseth.
Must be two Witnesses who are Citizens.   Willington Haiskonabbe
Gibson Kaniatubbee

Subscribed and sworn to before me this  21   day of   Jan   190 5

W.A. Shoney
Notary Public.

My commission expires:  Jan 10 1909

## Applications for Enrollment of Choctaw Newborn
## Act of 1905 Volume XIII

### AFFIDAVIT OF ATTENDING PHYSICIAN OR MIDWIFE

UNITED STATES OF AMERICA
INDIAN TERRITORY
Central DISTRICT

I, Helen[sic] Kaniatubbee a midwife on oath state that I attended on Mrs. Rosa Kaniatobe wife of Wilburn Kaniatobe on the $11^{th}$ day of March , 190 3 , that there was born to her on said date a female child, that said child is now living, and is said to have been named Rhoda Kaniatobe

Helen Kaniatubbee
Subscribed and sworn to before me this, the $21^{st}$ day of Jan 190 5

WITNESSETH: W.A. Shoney Notary Public.
Must be two witnesses who are citizens { Willington Haiskonabbe

Gibson Kaniatubbee

We hereby certify that we are well acquainted with Helen Kaniatubbee a and know to be reputable and of good standing in the community.

Willington Haiskonabbe _____

Gibson Kaniatubbee _____

BIRTH AFFIDAVIT.
### DEPARTMENT OF THE INTERIOR.
### COMMISSION TO THE FIVE CIVILIZED TRIBES.

IN RE APPLICATION FOR ENROLLMENT, as a citizen of the Choctaw Nation, of Rhoda Kaniatobe , born on the 11th day of March , 1903

Name of Father: Wilburn Kaniatobe a citizen of the Choctaw Nation.
Name of Mother: Rosa Kaniatobe a citizen of the Choctaw Nation.

Postoffice Idabel, Ind. Ter.

# Applications for Enrollment of Choctaw Newborn
## Act of 1905 Volume XIII

**AFFIDAVIT OF MOTHER.**

UNITED STATES OF AMERICA, Indian Territory, }
Central DISTRICT.

I, Rosa Kaniatobe, on oath state that I am 28 years of age and a citizen by blood, of the Choctaw Nation; that I am the lawful wife of Wilburn Kaniatobe, who is a citizen, by blood of the Choctaw Nation; that a female child was born to me on 11th day of March, 1903; that said child has been named Rhoda Kaniatobe, and was living March 4, 1905.

Rosa Kaniatobe

Witnesses To Mark:
{

Subscribed and sworn to before me this 11th day of April, 1905

Wirt Franklin
Notary Public.

---

**AFFIDAVIT OF ATTENDING PHYSICIAN OR MID-WIFE.**

UNITED STATES OF AMERICA, Indian Territory, }
Central DISTRICT.

I, Ellen Kaniatobe, a mid-wife, on oath state that I attended on Mrs. Rosa Kaniatobe, wife of Wilburn Kaniatobe on the 11th day of March, 1903; that there was born to her on said date a female child; that said child was living March 4, 1905, and is said to have been named Rhoda Kaniatobe

her
Ellen x Kaniatobe
mark

Witnesses To Mark:
{ Robert Anderson
  Vester Rose

Subscribed and sworn to before me this 11th day of April, 1905

Wirt Franklin
Notary Public.

## Applications for Enrollment of Choctaw Newborn
## Act of 1905 Volume XIII

Choc New Born 930
    Silena Moore  b. 8-9-03

7-NB-930.

Muskogee, Indian Territory, June 1, 1905.

John Moore,
    America, Indian Territory.

Dear Sir:

    Referring to the application for the enrollment of your infant child, Silena Moore, born August 9, 1903, it is noted from the affidavits heretofore filed in this office that you were the only one in attendance upon your wife at the time of birth of the applicant.

    In this event it will be necessary that you file in this office the affidavits of two persons, who are disinterested and not related to the applicant, who have actual knowledge of the facts that the child was born, the date of her birth; that she was living on March 4, 1905, and that Frances Moore is her mother.

    The affidavit of Johnson Cogswell to these facts has been filed. It will therefore be necessary that you secure the affidavit of another person to these facts.

Respectfully,

Chairman.

7 NB 930

Muskogee, Indian Territory, June 26, 1905.

John Moore,
    America, Indian Territory.

Dear Sir:

    Receipt is hereby acknowledged of the affidavit of Daniel Jefferson to the birth of Selina Moore, daughter of John and Francis Moore, August 9, 1903, and the same has been filed with our records in the matter of the enrollment of said child.

Respectfully,

Chairman.

Applications for Enrollment of Choctaw Newborn
Act of 1905 Volume XIII

7 NB 930

Muskogee, Indian Territory, June 29, 1905.

John Moore,
    America, Indian Territory.

Dear Sir:

    Receipt is hereby acknowledged of the affidavit of Daniel Jefferson to the birth of Selina Moore, daughter of John and Francis Moore, August 9, 1903, and the same has been filed with our records in the matter of the enrollment of said child.

    Respectfully,

Chairman.

# NEW BORN AFFIDAVIT

No ..........

## CHOCTAW ENROLLING COMMISSION

IN THE MATTER OF THE APPLICATION FOR ENROLLMENT as a citizen of the Choctaw Nation, of Salena[sic] Moore born on the 9th day of August 190 3

Name of father John Moore     a citizen of Choctaw Nation, final enrollment No. ..........

Name of mother Francis Moore     a citizen of Choctaw Nation, final enrollment No. ..........

America, I.T.     Postoffice.

**AFFIDAVIT OF MOTHER**

UNITED STATES OF AMERICA }
INDIAN TERRITORY
DISTRICT Central

    I Francis Moore , on oath state that I am 35 years of age and a citizen by blood of the Choctaw Nation, and as such have been placed upon the final roll of the Choctaw Nation, by the Honorable Secretary of the Interior my final enrollment number being .......... ; that I am the lawful wife of John Moore , who is

## Applications for Enrollment of Choctaw Newborn
## Act of 1905  Volume XIII

a citizen of the Choctaw Nation, and as such has been placed upon the final roll of said Nation by the Honorable Secretary of the Interior, his final enrollment number being .................. and that a female child was born to me on the 9$^{th}$ day of August 190 3; that said child has been named Salena Moore , and is now living.

                  her
WITNESSETH:                 Francis x Moore
Must be two witnesses { Johnson Coxwell     mark
who are citizens         Reuben Mclure[sic]

Subscribed and sworn to before me this, the 15 day of Feb , 190 5

                W.A. Shoney
                     Notary Public.
My Commission Expires:
      Jan 10 1909

## AFFIDAVIT OF ATTENDING PHYSICIAN OR MIDWIFE

UNITED STATES OF AMERICA
INDIAN TERRITORY
  Central      DISTRICT

    I, John Moore a Attendant on oath state that I attended on Mrs. Francis Moore wife of John Moore on the 9$^{th}$ day of August , 190 3 , that there was born to her on said date a female child, that said child is now living, and is said to have been named Salena Moore

                    John Moore
Subscribed and sworn to before me this, the 15 day of Feb 190 5

WITNESSETH:         W.A. Shoney     Notary Public.
Must be two witnesses { Johnson Coxwell
who are citizens
              Reuben MClure[sic]

    We hereby certify that we are well acquainted with John Moore a Attendant and know him to be reputable and of good standing in the community.

      Johnson Coxwell          _____

      Reuben McClure          _____

## Applications for Enrollment of Choctaw Newborn
## Act of 1905   Volume XIII

*(The affidavit below typed as given.)*

United States of America  
   Indian Territory    } ss  
Central Dist

        I Daniel Jefferson of Goodwater Indian Territory do solemnly swear that I am acquainted with Francis Moore wife of John Moore and that on the ninth day of August 1903 I visited John Moore's house and saw a baby girl that was born to Francis Moore that day. Which was named Silena and that the said child is now living at the house of John Moore.

Daniel Jefferson

Subscribed and sworn to before me this 21$^{st}$ day of June AD 1905

William Spencer<br>Notary Public

---

United States of America,   )  
                                  )  
Indian Territory,           ) ss.  
                                  )  
Central District.            )

        I, Johnson Cogswell, on oath state that I am twenty-six years of age and a citizen by blood of the Choctaw Nation; that my post office address is America, Indian Territory; that I am personally acquainted with Frances Moore, wife of John Moore, and have known said parties nearly all my life; that I know of my own knowledge that there was born to the said Frances Moore on or about the 9th day of August, 1903, a female child; that said child is now living and is said to have been names Silena Moore.

Johnson Cogswell

Subscribed and sworn to before me this 11th day of April, 1905.

Wirt Franklin<br>Notary Public.

## Applications for Enrollment of Choctaw Newborn
## Act of 1905   Volume XIII

BIRTH AFFIDAVIT.

### DEPARTMENT OF THE INTERIOR.
### COMMISSION TO THE FIVE CIVILIZED TRIBES.

IN RE APPLICATION FOR ENROLLMENT, as a citizen of the   Choctaw   Nation, of   Silena Moore   , born on the 9th   day of   August   , 1903

Name of Father: John Moore         a citizen of the   Choctaw   Nation.
Name of Mother: Frances Moore      a citizen of the   Choctaw   Nation.

Postoffice   America, Ind. Ter.

### AFFIDAVIT OF MOTHER.

UNITED STATES OF AMERICA, Indian Territory,}
Central    DISTRICT.

I, Frances Moore   , on oath state that I am   35   years of age and a citizen by   blood   , of the   Choctaw   Nation; that I am the lawful wife of   John Moore   , who is a citizen, by blood   of the   Choctaw   Nation; that a female   child was born to me on 9th   day of   August   , 1903; that said child has been named   Silena Moore   , and was living March 4, 1905. *and that no physician or midwife attended me at the birth of said child.*

                          her
                        Frances x Moore
Witnesses To Mark:      mark
{ Robert Anderson
  Vester W Rose

Subscribed and sworn to before me this   11th   day of   April   , 1905

                      Wirt Franklin
                      Notary Public.

### AFFIDAVIT OF ATTENDING PHYSICIAN OR MID-WIFE.

UNITED STATES OF AMERICA, Indian Territory,}
Central    DISTRICT.

I, John Moore   , ~~a~~ ..................., on oath state that I attended on Mrs.   Frances Moore   , ~~wife of~~ *my wife* on the   9th day of   August   , 1903; that there was born to her on said date a   female   child; that said child was living March 4, 1905, and ~~is said to have~~ *has* been named   Silena Moore; *and that no one else was present when said child was born*

## Applications for Enrollment of Choctaw Newborn
## Act of 1905 Volume XIII

Witnesses To Mark:
{
John Moore

Subscribed and sworn to before me this 11th day of April , 1905

Wirt Franklin
Notary Public.

---

Choc New Born 931
Lylie Colbert b. 4-6[sic]-04

**BIRTH AFFIDAVIT.**
### DEPARTMENT OF THE INTERIOR.
### COMMISSION TO THE FIVE CIVILIZED TRIBES.

**IN RE APPLICATION FOR ENROLLMENT,** as a citizen of the Choctaw Nation, of Lylie Colbert , born on the 16th day of April , 1904

Name of Father: Simpson Colbert     a citizen of the Choctaw Nation.
Name of Mother: Timesy Colbert     a citizen of the Choctaw Nation.

Postoffice    Eagletown, Ind. Ter.

**AFFIDAVIT OF MOTHER.**

UNITED STATES OF AMERICA, Indian Territory, }
Central     DISTRICT.

I, Timesy Colbert , on oath state that I am 33 years of age and a citizen by blood , of the Choctaw Nation; that I ~~am~~ was the lawful wife of Simpson Colbert, deceased , who ~~is~~ was a citizen, by blood of the Choctaw Nation; that a female child was born to me on 16th day of April , 1904; that said child has been named Lylie Colbert , and was living March 4, 1905.

her
Timesy x Colbert
mark

225

# Applications for Enrollment of Choctaw Newborn
## Act of 1905   Volume XIII

Witnesses To Mark:
{ Robert Anderson
  Vester W Rose

    Subscribed and sworn to before me this   11th  day of   April   , 1905

                        Wirt Franklin
                        Notary Public.

---

**AFFIDAVIT OF ATTENDING PHYSICIAN OR MID-WIFE.**

UNITED STATES OF AMERICA, Indian Territory,
   Central          DISTRICT.

    I,   Liney Wall   , a  mid-wife   , on oath state that I attended on Mrs.   Timesy Colbert   , wife of  Simpson Colbert   on the  16th   day of April , 1904; that there was born to her on said date a   female   child; that said child was living March 4, 1905, and is said to have been named  Lylie Colbert

                        her
                 Liney x Wall
Witnesses To Mark:        mark
{ Robert Anderson
  Vester W Rose

    Subscribed and sworn to before me this   11th  day of   April   , 1905

                        Wirt Franklin
                        Notary Public.

---

Choc New Born 932
    Ray Tonihka  b. 2-20-05

# Applications for Enrollment of Choctaw Newborn
# Act of 1905   Volume XIII

BIRTH AFFIDAVIT.

## DEPARTMENT OF THE INTERIOR.
## COMMISSION TO THE FIVE CIVILIZED TRIBES.

**IN RE APPLICATION FOR ENROLLMENT,** as a citizen of the Choctaw Nation, of Ray Tonihka, born on the 20th day of February, 1905

Name of Father: John Tonihka    a citizen of the Choctaw Nation.
Name of Mother: Betsy Tonihka    a citizen of the Choctaw Nation.

Postoffice   Eagletown, Ind. Ter.

### AFFIDAVIT OF MOTHER.

UNITED STATES OF AMERICA, Indian Territory,
Central   DISTRICT.

I, Betsy Tonihka, on oath state that I am 28 years of age and a citizen by blood, of the Choctaw Nation; that I am the lawful wife of John Tonihka, who is a citizen, by blood of the Choctaw Nation; that a male child was born to me on 20th day of February, 1904; that said child has been named Ray Tonihka, and was living March 4, 1905.

            her
          Betsy x Tonihka
Witnesses To Mark:      mark
 { Robert Anderson
   Vester W Rose

Subscribed and sworn to before me this 11th day of April, 1905

        Wirt Franklin
         Notary Public.

### AFFIDAVIT OF ATTENDING PHYSICIAN OR MID-WIFE.

UNITED STATES OF AMERICA, Indian Territory,
Central   DISTRICT.

I, Ellen Mambi, a mid-wife, on oath state that I attended on Mrs. Betsy Tonihka, wife of John Tonihka on the 20th day of February, 1905; that there was born to her on said date a male child; that said child was living March 4, 1905, and is said to have been named Ray Tonihka

           her
         Ellen x Mambi
          mark

Applications for Enrollment of Choctaw Newborn
Act of 1905  Volume XIII

Witnesses To Mark:
{ Robert Anderson
 Vester W Rose

Subscribed and sworn to before me this 11th day of April, 1905

Wirt Franklin
Notary Public.

---

Choc New Born 933
Lottie Willis  b. 2-24-03

**NEW-BORN AFFIDAVIT.**

Number..................

## Choctaw Enrolling Commission.

IN THE MATTER OF THE APPLICATION FOR ENROLLMENT, as a citizen of the Choctaw Nation, of    Lottie Willis

born on the  24  day of  February    190 3

Name of father   John Willis            a citizen of    Choctaw
Nation final enrollment No  1344
Name of mother    Sammie Willis      a citizen of    Choctaw
Nation final enrollment No   560

Postoffice    Garvin I.T.

**AFFIDAVIT OF MOTHER.**

UNITED STATES OF AMERICA, }
  INDIAN TERRITORY,
  ---------------------------------DISTRICT }

I            Sammie Willis                on oath state that I am  34  years of age and a citizen by  Intermarriage   of the  Choctaw   Nation, and as such have been placed upon the final roll of the   Choctaw   Nation, by the Honorable Secretary of the Interior my final enrollment number being  560   ; that I am the lawful wife of    John Willis       , who is a citizen of the   Choctaw   Nation, and as such has been placed upon the final roll of said Nation by the Honorable Secretary of the Interior, his final enrollment number being   1344   and that a   Female

228

## Applications for Enrollment of Choctaw Newborn
## Act of 1905   Volume XIII

child was born to me on the   24   day of   February   190 3 ; that said child has been named   Lottie Willis   , and is now living.

                                                her
                                      Sammie x Willis

WITNESSETH:                              mark

Must be two Witnesses who are Citizens.   }   Thomas L Lucas
                           Lyman Baker

Subscribed and sworn to before me this   22   day of   Feb   190 5

                                          W.A. Shoney
                                                    Notary Public.

My commission expires   Jan 10 1909

### *Affidavit of Attending Physician or Midwife*

UNITED STATES OF AMERICA,   }
     INDIAN TERRITORY,
Central      DISTRICT

I,   John Willis   a   Attendant on oath state that I attended on Mrs.   Sammie Willis   wife of   John Willis   on the   24   day of   Feb   , 190 3, that there was born to her on said date a   female   child, that said child is now living, and is said to have been named   Lottie Willis

                                       John Willis        ~~M.D.~~

Subscribed and sworn to before me this the   22   day of   Feb   1905

                                       W A Shoney
                                               Notary Public.

WITNESSETH:

Must be two witnesses who are citizens and know the child.   {   Thomas L Lucas
                              Lyman Baker

We hereby certify that we are well acquainted with   John Willis   a   attendant   and know   him   to be reputable and of good standing in the community.

                              Must be two citizen witnesses.   {   Thomas L Lucas
                                                                 Lyman Baker

## Applications for Enrollment of Choctaw Newborn
## Act of 1905  Volume XIII

BIRTH AFFIDAVIT.

## DEPARTMENT OF THE INTERIOR.
## COMMISSION TO THE FIVE CIVILIZED TRIBES.

IN RE APPLICATION FOR ENROLLMENT, as a citizen of the Choctaw Nation, of Lottie Willis, born on the 24th day of February, 1903

Name of Father: John Willis     a citizen of the Choctaw Nation.
Name of Mother: Sammie Willis     a citizen of the Choctaw Nation.

Postoffice   Garvin, Ind. Ter.

### AFFIDAVIT OF MOTHER.

UNITED STATES OF AMERICA, Indian Territory, }
Central          DISTRICT.

I, Sammie Willis, on oath state that I am 34 years of age and a citizen by marriage, of the Choctaw Nation; that I am the lawful wife of John Willis, who is a citizen, by blood of the Choctaw Nation; that a female child was born to me on 24th day of February, 1903; that said child has been named Lottie Willis, and was living March 4, 1905.

                             Sammie Willis

Witnesses To Mark:
{ Robert Anderson
   Vester W Rose

Subscribed and sworn to before me this 10th day of April, 1905

                             Wirt Franklin
                             Notary Public.

### AFFIDAVIT OF ATTENDING PHYSICIAN OR MID-WIFE.

UNITED STATES OF AMERICA, Indian Territory, }
Central          DISTRICT.

I, Susan John, a mid-wife, on oath state that I attended on Mrs. Sammie Willis, wife of John Willis on the 24th day of February, 1903; that there was born to her on said date a female child; that said child was living March 4, 1905, and is said to have been named Lottie Willis

                             her
                         Susan x John
                             mark

## Applications for Enrollment of Choctaw Newborn
## Act of 1905 Volume XIII

Witnesses To Mark:
{ Robert Anderson
{ Vester W Rose

Subscribed and sworn to before me this 10th day of April, 1905

Wirt Franklin
Notary Public.

---

Choc New Born 934
Ella Jefferson b. 9-19-04

**BIRTH AFFIDAVIT.**

**DEPARTMENT OF THE INTERIOR.**
**COMMISSION TO THE FIVE CIVILIZED TRIBES.**

IN RE APPLICATION FOR ENROLLMENT, as a citizen of the Choctaw Nation, of Ella Jefferson, born on the 19th day of September, 1904

Name of Father: Ellis Jefferson        a citizen of the Choctaw Nation.
Name of Mother: Lizzie Jefferson       a citizen of the Choctaw Nation.

Postoffice    Garvin, Ind. Ter.

**AFFIDAVIT OF MOTHER.**

UNITED STATES OF AMERICA, Indian Territory, }
Central           DISTRICT. }

I, Lizzie Jefferson, on oath state that I am 25 years of age and a citizen by blood, of the Choctaw Nation; that I am the lawful wife of Ellis Jefferson, who is a citizen, by blood of the Choctaw Nation; that a female child was born to me on 19th day of September, 1904; that said child has been named Ella Jefferson, and was living March 4, 1905.

Lizzie Jefferson

Witnesses To Mark:
{
{

# Applications for Enrollment of Choctaw Newborn
## Act of 1905   Volume XIII

Subscribed and sworn to before me this 10th day of April, 1905

Wirt Franklin
Notary Public.

---

**AFFIDAVIT OF ATTENDING PHYSICIAN OR MID-WIFE.**

UNITED STATES OF AMERICA, Indian Territory, }
Central           DISTRICT. }

I, Eleas Morrison, a mid-wife, on oath state that I attended on Mrs. Lizzie Jefferson, wife of Ellis Jefferson on the 19th day of September, 1904; that there was born to her on said date a female child; that said child was living March 4, 1905, and is said to have been named Ella Jefferson

Eleas x Morrison

Witnesses To Mark:
{ Robert Anderson
{ Vester W Rose

Subscribed and sworn to before me this 10th day of April, 1905

Wirt Franklin
Notary Public.

---

## *Affidavit of Attending Physician or Midwife*

UNITED STATES OF AMERICA, }
INDIAN TERRITORY, }
Central   DISTRICT }

I, Eleyis Morrison   a   midwife on oath state that I attended on Mrs. Lizzie Morrison   wife of Ellis Jefferson on the 19$^{th}$ day of Sept, 1904, that there was born to her on said date a female child, that said child is now living, and is said to have been named Ella Jefferson

her
Eleyis x Morrison   ~~M. D.~~
mark

Subscribed and sworn to before me this the 17$^{th}$ day of Feb   1905

W.A. Shoney
Notary Public.

WITNESSETH:
Must be two witnesses { Wilbon Cephus
who are citizens and  {
know the child.       { Mimy Holmes

## Applications for Enrollment of Choctaw Newborn
## Act of 1905  Volume XIII

We hereby certify that we are well acquainted with        Eleyis Morrison
a    midwife                       and know     her       to be reputable and of good standing in the community.

Must be two citizen { Wilbon Cephus
witnesses.            Mimy Holmes

# NEW BORN AFFIDAVIT

No ............

## CHOCTAW ENROLLING COMMISSION

IN THE MATTER OF THE APPLICATION FOR ENROLLMENT as a citizen of the Choctaw Nation, of      Ella Jefferson       born on the $19^{th}$ day of   September    190 4

Name of father   Ellis Jefferson       a citizen of    Choctaw    Nation, final enrollment No.  2629
Name of mother   Lizzie Morrison       a citizen of    Choctaw    Nation, final enrollment No.  1697

Garvin I.T.                    Postoffice.

**AFFIDAVIT OF MOTHER**

UNITED STATES OF AMERICA  }
INDIAN TERRITORY          }
DISTRICT    Central        }

I    Lizzie Morrison         , on oath state that I am   27   years of age and a citizen by    blood    of the    Choctaw    Nation, and as such have been placed upon the final roll of the   Choctaw    Nation, by the Honorable Secretary of the Interior my final enrollment number being   1697   ; that I am the lawful wife of   Ellis Jefferson  , who is a citizen of the    Choctaw    Nation, and as such has been placed upon the final roll of said Nation by the Honorable Secretary of the Interior, his final enrollment number being   2629   and that a   female   child was born to me on the   $19^{th}$   day of September   190 4; that said child has been named   Ella Jefferson   , and is now living.

                                                 her
WITNESSETH:                           Lizzie  x  Morrison
                                              mark
Must be two witnesses  { Wilbon Cephus
who are citizens       { Mimy Holmes

Applications for Enrollment of Choctaw Newborn
Act of 1905   Volume XIII

Subscribed and sworn to before me this, the 17<sup>th</sup> day of Feb , 190 5

W.A. Shoney
Notary Public.

My Commission Expires: Jan 10 1909

---

Choc New Born 935
    Racy McClure   b. 2-15-04

# NEW BORN AFFIDAVIT

No ............

## CHOCTAW ENROLLING COMMISSION

IN THE MATTER OF THE APPLICATION FOR ENROLLMENT as a citizen of the Choctaw Nation, of    Racie[sic] M<sup>c</sup>Clure    born on the 15<sup>th</sup> day of February  190 4

Name of father  Reuben M<sup>c</sup>Clure    a citizen of  Choctaw   Nation, final enrollment No.  3459
Name of mother  Ellen McClure    a citizen of  Choctaw   Nation, final enrollment No.  3460

Goodwater I.T.   Postoffice.

---

**AFFIDAVIT OF MOTHER**

UNITED STATES OF AMERICA
   INDIAN TERRITORY
DISTRICT    Central

I   Reuben McClure    , on oath state that I am  37  years of age and a citizen by  blood  of the  Choctaw  Nation, and as such have been placed upon the final roll of the  Choctaw  Nation, by the Honorable Secretary of the Interior my final enrollment number being  3469[sic]  ; that I am the lawful ~~wife~~ husband of   Ellen McClure deceased  , who ~~is was~~ a citizen of the  Choctaw   Nation, and as such has been placed upon the final roll of said Nation by the Honorable Secretary of the Interior, ~~his~~ her final enrollment number being  3460  and that a  female  child was born to ~~me~~ her

234

## Applications for Enrollment of Choctaw Newborn
## Act of 1905 Volume XIII

on the 15th day of Feb 190 4; that said child has been named Racie McClure, and is now living.

Reuben M<sup>c</sup>Clure

WITNESSETH:
Must be two witnesses who are citizens { Stephen M<sup>c</sup>Clure
Johnson Coxwell

Subscribed and sworn to before me this, the 15th day of Feb , 190 5

W A Shoney
Notary Public.

My Commission Expires:
Jan 10 1909

## AFFIDAVIT OF ATTENDING PHYSICIAN OR MIDWIFE

UNITED STATES OF AMERICA
INDIAN TERRITORY
.............................DISTRICT

I, Reuben M<sup>c</sup>Clure a Attendant on oath state that I attended on Mrs. Ellen M<sup>c</sup>Clure wife of Reuben M<sup>c</sup>Clure on the 15th day of February , 190 4 , that there was born to her on said date a female child, that said child is now living, and is said to have been named Racie M<sup>c</sup>Clure

Reuben M<sup>c</sup>Clure

Subscribed and sworn to before me this, the 15 day of Feb 190 5

WITNESSETH:
Must be two witnesses who are citizens { Stephen M<sup>c</sup>Clure
Johnson Coxwell

W.A. Shoney Notary Public.

We hereby certify that we are well acquainted with Reuben M<sup>c</sup>Clure a attendant and know him to be reputable and of good standing in the community.

Stephen McClure  _____

Johnson Coxwell  _____

## Applications for Enrollment of Choctaw Newborn
## Act of 1905   Volume XIII

United States of America,   )
                            )
Indian Territory,           )   ss.
                            )
Central District.           )

     I, Sally Fobb, on oath state that I am thirty-seven years of age and a citizen by blood of the Choctaw Nation; that my post office address is Goodwater, Indian Territory; that I was personally acquainted with Ellen McClure, deceased, formerly the wife of Reuben McClure, and have known said parties nearly all my life; that for the last six years I have lived within one mile of where they have lived, near Goodwater, Indian Territory; that there was born to the said Ellen McClure on or about the 15th day of February, 1904, a female child; that said child is now living and is said to have been named Racy McClure; and that the said Ellen McClure died on the 21st day of March, 1904.

                                                      her
                                          Sally x Fobb
                                            mark

Subscribed and sworn to before me this 10th day of April, 1905.

                                        Wirt Franklin
                                              Notary Public.

Witnesses to mark.
        Robert Anderson
        Vester W Rose

---

United States of America,   )
                            )
Indian Territory,           )   ss.
                            )
Central District.           )

     I, Eastman Fobb, on oath state that I am twenty-seven years of age and a citizen by blood of the Choctaw Nation; that my post office address is Goodwater, Indian Territory; that I was personally acquainted with Ellen McClure, deceased, formerly the wife of Reuben McClure, and have known said parties about twelve years, and for the last six years have resided within one mile of where they have resided, near Goodwater, Indian Territory; that on or about the 15$^{th}$ day of February, 1904, there was born to the said Ellen McClure a female child; that said child is now living and is said to have been named Racy McClure; and that the said Ellen McClure dies on the 21 day of March, 1904.

                                        Eastman Fobb

## Applications for Enrollment of Choctaw Newborn
## Act of 1905  Volume XIII

Subscribed and sworn to before me this 10th day of April, 1905.

          Wirt Franklin
          Notary Public.

---

**BIRTH AFFIDAVIT.**

      **DEPARTMENT OF THE INTERIOR.**
    **COMMISSION TO THE FIVE CIVILIZED TRIBES.**

---

  **IN RE APPLICATION FOR ENROLLMENT,** as a citizen of the  Choctaw  Nation, of  Racy McClure , born on the  15th  day of  February , 1904

Name of Father: Reuben McClure  a citizen of the  Choctaw  Nation.
Name of Mother: Ellen McClure, deceased  a citizen of the  Choctaw  Nation.

      Postoffice  Goodwater, Ind. Ter.

---

      **AFFIDAVIT OF MOTHER.**

**UNITED STATES OF AMERICA, Indian Territory,**
  Central    **DISTRICT.**

  I, Reuben McClure , on oath state that I am  36  years of age and a citizen by  blood , of the  Choctaw  Nation; that I ~~am~~ was the lawful ~~wife~~ husband of  Ellen McClure, deceased , who ~~is~~ was a citizen, by  blood  of the  Choctaw  Nation; that a  female  child was born to me on  15th  day of  February , 1904; that said child has been named  Racy McClure , and was living March 4, 1905.

         his
       Reuben x McClure
Witnesses To Mark:    mark
 { Robert Anderson
  Vester Rose

  Subscribed and sworn to before me this  10th  day of  April , 1905

         Wirt Franklin
         Notary Public.

## Applications for Enrollment of Choctaw Newborn
## Act of 1905   Volume XIII

**AFFIDAVIT OF ATTENDING PHYSICIAN OR MID-WIFE.**

UNITED STATES OF AMERICA, Indian Territory,
Central                  DISTRICT.

I, Reuben McClure , ~~a~~ ........................., on oath state that I attended on Mrs. Ellen McClure , ~~wife of~~ *my wife* on the 15th day of February, 1904; that there was born to her on said date a female child; that said child was living March 4, 1905, and is said to have been named Racy McClure *and that no one else was present when said child was born.*

                                                  his
                                      Reuben x McClure
Witnesses To Mark:                mark
   { Robert Anderson
     Vester Rose

Subscribed and sworn to before me this 10th day of April, 1905

                                            Wirt Franklin
                                            Notary Public.

---

<u>Choc New Born 936</u>
    Johnnie Watson   b. 12-23-03

                                                                    $W^m O.B.$

**COMMISSIONERS:**
TAMS BIXBY,
THOMAS B. NEEDLES,   **DEPARTMENT OF THE INTERIOR,**
C.R. BRECKINBRIDGE.   **COMMISSIONER TO THE FIVE CIVILIZED TRIBES.**

REFER IN REPLY TO THE FOLLOWING:

7-NB-936.

WM. O. BEALL
Secretary

       ADDRESS ONLY THE
COMMISSION TO THE FIVE CIVILIZED TRIBES.

                                Muskogee, Indian Territory, June 1, 1905.

Ananias Watson,
    Noah, Indian Territory.

Dear Sir:

    Referring to the application for the enrollment of your infant child, Johnnie Watson, born December 23, 1903, it is noted from the affidavits heretofore filed in this office that you were the only one in attendance upon your wife at the time of birth of the applicant.

## Applications for Enrollment of Choctaw Newborn
## Act of 1905   Volume XIII

In this event it will be necessary that you file in this office the affidavits of two persons, who are disinterested and not related to the applicant, who have actual knowledge of the facts that the child was born, the date of his birth; that he was living on March 4, 1905, and that Senie Watson is her mother.

The affidavit of Samuel Jefferson to these facts has been filed, so it will be necessary for you to secure the affidavit of another person.

                Respectfully,
                T.B. Needles
                Commissioner in Charge.

*(The affidavit below typed as given.)*

DEPARTMENT OF THE INTERIOR,
Commission to the Five Civilized Tribes.
**FILED**
JUN 28 1905
Tams Bixby CHAIRMAN.

Affidavits of Rayson John and
S.B. Noah

United Stats of Ammarica Ind Teritory[sic]
Central district
We Rayson John and S B Noah state that we ar acquainted with Johnney Watson and Senie Watson and know that Senie Watson is the mother of Johnney Watson. and that Johnney Watson was born to the said Senie Watson on 24 day of Decembr 1904 and was living March 4$^{th}$ 1905 and is living at this time

Witness          S. B. Noah  Bethel Ind. Ter.
                  Rayson John  Bethel Ind. Ter.

Subscribed and sworn to before me this 19 day of June 1905

        J.H. Matthews
my commission                 Notary Public
expires Feb 13=1909

## Applications for Enrollment of Choctaw Newborn
## Act of 1905   Volume XIII

7-NB-936.

Muskogee, Indian Territory, June 29, 1905.

Ananias Watson,
    Noah, Indian Territory.

Dear Sir:

    Receipt is hereby acknowledged of the joint affidavit of Rayson John and S. B. Noah to the birth of your infant child, Johnnie Watson.

    Your attention is called to the fact that the affidavits of yourself, your wife, Semie Watson, and Samuel Jefferson heretofore filed in this office gives the date of the birth of this child as December 23, 1903, while the affidavits of Rayson John and S. B. Noah, Indian Territory, above referred to, give it as December 24, 1904.

    It will therefore be necessary that you have Rayson John and S. B. Noah to re-execute their affidavits, for which purpose a blank is enclosed. You will please give this matter your immediate attention as no further action can be taken until these affidavits are filed with the Commission.

                     Respectfully,

DeB--2/29.                                            Chairman.

---

United States of America,  )
                                   )
Indian Territory,           )  ss.
                                   )
Central District.          )

    I, Samuel Jefferson, on oath state that I am twenty-one years of age and a citizen by blood of the Choctaw Nation; that my post office addres[sic] is Bethel, Indian Territory; that I am personally acquainted with Semi Watson, wife of Ananias Watson; that I know of my own knowledge that on or about the twenty-third day of December, 1903, there was born to the said Semie Watson a male child; that said child is now living and is said to have been named Johnnie Watson.

                                        Samuel Jefferson

Subscribed and sworn to before me this 6th day of April, 1905.

                                        Wirt Franklin
                                            Notary Public.

## Applications for Enrollment of Choctaw Newborn
## Act of 1905   Volume XIII

BIRTH AFFIDAVIT.

### DEPARTMENT OF THE INTERIOR.
### COMMISSION TO THE FIVE CIVILIZED TRIBES.

IN RE APPLICATION FOR ENROLLMENT, as a citizen of the Choctaw Nation, of Johnnie Watson, born on the 23rd day of December, 1903

Name of Father: Ananias Watson        a citizen of the Choctaw Nation.
Name of Mother: Semie Watson        a citizen of the Choctaw Nation.

Postoffice   Noah, Ind. Ter.

**AFFIDAVIT OF MOTHER.**

UNITED STATES OF AMERICA, Indian Territory, }
Central          DISTRICT.

I, Semie Watson, on oath state that I am 23 years of age and a citizen by blood, of the Choctaw Nation; that I am the lawful wife of Ananias Watson, who is a citizen, by blood of the Choctaw Nation; that a male child was born to me on 23rd day of December, 1903; that said child has been named Johnnie Watson, and was living March 4, 1905. *and that no physician or mid-wife attended me at the birth of said child*

                              her
                        Semie x Watson
Witnesses To Mark:            mark
  { Robert Anderson
  { Vester W Rose

Subscribed and sworn to before me this 6th day of April, 1905

                        Wirt Franklin
                           Notary Public.

**AFFIDAVIT OF ATTENDING PHYSICIAN OR MID-WIFE.**

UNITED STATES OF AMERICA, Indian Territory, }
Central          DISTRICT.

I, Ananias Watson, ~~a~~ , on oath state that I attended on Mrs. Semie Watson, ~~wife of~~ *my wife* on the 23rd day of December, 1903; that there was born to her on said date a male child; that said child was living March 4, 1905, and ~~is said to have~~ *has* been named Johnnie Watson *and that no one else present when said child was born*

241

## Applications for Enrollment of Choctaw Newborn
## Act of 1905 Volume XIII

                                        his
                                Ananias x Watson

Witnesses To Mark:                  mark
{ Robert Anderson
  Vester W Rose

Subscribed and sworn to before me this 6th day of April, 1905

                              Wirt Franklin
                              Notary Public.

**BIRTH AFFIDAVIT.**

### DEPARTMENT OF THE INTERIOR.
### COMMISSION TO THE FIVE CIVILIZED TRIBES.

**IN RE APPLICATION FOR ENROLLMENT**, as a citizen of the Choctaw Nation, of Johnnie Watson, born on the 23 day of December, 1903

Name of Father: Annias[sic] Watson    a citizen of the Choctaw Nation.
Name of Mother: Sennie[sic] Watson   a citizen of the Choctaw Nation.

                        Postoffice    Noah Ind Teritory[sic]

### AFFIDAVIT OF MOTHER.

**UNITED STATES OF AMERICA, Indian Territory,**
**Central DISTRICT.**

I, S B Noah, on oath state that I am acquainted ~~years of age and a citizen by~~ with, ~~of the~~ Sennie Watson ~~Nation; that I am the~~ lawful wife of Ananias Watson, who is a citizen, by Blood of the Choctaw Nation; that a male child was born to ~~me~~ her on 23 day of December, 1903; that said child has been named Johnnie Watson, and was living March 4, 1905.

                              S.B. Noah

Witnesses To Mark:
{ Bud Stephens Noah I.T.
  Esais Morris Tushkahoma[sic] I.T.

Subscribed and sworn to before me this 17 day of July, 1905

                              J H Matthews
                              Notary Public.

## Applications for Enrollment of Choctaw Newborn
## Act of 1905   Volume XIII

### AFFIDAVIT OF ATTENDING PHYSICIAN OR MID-WIFE.

UNITED STATES OF AMERICA, Indian Territory, }
Central                DISTRICT.

am acquainted with

I,  Rayson John  ~~, a~~  , on oath state that I ~~attended on~~ Mrs.  Semie Watson , wife of  Ananias Watson  that  on the  23  day of Dec.  , 1903; that there was born to her on said date a  male  child; that said child was living March 4, 1905, and is said to have been named  Johnnie Watson

Rayson John Bethel I.T.

Witnesses To Mark:
{ Bud Stephens   Noah I.T.
{ Esais Morris   Tushkahoma[sic] I.T.

Subscribed and sworn to before me this  17  day of  July  , 1905

J H Matthews
Notary Public.

---

Choc New Born 937
   Jonas Jacob  b. 6-22-04

Simeon Jacob
roll No. 1220

Sophie Jacob,
No. 1221

### NEW-BORN AFFIDAVIT.

Number

...Choctaw Enrolling Commission...

IN THE MATTER OF THE APPLICATION FOR ENROLLMENT, as a citizen of the Choctaw  Nation, of  Jonas Jacob

born on the  22  day of  June  190 4

243

# Applications for Enrollment of Choctaw Newborn
## Act of 1905   Volume XIII

Name of father   Simeon Jacob            a citizen of   Choctaw
Nation final enrollment No.   1220
Name of mother   Sophie Jacob            a citizen of   Choctaw
Nation final enrollment No.   1221

Postoffice   Valliant, I.T.

## AFFIDAVIT OF MOTHER.

UNITED STATES OF AMERICA
INDIAN TERRITORY
Central   DISTRICT

I   Sophie Jacob   , on oath state that I am 27 years of age and a citizen by   blood   of the   Choctaw   Nation, and as such have been placed upon the final roll of the   Choctaw   Nation, by the Honorable Secretary of the Interior my final enrollment number being   1221 ; that I am the lawful wife of   Simeon Jacob   , who is a citizen of the   Choctaw   Nation, and as such has been placed upon the final roll of said Nation by the Honorable Secretary of the Interior, his final enrollment number being   1220   and that a   male   child was born to me on the 22   day of   June   190 4; that said child has been named   Jonas Jacob   , and is now living.

Sophie Jacob

Witnesseth.
Must be two ⎫  Willie Caldwell
Witnesses who ⎬
are Citizens. ⎭  Nicholas Jackson

Subscribed and sworn to before me this   22   day of   Feb   190 5

W.A. Shoney
Notary Public.

My commission expires:   Jan 10, 1909

## AFFIDAVIT OF ATTENDING PHYSICIAN OR MIDWIFE

UNITED STATES OF AMERICA
INDIAN TERRITORY
Central   DISTRICT

I,   Rhoda Jacob   a   midwife   on oath state that I attended on Mrs.   Sophie Jacob   wife of   Simeon Jacob   on the 22$^{nd}$   day of   June , 190 4, that there was born to her on said date a   male   child, that said child is now living, and is said to have been named   Jonas Jacob

her
Rhoda x Jacob   ~~M.D~~.
mark

# Applications for Enrollment of Choctaw Newborn
## Act of 1905 Volume XIII

**WITNESSETH:**

Must be two witnesses who are citizens and know the child. { Willie Caldwell

Nicholas Jackson

Subscribed and sworn to before me this, the 22 day of Feb 1905

W.A. Shoney    Notary Public.

We hereby certify that we are well acquainted with Rhoda Jacob a midwife and know her to be reputable and of good standing in the community.

{ Willie Caldwell

Nicholas Jackson

---

**BIRTH AFFIDAVIT.**

## DEPARTMENT OF THE INTERIOR.
## COMMISSION TO THE FIVE CIVILIZED TRIBES.

---

**IN RE APPLICATION FOR ENROLLMENT,** as a citizen of the Choctaw Nation, of Jonas Jacob, born on the 22 day of June, 1904

Name of Father: Simeon Jacob    a citizen of the Choctaw Nation.
Name of Mother: Sophie Jacob    a citizen of the Choctaw Nation.

Postoffice    Valliant, Ind. Ter.

---

**AFFIDAVIT OF MOTHER.**

UNITED STATES OF AMERICA, Indian Territory,
Central    DISTRICT.

I, Sophie Jacob, on oath state that I am 30 years of age and a citizen by blood, of the Choctaw Nation; that I am the lawful wife of Simeon Jacob, who is a citizen, by blood of the Choctaw Nation; that a male child was born to me on 22nd day of June, 1904; that said child has been named Jonas Jacob, and was living March 4, 1905.

her
Sophie x Jacob
mark

Witnesses To Mark:
{ Robert Anderson
Vester W Rose

## Applications for Enrollment of Choctaw Newborn
## Act of 1905  Volume XIII

Subscribed and sworn to before me this 10th day of April, 1905

                                Wirt Franklin
                                Notary Public.

**AFFIDAVIT OF ATTENDING PHYSICIAN OR MID-WIFE.**

UNITED STATES OF AMERICA, Indian Territory, }
   Central               DISTRICT. }

I, Rhoda Jacob, a mid-wife, on oath state that I attended on Mrs. Sophie Jacob, wife of Simeon Jacob on the 22nd day of June, 1904; that there was born to her on said date a male child; that said child was living March 4, 1905, and is said to have been named Jonas Jacob

                            her
                     Rhoda x Jacob
Witnesses To Mark:       mark
 { Robert Anderson
 { Vester W Rose

Subscribed and sworn to before me this 10th day of April, 1905

                                Wirt Franklin
                                Notary Public.

---

Choc New Born 938
    Jesse Taylor  b. 2-16-03

## Applications for Enrollment of Choctaw Newborn
## Act of 1905   Volume XIII

**NEW-BORN AFFIDAVIT.**

Number..............

## ...Choctaw Enrolling Commission...

IN THE MATTER OF THE APPLICATION FOR ENROLLMENT, as a citizen of the Choctaw Nation, of Jesse Taylor

born on the 16$^{th}$ day of __February__ 190 3

Name of father   John Taylor           a citizen of   Choctaw
Nation final enrollment No.   897
Name of mother   Catherine Taylor      a citizen of   Choctaw
Nation final enrollment No.   898

Postoffice   Idabel I.T.

**AFFIDAVIT OF MOTHER.**

UNITED STATES OF AMERICA
INDIAN TERRITORY
   Central         DISTRICT

I   Catherine Taylor   , on oath state that I am 37 years of age and a citizen by blood of the Choctaw Nation, and as such have been placed upon the final roll of the Choctaw Nation, by the Honorable Secretary of the Interior my final enrollment number being 898 ; that I am the lawful wife of John Taylor , who is a citizen of the Choctaw Nation, and as such has been placed upon the final roll of said Nation by the Honorable Secretary of the Interior, his final enrollment number being 897 and that a Male child was born to me on the 16$^{th}$ day of February 190 3; that said child has been named Jesse Taylor , and is now living.

                                               her
                              Catherine Taylor  x
Witnesseth.                                    mark
   Must be two  } Simpson Tushka
   Witnesses who
   are Citizens.   W.S. Ward

Subscribed and sworn to before me this   21   day of   Jan   190 5

W.A. Shoney
Notary Public.

My commission expires:

## Applications for Enrollment of Choctaw Newborn
## Act of 1905   Volume XIII

## AFFIDAVIT OF ATTENDING PHYSICIAN OR MIDWIFE

UNITED STATES OF AMERICA
INDIAN TERRITORY
Central   DISTRICT

I, Patsey Clay  a  midwife on oath state that I attended on Mrs. Catherine Clay[sic]   wife of John Taylor on the 16th day of February, 1903, that there was born to her on said date a male child, that said child is now living, and is said to have been named Jesse Taylor

                                          her
                                Patsey Clay  x
Subscribed and sworn to before me this, the  mark  21st  day of Jan  1905

WITNESSETH:                    W.A. Shoney   Notary Public.
Must be two witnesses { Impson Tushka
who are citizens
                 W.S. Ward

We hereby certify that we are well acquainted with  Patsey Clay  a  midwife  and know  her  to be reputable and of good standing in the community.

       Impson Tushka                 _____

       W.S. Ward                       _____

BIRTH AFFIDAVIT.
## DEPARTMENT OF THE INTERIOR.
## COMMISSION TO THE FIVE CIVILIZED TRIBES.

IN RE APPLICATION FOR ENROLLMENT, as a citizen of the  Choctaw  Nation, of Jesse Taylor, born on the 16th day of February, 1903

Name of Father: John Taylor         a citizen of the  Choctaw  Nation.
Name of Mother: Catherine Taylor    a citizen of the  Choctaw  Nation.

                          Postoffice   Idabel, Indian Territory

# Applications for Enrollment of Choctaw Newborn
## Act of 1905   Volume XIII

### AFFIDAVIT OF MOTHER.

UNITED STATES OF AMERICA, Indian Territory,  
Central                        DISTRICT.

I, Catherine Taylor, on oath state that I am 39 years of age and a citizen by blood, of the Choctaw Nation; that I ~~am~~ was the lawful wife of John Taylor, deceased, who ~~is~~ was a citizen, by blood of the Choctaw Nation; that a male child was born to me on 16th day of February, 1903; that said child has been named Jesse Taylor, and was living March 4, 1905.

                                            her  
                                    Catherine x Taylor  
Witnesses To Mark:              mark  
  Robert Anderson  
  Vester Rose

Subscribed and sworn to before me this 10th day of April, 1905

                                    Wirt Franklin  
                                    Notary Public.

### AFFIDAVIT OF ATTENDING PHYSICIAN OR MID-WIFE.

UNITED STATES OF AMERICA, Indian Territory,  
Central                        DISTRICT.

I, Betsy Clay, a mid-wife, on oath state that I attended on Mrs. Catherine Taylor, wife of John Taylor, deceased on the 16th day of February, 1903; that there was born to her on said date a male child; that said child was living March 4, 1905, and is said to have been named Jesse Taylor

                                            her  
                                    Betsy x Clay  
Witnesses To Mark:              mark  
  Robert Anderson  
  Vester Rose

Subscribed and sworn to before me this 10th day of April, 1905

                                    Wirt Franklin  
                                    Notary Public.

## Applications for Enrollment of Choctaw Newborn
## Act of 1905 Volume XIII

Choc New Born 939
Ida Jones b. 11-8-02

**BIRTH AFFIDAVIT.**

## DEPARTMENT OF THE INTERIOR.
## COMMISSION TO THE FIVE CIVILIZED TRIBES.

IN RE APPLICATION FOR ENROLLMENT, as a citizen of the Choctaw Nation, of Ida Jones, born on the 8th day of November, 1902

Name of Father: Isaac Jones       a citizen of the Choctaw Nation.
Name of Mother: Artie Ann Jones   a citizen of the Choctaw Nation.

Postoffice   Alikchi, Ind Ter

**AFFIDAVIT OF MOTHER.**

UNITED STATES OF AMERICA, Indian Territory, }
Central           DISTRICT. }

I, Artie Ann Jones, on oath state that I am about 30 years of age and a citizen by blood, of the Choctaw Nation; that I am the lawful wife of Isaac Jones, who is a citizen, by blood of the Choctaw Nation; that a female child was born to me on 8th day of November, 1902; that said child has been named Ida Jones, and was living March 4, 1905.

                                        her
                              Artie Ann x Jones
Witnesses To Mark:               mark
{ Robert Anderson
{ Vester W Rose

Subscribed and sworn to before me this 6th day of April, 1905

                              Wirt Franklin
                              Notary Public.

**AFFIDAVIT OF ATTENDING PHYSICIAN OR MID-WIFE.**

UNITED STATES OF AMERICA, Indian Territory, }
Central           DISTRICT. }

I, Adaline Jefferson, a mid-wife, on oath state that I attended on Mrs. Artie Ann Jones, wife of Isaac Jones on the 8th day of November,

## Applications for Enrollment of Choctaw Newborn
## Act of 1905 Volume XIII

1902; that there was born to her on said date a female child; that said child was living March 4, 1905, and is said to have been named Ida Jones

                                                her
                                     Adaline x Jefferson

Witnesses To Mark:                       mark
   { Robert Anderson
   { Vester W Rose

Subscribed and sworn to before me this 6th day of April, 1905

                                        Wirt Franklin
                                          Notary Public.

---

<u>Choc New Born 940</u>
    Helen Jefferson b. 5-26-04

BIRTH AFFIDAVIT.
### DEPARTMENT OF THE INTERIOR.
### COMMISSION TO THE FIVE CIVILIZED TRIBES.

**IN RE APPLICATION FOR ENROLLMENT,** as a citizen of the Choctaw Nation, of Helen Jefferson, born on the 26th day of May, 1904

Name of Father: Samuel Jefferson       a citizen of the Choctaw Nation.
Name of Mother: Emiline Jefferson     a citizen of the Choctaw Nation.

                            Postoffice   Bethel, Ind. Ter.

### AFFIDAVIT OF MOTHER.

UNITED STATES OF AMERICA, Indian Territory, }
    Central                   DISTRICT. }

    I, Emiline Jefferson, on oath state that I am 19 years of age and a citizen by blood, of the Choctaw Nation; that I am the lawful wife of Samuel Jefferson, who is a citizen, by blood of the Choctaw Nation; that a female child was born to me on 26th day of May, 1904; that said child has been named Helen Jefferson, and was living March 4, 1905.

                                        her
                               Emiline x Jefferson
                                   mark

# Applications for Enrollment of Choctaw Newborn
## Act of 1905    Volume XIII

Witnesses To Mark:
   { Robert Anderson
     Vester W Rose

Subscribed and sworn to before me this 6th day of April, 1905

                         Wirt Franklin
                         Notary Public.

---

### AFFIDAVIT OF ATTENDING PHYSICIAN OR MID-WIFE.

UNITED STATES OF AMERICA, Indian Territory, }
    Central                 DISTRICT.

I, Adaline Jefferson, a mid-wife, on oath state that I attended on Mrs. Emiline Jefferson, wife of Samuel Jefferson on the 26th day of May, 1904; that there was born to her on said date a female child; that said child was living March 4, 1905, and is said to have been named Helen Jefferson

                         her
                 Adaline x Jefferson
Witnesses To Mark:       mark
   { Robert Anderson
     Vester W Rose

Subscribed and sworn to before me this 6th day of April, 1905

                         Wirt Franklin
                         Notary Public.

---

Choc New Born 941
       Foster Jefferson   b. 3-1-05

---

BIRTH AFFIDAVIT.
### DEPARTMENT OF THE INTERIOR.
### COMMISSION TO THE FIVE CIVILIZED TRIBES.

---

**IN RE APPLICATION FOR ENROLLMENT,** as a citizen of the Choctaw Nation, of Foster Jefferson, born on the 1st day of March, 1905

Name of Father: Hickson Jefferson     a citizen of the Choctaw Nation.
Name of Mother: Adeline Jefferson     a citizen of the Choctaw Nation.

## Applications for Enrollment of Choctaw Newborn
## Act of 1905   Volume XIII

Postoffice   Bethel, Ind. Ter.

---

**AFFIDAVIT OF MOTHER.**

UNITED STATES OF AMERICA, Indian Territory, }
Central                DISTRICT.

I, Adeline Jefferson, on oath state that I am about 40 years of age and a citizen by blood, of the Choctaw Nation; that I am the lawful wife of Hickson Jefferson, who is a citizen, by blood of the Choctaw Nation; that a male child was born to me on 1st day of March, 1905; that said child has been named Foster Jefferson, and was living March 4, 1905. *and that said child died on March 6, 1905.*

                                              her
                                    Adeline x Jefferson

Witnesses To Mark:                  mark
{ Robert Anderson
{ Vester W Rose

Subscribed and sworn to before me this 6th day of April, 1905

                                  Wirt Franklin
                                  Notary Public.

---

**AFFIDAVIT OF ATTENDING PHYSICIAN OR MID-WIFE.**

UNITED STATES OF AMERICA, Indian Territory, }
Central                DISTRICT.

I, Emiline Jefferson, a mid-wife, on oath state that I attended on Mrs. Adeline Jefferson, wife of Hickson Jefferson on the 1st day of March, 1905; that there was born to her on said date a male child; that said child was living March 4, 1905, and is said to have been named Foster Jefferson *and that said child died on March 6, 1905*

                                              her
                                    Emiline x Jefferson

Witnesses To Mark:                  mark
{ Robert Anderson
{ Vester W Rose

Subscribed and sworn to before me this 6th day of April, 1905

                                  Wirt Franklin
                                  Notary Public.

# Applications for Enrollment of Choctaw Newborn
## Act of 1905   Volume XIII

Choc New Born 942
    Sudie Robert  b. 2-8-03

---

7-NB-942

                         Muskogee, Indian Territory, February 7, 1906.

Litcey[sic] Robert,
    Smithville, Indian Territory.

Dear Sir[sic]:

    Receipt is hereby acknowledged of your letter of January 29, 1906, asking if your child Sudy[sic] Robert has been enrolled and approved.

    In reply to your letter you are advised that the enrollment of your child Sudie Robert as a new born citizen of the Choctaw Nation was approved by the Secretary of the Interior, July 23, 1905.

                      Respectfully,

                                      Acting Commissioner.

---

United States of America,  )
                              )
Indian Territory,          )   ss.
                              )
Central District.          )

    I, Sinsie J. Johnson, on oath state that I am about twenty years of age and a citizen by blood of the Choctaw Nation; that my post office address is Smithville, Indian Territory; that I am personally acquainted with Litsey Robert; that I have known her all my life and have lived within three miles of where she lives, near Smithville, Indian Territory, for about the last ten years; that there was born to her on or about the 8th day of February, 1903, a female child; that said child has been named Sudie Robert and is now living, and that it is commonly reported that the father of said child is Holman McCoy.

                                      Sinsie J Johnson

Subscribed and sworn to before me this 6th day of April, 1905.

                                      Wirt Franklin
                                        Notary Public.

Witnesses to mark.
    -------------------------------
    -------------------------------

## Applications for Enrollment of Choctaw Newborn
## Act of 1905   Volume XIII

United States of America, )
)
Indian Territory, ) ss.
)
Central District. )

    I, Sallie Hudson, on oath state that I am twenty years of age and a citizen by blood of the Choctaw Nation; that I am personally acquainted with Litsey Robert; that I have known her all my life and have lived within two miles of where she lives, near Smithville, Indian Territory, for the last three years; that there was born to her on or about the eight day of February, 1903, a female child; that said child has been named Sudie Robert and is now living, and that it is commonly reported that the father of said child is Holman McCoy.

                                                         her
                                                  Sallie x Hudson
                                                     mark

Subscribed and sworn to before me this 6th day of April, 1905.

                                                   Wirt Franklin
                                                   Notary Public.

Witnesses to mark.
    Robert Anderson
    Vester W Rose

---

**BIRTH AFFIDAVIT.**
### DEPARTMENT OF THE INTERIOR.
### COMMISSION TO THE FIVE CIVILIZED TRIBES.

---

    **IN RE APPLICATION FOR ENROLLMENT,** as a citizen of the     Choctaw    Nation, of Sudie Robert    , born on the 8th    day of    February    , 1903

Name of Father: Holman McCoy        a citizen of the    Choctaw    Nation.
Name of Mother: Litsey Robert         a citizen of the    Choctaw    Nation.

                                      Postoffice    Smithville, Ind. Ter.

---

**AFFIDAVIT OF MOTHER.**

UNITED STATES OF AMERICA, Indian Territory, }
    Central                    DISTRICT. }

    I, Litsey Robert    , on oath state that I am    about 28    years of age and a citizen by    blood    , of the    Choctaw    Nation; that I am not the lawful wife of Holman McCoy    , who is a citizen, by    blood    of the    Choctaw    Nation;

## Applications for Enrollment of Choctaw Newborn
## Act of 1905   Volume XIII

that a   female   child was born to me on   8th   day of   February   , 1903; that said child has been named   Sudie Robert   , and was living March 4, 1905.

Litsey Robert

Witnesses To Mark:
{

Subscribed and sworn to before me this   30th   day of   March   , 1905

Wirt Franklin<br>Notary Public.

---

Choc New Born 943
    Ethel Bohanan   b. 1-7-05

7-NB-943

Muskogee, Indian Territory, July 24, 1905.

Sallie Ann Bohanan,
    Smithville, Indian Territory.

Dear Madam:

    Receipt is hereby acknowledged of your letter of July 18, 1905, asking if your baby Ethel Bohanan has been listed as a citizen by blood of the Choctaw Nation.

    In reply to your letter you are advised that the name of your child Ethel Bohanan has been placed upon a schedule of citizens by blood of the Choctaw Nation which has been forwarded the Secretary of the Interior but this office has not yet been notified of Departmental action thereon.

Respectfully,

Commissioner.

## Applications for Enrollment of Choctaw Newborn
## Act of 1905 Volume XIII

BIRTH AFFIDAVIT.

## DEPARTMENT OF THE INTERIOR.
## COMMISSION TO THE FIVE CIVILIZED TRIBES.

IN RE APPLICATION FOR ENROLLMENT, as a citizen of the Choctaw Nation, of Ethel Bohanan, born on the 7th day of January, 1905

Name of Father: Lartin S. Bohanan     a citizen of the Choctaw Nation.
Name of Mother: Sally Ann Bohanan     a citizen of the Choctaw Nation.

Postoffice    Smithville, Ind. Ter.

**AFFIDAVIT OF MOTHER.**

UNITED STATES OF AMERICA, Indian Territory, }
Central      DISTRICT.

I, Sally Ann Bohanan, on oath state that I am 37 years of age and a citizen by blood, of the Choctaw Nation; that I am the lawful wife of Lartin S Bohanan, who is a citizen, by blood of the Choctaw Nation; that a female child was born to me on 7th day of January, 1905; that said child has been named Ethel Bohanan, and was living March 4, 1905.

Sally Ann Bohanon[sic]

Witnesses To Mark:
{

Subscribed and sworn to before me this 4th day of April, 1905

Wirt Franklin
Notary Public.

**AFFIDAVIT OF ATTENDING PHYSICIAN OR MID-WIFE.**

UNITED STATES OF AMERICA, Indian Territory, }
Central      DISTRICT.

I, Agnes James, a mid-wife, on oath state that I attended on Mrs. Sally Ann Bohanan, wife of Lartin S Bohanan on the 7th day of January, 1905; that there was born to her on said date a female child; that said child was living March 4, 1905, and is said to have been named Ethel Bohanan

Agnes James

Witnesses To Mark:
{

# Applications for Enrollment of Choctaw Newborn
## Act of 1905   Volume XIII

Subscribed and sworn to before me this 4th day of April, 1905

Wirt Franklin<br>
Notary Public.

---

Choc New Born 944
    Roosevelt Easton Hudson   b. 2-5-03

7-NB-944.

Muskogee, Indian Territory, June 1, 1905.

Rufus Hudson,
    Smithville, Indian Territory.

Dear Sir:

    Referring to the applicant for the enrollment of your infant child, Roosevelt Easton Hudson, born February 5, 1903, it is noted from the affidavits heretofore filed in this office that you were the only one in attendance upon your wife at the time of birth of the applicant.

    In this event it will be necessary that you file in this office the affidavits of two persons, who are disinterested and not related to the applicant, who have actual knowledge of the facts that the child was born, the date of his birth; that he was living on March 4, 1905, and that Sallie Hudson is his mother. The affidavit of Wilmon J. Johnson to these facts has been filed, so it will be necessary for you to secure a similar affidavit from another person.

                      Respectfully,

                                            Chairman.

# Applications for Enrollment of Choctaw Newborn
# Act of 1905 Volume XIII

Choctaw N B 944.

Muskogee, Indian Territory, June 29, 1905.

Rufus Hudson,
    Smithville, Indian Territory.

Dear Sir:

    Receipt is hereby acknowledged of the affidavit of Joseph Johnson to the birth of Roosevelt Easton Hudson and the same has been filed with our records in the matter of the enrollment of said child.

Respectfully,

Chairman.

---

United States of America
Indian Territory
Central District
Affidavit of Acquaintance

    I, Joseph Johnson on oath state that I am 53 years of age and a citizen by blood of the Choctaw Nation, that my post office address is Smithville, Indian Territory, that I am not related to the applicant, who is a citizen by blood of the Choctaw Nation, that I am personally acquainted with Sallie Hudson, wife of Rufus Hudson, who is a citizen by blood of the Choctaw Nation, and that a male child was born to Sallie Hudson on the 5$^{th}$ day of February 1903, and that said male child has been named Rosevelt[sic] Easton Hudson and that said Rosevelt Easton Hudson was living on the 4$^{th}$ day of March 1905. and I have personal knowledge that Sallie Hudson is the mother of said Rosevelt Easton Hudson.

                                  his
                          Joseph x Johnson
                                 mark

Witness to mark
1 Larsen Watson
2 George Watson

Subscribed and sworn to before me this 19$^{th}$ day of June 1905

WH. McKinney
Notary Public.

My commission expires Mrch 30-1909

## Applications for Enrollment of Choctaw Newborn
## Act of 1905   Volume XIII

United States of America,   )
)
Indian Territory,   )   ss.
)
Central District.   )

I, Wilmon J. Johnson, on oath state that I am twenty-eight years of age and a citizen by blood of the Choctaw Nation; that I am personally acquainted with Sallie Hudson, wife of Rufus Hudson; that for the last five years I have known said parties and during this time since their marriage that have lived within two miles of where I have lived, near Smithville, Indian Territory; that on or about February 5, 1903, there was born to the said Sallie Hudson a male child; that said child is now living and is said to have been named Roosevelt Easton Hudson.

Wilson J. Johnson

Subscribed and sworn to before me this 6th day of April, 1905.

Wirt Franklin<br>Notary Public.

**BIRTH AFFIDAVIT.**

### DEPARTMENT OF THE INTERIOR.
### COMMISSION TO THE FIVE CIVILIZED TRIBES.

**IN RE APPLICATION FOR ENROLLMENT**, as a citizen of the   Choctaw   Nation, of Roosevelt Easton Hudson   , born on the 5th   day of  February   , 1903

Name of Father: Rufus Hudson         a citizen of the   Choctaw   Nation.
Name of Mother: Sallie Hudson         a citizen of the   Choctaw   Nation.

Postoffice   Smithville, Ind.Ter.

**AFFIDAVIT OF MOTHER.**

UNITED STATES OF AMERICA, Indian Territory, }
  Central           DISTRICT.   }

I, Sallie Hudson   , on oath state that I am   about 20   years of age and a citizen by   blood   , of the   Choctaw   Nation; that I am the lawful wife of Rufus Hudson   , who is a citizen, by blood   of the   Choctaw   Nation; that a   male   child was born to me on 5th   day of   February   , 1903; that said child has been named   Roosevelt Easton Hudson   , and was living March 4, 1905. *and that no physician or midwife attended me at the birth of said child*

260

# Applications for Enrollment of Choctaw Newborn
## Act of 1905   Volume XIII

Witnesses To Mark:
{ Robert Anderson
  Vester W Rose

           her
Sallie x Hudson
          mark

Subscribed and sworn to before me this 6th day of April, 1905

                Wirt Franklin
                Notary Public.

---

**AFFIDAVIT OF ATTENDING PHYSICIAN OR MID-WIFE.**

UNITED STATES OF AMERICA, Indian Territory, }
Central            DISTRICT. }

I, Rufus Hudson, ~~a~~ _____, on oath state that I attended on Mrs. Sallie Hudson, ~~wife of~~ *my wife* on the 5th day of February, 1903; that there was born to her on said date a male child; that said child was living March 4, 1905, and is said to have been named Roosevelt Easton Hudson *and that no one else was present when said child was born*

                Rufus Hudson

Witnesses To Mark:
{

Subscribed and sworn to before me this 6th day of April, 1905

                Wirt Franklin
                Notary Public.

---

Choc New Born 945
    Norman Joseph Johnson   b. 9-30-04

**BIRTH AFFIDAVIT.**

### DEPARTMENT OF THE INTERIOR.
### COMMISSION TO THE FIVE CIVILIZED TRIBES.

**IN RE APPLICATION FOR ENROLLMENT,** as a citizen of the Choctaw Nation, of Norman Joseph Johnson, born on the 30th day of September, 1904

Name of Father: Wilmon J. Johnson     a citizen of the Choctaw Nation.
Name of Mother: Sinsie J Johnson     a citizen of the Choctaw Nation.

## Applications for Enrollment of Choctaw Newborn
## Act of 1905  Volume XIII

Postoffice   Smithville, Ind. Ter.

---

**AFFIDAVIT OF MOTHER.**

UNITED STATES OF AMERICA, Indian Territory, }
Central           DISTRICT.

I, Sinsie J. Johnson, on oath state that I am about 20 years of age and a citizen by blood, of the Choctaw Nation; that I am the lawful wife of Wilmon J Johnson, who is a citizen, by blood of the Choctaw Nation; that a male child was born to me on 30th day of September, 1904; that said child has been named Norman Joseph Johnson, and was living March 4, 1905.

Sinsie J. Johnson

Witnesses To Mark:
{

Subscribed and sworn to before me this 6th day of April, 1905

Wirt Franklin
Notary Public.

---

**AFFIDAVIT OF ATTENDING PHYSICIAN OR MID-WIFE.**

UNITED STATES OF AMERICA, Indian Territory, }
Central           DISTRICT.

I, Louina Plumbbi, a mid-wife, on oath state that I attended on Mrs. Sinsie J Johnson, wife of Wilmon J Johnson on the 30th day of September, 1904; that there was born to her on said date a male child; that said child was living March 4, 1905, and is said to have been named Norman Joseph Johnson

                                              her
                                    Louina x Plumbbi

Witnesses To Mark:                  mark
{ Robert Anderson
  Vester W Rose

Subscribed and sworn to before me this 6th day of April, 1905

Wirt Franklin
Notary Public.

## Applications for Enrollment of Choctaw Newborn
## Act of 1905 Volume XIII

Choc New Born 946
Lindsy Whale  b. 5-10-03

BIRTH AFFIDAVIT.

DEPARTMENT OF THE INTERIOR.
## COMMISSION TO THE FIVE CIVILIZED TRIBES.

IN RE APPLICATION FOR ENROLLMENT, as a citizen of the Choctaw Nation, of Lindsy Whale, born on the 10th day of May, 1903

Name of Father: David Whale       a citizen of the Choctaw Nation.
Name of Mother: Elmira Whale      a citizen of the Choctaw Nation.

Postoffice  Smithville, Ind. Ter.

AFFIDAVIT OF MOTHER.

UNITED STATES OF AMERICA, Indian Territory,
Central            DISTRICT.

I, Elmira Whale, on oath state that I am 34 years of age and a citizen by blood, of the Choctaw Nation; that I am the lawful wife of David Whale, who is a citizen, by blood of the Choctaw Nation; that a male child was born to me on 10th day of May, 1903; that said child has been named Lindsy Whale, and was living March 4, 1905.

                            her
                        Elmira x Whale
Witnesses To Mark:          mark
  { Robert Anderson
    Vester W Rose

Subscribed and sworn to before me this 6th day of April, 1905

                        Wirt Franklin
                          Notary Public.

AFFIDAVIT OF ATTENDING PHYSICIAN OR MID-WIFE.

UNITED STATES OF AMERICA, Indian Territory,
Central            DISTRICT.

I, Podema Watson, a mid-wife, on oath state that I attended on Mrs. Elmira Whale, wife of David Whale on the 10th day of May, 1903;

## Applications for Enrollment of Choctaw Newborn
## Act of 1905   Volume XIII

that there was born to her on said date a    male    child; that said child was living March 4, 1905, and is said to have been named Lindsy Whale

Podema Watson

Witnesses To Mark:
{

Subscribed and sworn to before me this 6th day of April , 1905

Wirt Franklin
Notary Public.

---

Choc New Born 947
    Willis Bohanan   b. 12-6-04

7--NB--947

Muskogee, Indian Territory, June 1, 1905.

Jonas Bohanan,
    Smithville, Indian Territory.

Dear Sir:

    Referring to the application for the enrollment of your infant child, Willis Bohanan, born December 6, 1904, it is noted from the affidavits heretofore filed in this office that you were the only one in attendance upon your wife at the time of the birth of the applicant.

    In this event it will be necessary that the affidavits of two persons, who are disinterested and not related to the applicant, who have actual knowledge of the facts that the child was born, the date of his birth; that he was living on March 4, 1905, and that Lucinda Bohanan is his mother be filed in this office.

    The affidavit of Allen W. James to these facts has been filed. It will, therefore, be necessary that you secure a similar affidavit from another person.

    This matter should receive your immediate attention as no further action can be taken relative to the enrollment of your child until this affidavit is receive by the Commission.

                Respectfully,

                          Chairman.

# Applications for Enrollment of Choctaw Newborn
## Act of 1905  Volume XIII

7-NB-947.

Muskogee, Indian Territory, June 20, 1905.

Jonas Bohanan,
Smithville, Indian Territory.

Dear Sir:

Receipt is hereby acknowledged of the affidavit of Thompson Taylor to the birth of your infant child, Willis Bohanan, and the same is returned herewith for the reason that the year of the child's birth is omitted. It will therefore be necessary that you have this affidavit re-executed and filed in this office as no further action can be taken in this matter until it is received.

Respectfully,

Chairman.

DeB--1/19

7-NB-947

Muskogee, Indian Territory, July 1, 1905.

James Bohanan,
Beach, Indian Territory.

Dear Sir:

Receipt is hereby acknowledged of the affidavit of Jamison Lewis to the birth of Willis Bohanan, son of Jonas and Lucinda Bohanan December 6, 1904, and the same has been filed with our records in the matter of the enrollment of said child.

Respectfully,

Commissioner.

## Applications for Enrollment of Choctaw Newborn
## Act of 1905   Volume XIII

**AFFIDAVIT OF ATTENDING PHYSICIAN OR MID-WIFE.**

UNITED STATES OF AMERICA, Indian Territory,
Central            DISTRICT.

*know*

I, Jamison Lewis, a ................., on oath state that I ~~attended on~~ Mrs. Lucinda Bohanan, wife of Jonas Bohanan on the 6 day of December, 1904; that there was born to her on said date a male child; that said child was living March 4, 1905, and is said to have been named Willis Bohanan

Jamison Lewis

Witnesses To Mark:

Subscribed and sworn to before me this 24 day of June, 1905

C.L. Lester
Notary Public.

---

United States of America,   )
                            )
Indian Territory,           )  ss.
                            )
Central District.           )

I, Allen W. James, on oath state that I am forty one years of age and a citizen by blood of the Choctaw Nation; that I am personally acquainted with Lucinda Bohanan, wife of Jonas Bohanan; that said parties live about one and a half miles from me, near Beach, Indian Territory; that there was born to said Lucinda Bohanan on the 6th day of December, 1904; a male child; that said child is now living and is said to have been named Willis Bohanan.

Allen W. James

Subscribed and sworn to before me this 4th day of April, 1904[sic].

Wirt Franklin
Notary Public.

# Applications for Enrollment of Choctaw Newborn
## Act of 1905   Volume XIII

BIRTH AFFIDAVIT.

## DEPARTMENT OF THE INTERIOR.
## COMMISSION TO THE FIVE CIVILIZED TRIBES.

---

IN RE APPLICATION FOR ENROLLMENT, as a citizen of the Choctaw Nation, of Willis Bohanan, born on the 6th day of December, 1904

Name of Father: Jonas Bohanan     a citizen of the Choctaw Nation.
Name of Mother: Lucinda Bohanan    a citizen of the Choctaw Nation.

Postoffice   Smithville, Ind. Ter.

---

### AFFIDAVIT OF MOTHER.

UNITED STATES OF AMERICA, Indian Territory, }
Central   DISTRICT.

I, Lucinda Bohanan, on oath state that I am 21 years of age and a citizen by blood, of the Choctaw Nation; that I am the lawful wife of Jonas Bohanan, who is a citizen, by blood of the Choctaw Nation; that a male child was born to me on 6th day of December, 1904; that said child has been named Willis Bohanan, and was living March 4, 1905. *and that no physician or midwife attended me at the birth of said child*

her<br>
Lucinda x Bohanan<br>
mark

Witnesses To Mark:
{ Vester W Rose
{ Robert Anderson

Subscribed and sworn to before me this 4th day of April, 1905

Wirt Franklin
Notary Public.

---

### AFFIDAVIT OF ATTENDING PHYSICIAN OR MID-WIFE.

UNITED STATES OF AMERICA, Indian Territory, }
Central   DISTRICT.

I, Jonas Bohanan, ~~a~~ .................., on oath state that I attended on Mrs. Lucinda Bohanan, ~~wife of~~ *my wife* on the 6th day of December, 1904; that there was born to her on said date a male child; that said child was living March 4, 1905, and ~~is said to have~~ *has* been named Willis Bohanan

# Applications for Enrollment of Choctaw Newborn
## Act of 1905   Volume XIII

                                           his
                             Jonas x Bohanan

Witnesses To Mark:                mark
  { Vester W Rose
    Robert Anderson

Subscribed and sworn to before me this   4th day of   April   , 1905

                                 Wirt Franklin
                                 Notary Public.

---

Choc New Born 948
    Austin Bathest   b. 9-18-03

                                      7-NB-948

              Muskogee, Indian Territory, June 1, 1905.

Allington Bathest,
    Bethel, Indian Territory.

Dear Sir:

    Referring to the application for the enrollment of your infant child, Austin Bathest, born September 18, 1903, it is noted from the affidavits heretofore filed in this office that you were the only one in attendance upon your wife at the time of the birth of the applicant.

    In this event it will be necessary that the affidavits of two persons, who are disinterested and not related to the applicant, who have actual knowledge of the facts that the child was born, the date of his birth; that he was living on March 4, 1905, and that Melwissie Bathest is his mother be filed in this office.

    The affidavit of Simeon Noah to these facts has been filed. It will, therefore, be necessary that you secure a simular[sic] affidavit from another person.

    This matter should receive your immediate attention as no further action can be taken relative to the enrollment of your child until this affidavit is received.

                           Respectfully,

                               Chairman.

## Applications for Enrollment of Choctaw Newborn
## Act of 1905 Volume XIII

7 NB 948

Muskogee, Indian Territory, June 19, 1905.

Allington Battiest[sic],
    Bethel, Indian Territory.

Dear Sir:

    Receipt is hereby acknowledged of the affidavit of Cephus Hicks to the birth of Austin Battiest[sic], son of Allington and Melwissie Battiest, September 18, 1903, and the same has been filed with our records in the matter of the enrollment of said child.

Respectfully,

Chairman.

United States of America
Indian Territory
Central District
Affidavit of Acquaintance

    I Cephus Hicks on oath state that I am 35 years of age and a citizen by blood of the Choctaw Nation, that my post office address is Bethel, Ind. Ter. that I am not related to the applicant, who is a citizen by blood of the Choctaw Nation, that I am personally acquainted with Melwissie Battiest wife of Allington Battiest, who is a citizen by blood of the Choctaw Nation, and that a male child was born to Melwissie Battiest on the 18$^{th}$ day of September 1903 and that the said male child has been named Austin Battiest and the said Austin Battiest was living on the 11$^{th}$ day of March 1905, and that I have personal knowledge that Melwissie Battiest is the mother of said Austin Battiest.

                                                                     his
                                            Cephus x Hicks
Witness to mark.                            mark
    Morton Edwards
    *(Name Illegible)*

Subscribed and sworn to before me this 12$^{th}$ day of June 1905

W.H. McKinney
Notary Public

My commission expires on the 30$^{th}$ day of March 1909

DEPARTMENT OF THE INTERIOR,
Commission to the Five Civilized Tribes.
**FILED**
JUN 19 1905

# Applications for Enrollment of Choctaw Newborn
## Act of 1905   Volume XIII

United States of America, )
)
Indian Territory, ) ss.
)
Central District. )

I, Simeon Noah, Indian Territory, on oath state that I am thirty-four years of age and a citizen by blood of the Choctaw Nation; that I am personally acquainted with Melwissie Bathest, wife of Allington Bathest; that I have known said parties over twenty years; that said parties live about four miles from me near Bethel, Indian Territory; that there was born to the said Melwissie Bathest on the 18th day of September, 1903, a male child; that said child is now living and is said to have been named Austin Bathest.

Simeon Noah

Subscribed and sworn to before me this 5th day of April, 1905.

Wirt Franklin
Notary Public.

**BIRTH AFFIDAVIT.**

### DEPARTMENT OF THE INTERIOR.
### COMMISSION TO THE FIVE CIVILIZED TRIBES.

**IN RE APPLICATION FOR ENROLLMENT**, as a citizen of the   Choctaw   Nation, of Austin Bathest   , born on the 18th   day of   September   , 1903

Name of Father: Allington Bathest    a citizen of the   Choctaw   Nation.
Name of Mother: Melwissie Bathest    a citizen of the   Choctaw   Nation.

Postoffice   Bethel, Ind. Ter.

**AFFIDAVIT OF MOTHER.**

UNITED STATES OF AMERICA, Indian Territory, }
Central       DISTRICT. }

I, Melwissie Bathest   , on oath state that I am   26   years of age and a citizen by   blood   , of the   Choctaw   Nation; that I am the lawful wife of Allington Bathest   , who is a citizen, by blood   of the   Choctaw   Nation; that a   male   child was born to me on   18th   day of   September   , 1903; that

# Applications for Enrollment of Choctaw Newborn
## Act of 1905   Volume XIII

said child has been named   Austin Bathest   , and was living March 4, 1905. *and that no physician or midwife attended me at the birth of said child.*

                                                   her
                               Melwissie x Bathest
Witnesses To Mark:              mark
    { Vester W Rose
      Robert Anderson

    Subscribed and sworn to before me this   5th   day of   April   , 1905

                                          Wirt Franklin
                                          Notary Public.

---

**AFFIDAVIT OF ATTENDING PHYSICIAN OR MID-WIFE.**

**UNITED STATES OF AMERICA, Indian Territory,** }
   Central                  **DISTRICT.**

    I,   Allington Bathest   , ~~a~~ ........................, on oath state that I attended on Mrs.   Melwissie Bathest   , ~~wife of~~ *my wife*   on the 18th   day of September , 1903; that there was born to her on said date a   male   child; that said child was living March 4, 1905, and is said to have been named   Austin Bathest *and that no one else was present when said child was born*

                                          Allington Bathest
Witnesses To Mark:
    {

    Subscribed and sworn to before me this   5th   day of   April   , 1905

                                          Wirt Franklin
                                          Notary Public.

---

<u>Choc New Born 949</u>
       Clifford Harris   b. 5-11-04

       Granted April 16, 1906

## Applications for Enrollment of Choctaw Newborn
## Act of 1905   Volume XIII

DEPARTMENT OF THE INTERIOR,
COMMISSIONER TO THE FIVE CIVILIZED TRIBES.
CHOCTAW-CHICKASAW DIVISION.
Antlers, Indian Territory, February 24, 1906.

---

949. In the matter of the enrollment of Clifford Harris, Choctaw New Born, Number

Testimony taken twelve miles west of Talihina, Indian Territory, on February 13, 1906.

WILLIAM HARRIS, being first duly sworn, testified as follows:

BY THE COMMISSIONER:

Q  What is your name?  A  William Harris.
Q  How old are you?  A  28 years old.
Q  What is tour[sic] post office address?  A  Talihina, I.T.
Q  Are you a citizen by blood of the Choctaw Nation?  A  Yes, sir.
Q  The records of the Five Tribes Commission show that you were married to Annie Ford, of Talihina, Indian Territory, on April 18, 1904, and that on May 11, 1904, there was born to Annie Harris (nee Ford) a male child, who was named Clifford Harris: Are you the father of Clifford Harris?
A  As far as I know, yes, sir.
Q  Were you positive at the time of Clifford Harris' birth that you were the child's father?
A  As far as I know, yes, sir.

Witness Excused.

---

ANNIE HARRIS, being first duly sworn, testified as follows:

BY THE COMMISSIONER:
Q  What is your name?  A  Annie Harris.
Q  What was your name before you married?  A  Annie Ford.
Q  How old are you?  A  21 years old.
Q  What is your post office address?  A  Talihina, I.T.
Q  Were you at the time of your marriage a citizen of the Choctaw Nation or non-citizen?
A  Non-citizen.
Q  The records of the Five Tribes Commission show that on April 18, 1904, you married William Harris, a citizen by blood of the Choctaw Nation of the Choctaw Nation, and that on May 11, 1904, there was born to you a male child, since named Clifford Harris: Who was the father of Clifford Harris?  A  William Harris.
Q  You state upon oath and positively that William Harris is the father of said child, Clifford Harris?  A  Yes, sir.

---

## Applications for Enrollment of Choctaw Newborn
## Act of 1905  Volume XIII

W.P. Covington, being first duly sworn, states that the above and foregoing is a full, true and correct transcript of his stenographic notes taken in said case on said date.

W.P. Covington

Subscribed and sworn to before me, this   24   day of   Feby   1906.

Lacey P Bobo<br>Notary Public.

---

7-NB-949.

DEPARTMENT OF THE INTERIOR,<br>COMMISSIONER TO THE FIVE CIVILIZED TRIBES.

In the matter of the application for the enrollment of Clifford Harris as a citizen by blood of the Choctaw Nation.

D E C I S I O N.

It appears from the record herein that on April 15, 1905, application was made to the Commission to the Five Civilized Tribes for the enrollment of Clifford Harris as a citizen by blood of the Choctaw Nation.

It further appears from the record herein and from the records of the said Commission that the applicant was born on May 11, 1904, and is the son of William Harris, a recognized and enrolled citizen by blood of the Choctaw Nation, whose name appears as number 6584 upon the final roll of citizens by blood of the Choctaw Nation, approved by the Secretary of the Interior January 17, 1903, and Annie Harris, a non-citizen white woman; that said parents were married on April 18, 1904; and that said applicant was living on March 4, 1905.

The Act of Congress approved March 3, 1905 (33 Stats., 1070) provides:

> "That the Commission to the Five Civilized Tribes is authorized for sixty days after the date of the approval of this act to receive and consider applications for enrollment of children born subsequent to September twenty-fifth, nineteen hundred and two, and prior to March fourth, nineteen hundred and five, and who were living on said latter date, to citizens by blood of the Choctaw and Chickasaw tribes of Indians whose enrollment has been approved by the Secretary of the Interior prior to the date of the approval of this act; and to enroll and make allotments to such children."

I am, therefore, of the opinion that Clifford Harris should be enrolled as a citizen by blood of the Choctaw Nation in accordance with the provisions of law above quoted, and it is so ordered.

Tams Bixby  Commissioner.

Muskogee, Indian Territory.
  APR 16 1906

## Applications for Enrollment of Choctaw Newborn
## Act of 1905 Volume XIII

7-NB-949

Muskogee, Indian Territory, April 16, 1906.

William Harris,                      **COPY**
    Talihina, Indian Territory.

Dear Sir:

    Inclosed herewith you will find a copy of the decision of the Commissioner to the Five Civilized Tribes, rendered April 16, 1906, granting the application for the enrollment of your minor child Clifford Harris, as a citizen by blood of the Choctaw Nation.

    The attorneys for the Choctaw and Chickasaw Nations have been furnished a copy of this decision and have been allowed fifteen days from the date of this notice within which to file protest against his enrollment. If at the expiration of that time no protest has been filed, the name of Clifford Harris will be placed upon the final roll of new born citizens of the Choctaw Nation to be submitted to the Secretary of the Interior for his approval.

                                              Respectfully,
                                              SIGNED
                                              Wm. O. Beall
Registered.                                       Acting Commissioner.

Incl. 7-NB-949

---

7-NB-949

Muskogee, Indian Territory, April 16, 1906.

Mansfield, McMurray & Cornish,
    Attorneys for Choctaw and Chickasaw Nations,
        South McAlester, Indian Territory.

Gentlemen:

    Inclosed herewith you will find a copy of the decision of the Commissioner to the Five Civilized Tribes, rendered April 16, 1906, granting the application for the enrollment of your minor child Clifford Harris, as a citizen by blood of the Choctaw Nation.

# Applications for Enrollment of Choctaw Newborn
## Act of 1905  Volume XIII

You are hereby advised that you will be allowed fifteen days from the date of this notice within which to file protest against his enrollment. If at the expiration of that time no protest has been filed, the name of Clifford Harris will be placed upon the final roll of new born citizens of the Choctaw Nation to be submitted to the Secretary of the Interior for his approval.

Respectfully,
SIGNED
Wm. O. Beall

Registered.　　　　　　　　　　　　　　　　　　　　Acting Commissioner.

Incl. 7-NB-949

BIRTH AFFIDAVIT.

### DEPARTMENT OF THE INTERIOR.
### COMMISSION TO THE FIVE CIVILIZED TRIBES.

IN RE APPLICATION FOR ENROLLMENT, as a citizen of the Choctaw Nation, of Clifford Harris, born on the 11 day of May, 1904

Name of Father: William Harris　　　a citizen of the Choctaw Nation.
Name of Mother: Annie Harris　　　a citizen of the Choctaw Nation.

Postoffice　Talihina I.T.

**AFFIDAVIT OF MOTHER.**

UNITED STATES OF AMERICA, Indian Territory, }
Central　　　　　DISTRICT.

I, Annie Harris, on oath state that I am 21 years of age and a citizen by ————, of the United States Nation; that I am the lawful wife of William Harris, who is a citizen, by blood of the Choctaw Nation; that a male child was born to me on 11 day of May, 1904; that said child has been named Clifford Harris, and was living March 4, 1905.

Annie Harris

Witnesses To Mark:
{

Subscribed and sworn to before me this 11 day of April, 1905

OL Johnson
Notary Public.

## Applications for Enrollment of Choctaw Newborn
## Act of 1905   Volume XIII

**AFFIDAVIT OF ATTENDING PHYSICIAN OR MID-WIFE.**

UNITED STATES OF AMERICA, Indian Territory, }
Central                  DISTRICT.

I, Hetty Ford, a midwife, on oath state that I attended on Mrs. Annie Harris, wife of William Harris on the 11 day of May, 1904; that there was born to her on said date a male child; that said child was living March 4, 1905, and is said to have been named Clifford Harris

                          her
                      Hetty x Ford

Witnesses To Mark:         mark
{ Chas T Difendafer
  OL Johnson

Subscribed and sworn to before me this 11 day of April, 1905

                          OL Johnson
                          Notary Public.

No. 788

# MARRIAGE LICENSE

United States of America,                The Indian Territory,
                                    Central   DISTRICT, SS.

**To any Person Authorized by Law to Solemnize Marriage, Greeting:**

*You are hereby commanded to Solemnize the Rite and publish the Banns of Matrimony between Mr.* W.A. Harris
*of* Tallihina[sic] *in the Indian Territory, aged* 25 *years, and M iss* Annie Ford *of* Tallihina *in the Indian Territory., aged* 19 *years, according to law, and do you officially sign and return this License to the parties therein named.*

        WITNESS *my hand and official seal, this* 9th *day of* April *A. D. 190* 4

                          E.J. Fannin
                *Clerk of the United States Court.*
    *(Name Illegible)*        Deputy

## Applications for Enrollment of Choctaw Newborn
## Act of 1905   Volume XIII

### Certificate of Marriage.

United States of America,  
**The Indian Territory,** } ss.  
................................ District.

I,   J.L. Gates   *a*   minister   , *do hereby certify, that on the*   18   *day of*   April   *A. D. 190* 4 *, I did, duly and according to law, as commanded in the foregoing License, solemnize the Rite and publish the Banns of Matrimony between the parties therein named.*

*Witness my hand, this*   19   *day of*   April   *A. D. 190* 4

My credentials are recorded in the office of the Clerk of the United States Court in the Indian Territory, Central District, Book   B   , Page   80

J. L. Gates  
*a*   minister

---

No. 788

### Certificate of Record of Marriages.

United States of America,  
**The Indian Territory,** } sct.  
Central   District.

I,   E. J. Fannin   Clerk of the United States Court, in the Indian Territory and District aforesaid, do hereby CERTIFY, that the License for and Certificate of the Marriage of

Mr.   W.A. Harris   and  
Miss Annie Ford   was

filed in my office in said Territory and District the   30   day of   April   A.D., 190 4 , and duly recorded in Book   I   of Marriage Record, Page   395

WITNESS my hand and Seal of said Court, at ANTLERS  
this   30   day of   April   A.D. 190 4

*E. J. Fannin*   Clerk.  
By   *(Name Illegible)*   Deputy.

**P. O.**   Tallihina[sic]

DEPARTMENT OF THE INTERIOR,  
COMMISSION TO THE FIVE CIVILIZED TRIBES.  
**FILED**  
APR 19 1905  
*Tams Bixby* CHAIRMAN.

## Applications for Enrollment of Choctaw Newborn
## Act of 1905   Volume XIII

REFER IN REPLY TO THE FOLLOWING:

7-NB-949.

**DEPARTMENT OF THE INTERIOR,**
**COMMISSIONER TO THE FIVE CIVILIZED TRIBES.**

Muskogee, Indian Territory, November 24, 1905.

William Harris,
    Talihina, Indian Territory.

Dear Sir:

    Receipt is hereby acknowledged of your letter of November 18, 1905, stating that you are ill and unable to appear at this office to testify relative to the right to enrollment of Clifford Harris and you do not know whether you will recover; you therefore ask if you can introduce evidence as to the rights of this child.

    In reply to your letter you are advised that if you will forward your affidavit to the effect that Clifford Harris is your child, stating the name of his mother and the date of his birth and also incorporating therein the fact of your illness and inability to appear at this office, the same will be filed with the record in the matter of the enrollment of said child.

                     Respectfully,

                Annie[sic] Harris      Geo D Rodgers
                Born May 11 1904    Acting Commissioner.

*(The affidavit below typed as given.)*

Indian Territory,
Central District.

William Harris, being duly sworn, deposes and says, my name is William Harris, my age is twenty-eight years, my post office is Talihina, I. T.

I have a wife and one child. My wife is named Annie Harris. My child is named Clifford Harris. He was born on the 11th day of May 1904.

    I am a consumptive, and am much of the time unable to be out of doors. I am unable to go to the office at Muskogee to appear in the matter of the enrollment of my child.

    I have heretofore made application for the inrolement of my child Clifford Harris, and my illness has been and is the cause of my failure to appear at Muskogee in the matter.

## Applications for Enrollment of Choctaw Newborn
## Act of 1905   Volume XIII

In witness of which I hereunto sign my name.

Witnesses.
*(Name Illegible)*
R J Stow

his
William x Harris
mark

Subscribed and sworn to before me this the 6$^{th}$ day of December 1905.

My commission expires
Feb. 4/ 1908

T.B. Lunsford
Notary Public.

---

7-NB-949

**COPY**

Muskogee, Indian Territory, September 29, 1905

William Harris,
    Talihina, Indian Territory.

Dear Sir:

    Receipt is hereby acknowledged of your letter of September 22, 1905, in which you request to be advised as to the cause of delay in enrolling your minor son, Clifford Harris, as a citizen by blood of the Choctaw Nation, an application for whom was made by you at Tuskahoma on April 11, 1905.

    It appears from the record in this case that whatever rights said child possesses as a citizen by blood of the Choctaw Nation he derives through you, his mother being a noncitizen. It also appears from your marriage license and certificate, which is now on file, that you were married to Annie Harris, the mother of said child, on April 18, 1904, and from the proof of birth, on file in said case, that said Clifford Harris was born May 11, 1904 less than one month after your marriage.

    You are further advised that before the rights of your said son as a citizen by blood of the Choctaw Nation can be finally determined it will be necessary for you to appear in person at this office in Muskogee, Indian Territory for the purpose of giving your sworn testimony.

Respectfully,
SIGNED   *Tams Bixby*
Commissioner.

## Applications for Enrollment of Choctaw Newborn
## Act of 1905   Volume XIII

Choctaw 2272.

Muskogee, Indian Territory, April 19, 1905.

W. A. Harris,
    Talihina, Indian Territory.

Dear Sir:

    Receipt is hereby acknowledged of your letter of April 14, enclosing the marriage license and certificate between W. A. Harris and Annie Ford, which you offer in support of the application for the enrollment of your child, Clifford Harris, and the same has been filed in the matter of the enrollment of your child.

        Respectfully,

                Chairman.

---

7-NB-949

Muskogee, Indian Territory, October 30, 1905.

William Harris,
    Talihina, Indian Territory.

Dear Sir:

    Receipt is hereby acknowledged of your letter of October 11, 1905, stating that you are ill and cannot appear for the purpose of testifying relative to the matter of the enrollment of your son Clifford Harris, and you ask if your affidavit will be sufficient.

    In reply to your letter you are advised that it is desired that you appear in person for the purpose of testifying relative to the right to enrollment of your son Clifford Harris and if you are ill at this time and unable to appear, you are requested to make such appearance at the earliest practicable date.

        Respectfully,

                Commissioner.

## Applications for Enrollment of Choctaw Newborn
## Act of 1905   Volume XIII

7-NB-949

Muskogee, Indian Territory, November 11, 1905.

William Harris,
    Talihina, Indian Territory.

Dear Sir:

On September 29, 1905, you were advised that it would be necessary for you to appear in person at this office for the purpose of giving your sworn testimony in the matter of the right of your son Clifford Harris to enrollment as a citizen of the Chickasaw[sic] Nation.

This matter is again invited to your attention and you are requested to appear at as early a date as practicable for the purpose of testifying in yes case in order that disposition may be made of the application for the enrollment of said child.

Respectfully,

Commissioner.

---

7-NB-949

Muskogee, Indian Territory, December 11, 1905.

William Harris,
    Talihina, Indian Territory.

Dear Sir:

Receipt is hereby acknowledged of your affidavit relative to the birth of your child Clifford Harris and the same has been filed with the records of this office in the matter of the enrollment of said child.

Respectfully,

Acting Commissioner.

## Applications for Enrollment of Choctaw Newborn
## Act of 1905   Volume XIII

7-NB-949

Muskogee, Indian Territory, February 3, 1906.

William Harris,
   Talihina, Indian Territory.

Dear Sir:

    Receipt is hereby acknowledged of your letter of January 26, 1906, asking whey the enrollment of your child Clifford Harris has been delayed.

    In reply to your letter you are advised that the application of Clifford Harris for enrollment as a new born citizen of the Choctaw Nation has not yet been passed on, but you will be notified of such action as is taken in this case.

    Respectfully,

    Acting Commissioner.

---

7-NB-949

Muskogee, Indian Territory, February 6, 1906.

William Harris,
   Talihina, Indian Territory.

Dear Sir:

    Receipt is hereby acknowledged of your letter of January 26, 1906, asking why the enrollment of your child Clifford Harris has been delayed.

    In reply to your letter you are advised that it will be necessary that your testimony be taken in the matter of the enrollment of your child, Clifford Harris. Inasmuch, however, as you are physically unable to appear at this office for that purpose, a representative of the Commissioner to the Five Civilized Tribes who is now in the Choctaw Nation will be directed to proceed to Talihina as early as practicable for the purpose of securing your testimony.

    Respectfully,

    Acting Commissioner.

## Applications for Enrollment of Choctaw Newborn
## Act of 1905   Volume XIII

7-NB-949

Muskogee, Indian Territory, June 12, 1906.

William Harris,
    Talihina, Indian Territory.

Dear Sir:

    Receipt is hereby acknowledged of your letter of June 4, 1906, in which you ask the status of the application for the enrollment of your child Clifford Harris.

    In reply to your letter you are advised that on April 16, 1906, a decision was rendered granting the application of Clifford Harris for enrollment as a citizen by blood of the Choctaw Nation and his name will be placed upon the next schedule of new born citizens under the act of Congress approved March 3, 1905, which was prepared for forwarding to the Secretary of the Interior.

                  Respectfully,

                                Commissioner.

4711

## Department of the Interior
### United States Indian Service

OFFICE OF
DISTRICT AGENT.

Hugo, Okla., Jan. 24, 1912.

Subject: In re the ~~allot~~ enrollment of Wm. Harris, and
Clifford Harris. . . . . . . .

Honorable Dana M. Kelsey,
    United States Indian Superintendent,
        Muskogee, Oklahoma.

Sir:

    I am enclosing you herewith, copy of a decision of Commissioner to the Five Civilized Tribes, dated April 16, 1906, granting the application for enrollment of Clifford Harris, Choctaw New Born, Roll No. 1564, also letter transmitting this copy of the decision to William Harris, Talihina, Oklahoma, father of Clifford Harris.

## Applications for Enrollment of Choctaw Newborn
## Act of 1905   Volume XIII

You will note that the decision refers to "William Harris, a recognized and enrolled citizen of the Choctaw Nation, whose name appears as Number 6584 upon the final rolls of citizens by blood of the Choctaw Nation."

While at Tushkahoma[sic] recently, Mr. Harris, the father of Clifford Harris, called on me to assist him in making application for the per capita payment for himself and his son, and in doing so, I discovered that in all probability the correct roll number of William Harris, the father of Clifford Harris, is 15415, and that the copy of decision refers to another William Harris as being the father of the child, Clifford Harris, and I presume that the records of the Commissioner do not show the correct party as father of this child.

I am enclosing you herewith, a copy of the testimony of William Harris, whom I identify as Choctaw by blood, Roll No. 15415, from which you will note that he does not know any of the parties enrolled on the same card with William Harris, Choctaw by blood, roll number 6584, or on the card with William Harris, Choctaw by blood, Roll No. 2906. The last two named William Harris also appear to be of different age and different degree of Indian blood from the father of Clifford Harris, who claims to be 1/16 blood Choctaw, and 34 years of age.

Mr. Harris is quite an intelligent man, and I believe knows what he is talking about, and he desires if a mistake has been made as to the father of Clifford Harris, that the records be corrected.

I am also transmitting herewith, the application of William Harris, whom I identify as Choctaw by blood, roll No. 15415 for the per capita payment to him.

CB/ARM

Respectfully,
Chas Bozarth
District Agent.

4711 *AB*

REFER IN REPLY TO THE FOLLOWING:

7-NB-949

**DEPARTMENT OF THE INTERIOR,**
**COMMISSIONER TO THE FIVE CIVILIZED TRIBES.**

Muskogee, Indian Territory, April 16, 1906.

William Harris,
   Talihina, Indian Territory.

Dear Sir:

Inclosed herewith you will find a copy of the decision of the Commissioner to the Five Civilized Tribes, rendered April 16, 1906, granting the application for the

## Applications for Enrollment of Choctaw Newborn
## Act of 1905   Volume XIII

enrollment of your minor child Clifford Harris, as a citizen by blood of the Choctaw Nation.

The attorneys for the Choctaw and Chickasaw Nations have been furnished a copy of this decision and have been allowed fifteen days from the date of this notice within which to file protest against his enrollment. If at the expiration of that time no protest has been filed, the name of Clifford Harris will be placed upon the final roll of new born citizens of the Choctaw Nation to be submitted to the Secretary of the Interior for is approval.

Respectfully,<br>
W$^m$ O. Beall<br>
Acting Commissioner.

Registered.

Incl. 7-NB-949

4711

In the matter of the enrollment of
Clifford Harris, Choctaw New Born,
Roll No. 1564.

William Harris, being first duly sworn testified as follows:

Examination by the Commission by Chas Bozarth:

Q What is your name, age and post office address?
A William Harris, age 34, P. O. is Sardis, Okla.
Q What day, year and month were you born? [sic] October 30, 1877.
Q Are you enrolled as a member of the Choctaw tribe of Indans[sic]?
A Yes sir.
Q Do you know your correct roll number?
A I was led to believe by a decision of the Commissioner advising me of the enrollment of Clifford Harris, as a Choctaw Newborn that my roll No. was 6584 but on investigation I am satisfied that I am not the William Harris enrolled opposite that number.
Q Are you the father of Clifford Harris, Choctaw New Born, roll No. 1564? A Yes sir.
Q What is the name of your wife? A Annie L. Harris.
Q Is Annie L. Harris enrolled? [sic] No, she is a non-citizen.
Q What degree of Indian blood are you? A About one-sixteenth.
   (Note) Witness appears to have <u>very</u> little Indian blood)
Q Are [sic] acquainted with Abel, Henry, Ruthie, Thomas, Zado, James, Elizabeth or Everette J. Harris, who appear to be enrolled on the same care with William Harris, roll No. 6584?
A No sir, I don't know any of them.
[sic] Please state the names of the members of your family?
A Just my wife, myself and Clifford Harris.

## Applications for Enrollment of Choctaw Newborn
## Act of 1905   Volume XIII

Q Were there any other members of your family enrolled at the same time you were? A No, I think I am the only member of the family enrolled at that time. I have two sisters, Fannie Fry and Annie Holt enrolled but they were married and not enrolled with me, and my mother was dead and my father was never enrolled.
Q If the records of the Commissioner show Clifford Harris to be the son of William Harris, roll No. 6584, and one Annie Harris, is that correct or not?
A I suppose from the fact that I do not know any of the persons enrolled on the same card with William Harris, roll No. 6584, and as I am the father of Clifford Harris, that that is not correct.
Q Have you any idea as to what your correct roll No. is?
A I think that my name appears opposite roll No. 15415 as that corresponds with my age and degree of Indian blood.
Q What is the name of the mother of Clifford Harris? A Annie L. Harris.
Q What is the age of Clifford Harris? A Eight years.
Q Do you know what day, year and month Clifford was born.[sic]
A May 11, 1904.
Q Are you acquainted with Walter C., Henry C., Maggie E., Mattie M., Bessie L or Nettie Ella Harris, being the persons enrolled on the care with William Harris, roll No. 2906?
A Don't know none of them, except I have heard of a William Harris that lives at Talihina.
Q If there appears to be a mistake about this matter do you wish it corrected? A Yes sir.

Witness Excused.

Tuskahoma, Okla. Jany. 22, 1912.

Q What was your post office address at the time you were enrolled? A I lived at Talihina then.
Q What was your father's name? A Charlie Harris.
Q What was your mother's name? A Sarah Harris.

*(End of file)*

---

Choc New Born 950
      Lorena Baker   b. 8-24-03

Applications for Enrollment of Choctaw Newborn
Act of 1905   Volume XIII

BIRTH AFFIDAVIT.

## DEPARTMENT OF THE INTERIOR.
## COMMISSION TO THE FIVE CIVILIZED TRIBES.

IN RE APPLICATION FOR ENROLLMENT, as a citizen of the Choctaw Nation, of Lorena Baker, born on the 24th day of August, 1903

Name of Father: Isham Baker a citizen of the Choctaw Nation.
Name of Mother: Minnie Baker a citizen of the Choctaw Nation.

Postoffice   Bethel, Ind. Ter.

### AFFIDAVIT OF MOTHER.

UNITED STATES OF AMERICA, Indian Territory,
Central   DISTRICT.

I, Minnie Baker, on oath state that I am 18 years of age and a citizen by blood, of the Choctaw Nation; that I am the lawful wife of Isham Baker, who is a citizen, by blood of the Choctaw Nation; that a female child was born to me on 24th day of August, 1903; that said child has been named Lorena Baker, and was living March 4, 1905.

                                              her
                                     Minnie x Baker
Witnesses To Mark:                    mark
  { Robert Anderson
    Vester W Rose

Subscribed and sworn to before me this 5th day of April, 1905

                                      Wirt Franklin
                                      Notary Public.

### AFFIDAVIT OF ATTENDING PHYSICIAN OR MID-WIFE.

UNITED STATES OF AMERICA, Indian Territory,
Central   DISTRICT.

*was present with*

I, Loston Wallace, a _____, on oath state that I ~~attended on~~ Mrs. Minnie Baker, wife of Isham Baker on the 24th day of August, 1903; that there was born to her on said date a female child; that said child was living March 4, 1905, and is said to have been named Lorena Baker

                                        Loston Wallace

# Applications for Enrollment of Choctaw Newborn
## Act of 1905   Volume XIII

Witnesses To Mark:

{

    Subscribed and sworn to before me this   5th  day of    April         , 1905

                                   Wirt Franklin
                                   Notary Public.

---

Choc New Born 951
    James Bathest   b. 6-3-03

7-NB-951

                        Muskogee, Indian Territory, August 9, 1905.

Delilah Jacobs[sic],
    Bethel, Indian Territory.

Dear Madam:

    Receipt is hereby acknowledged of your affidavit and the joint affidavit of Wesley Baker and Charley Noah to the birth of James Bathest, son of Pitchlynn Bathest and Delilah Jacob, June 3, 1903. The same are returned herewith and you are requested to have the Notary Public J. H. Matthews fill in the year in which the joint affidavit of Wesley Baker and Charley Noah was acknowledged before him.

                      Respectfully,

                                      Acting Commissioner.

LM 5-28

## Applications for Enrollment of Choctaw Newborn
## Act of 1905   Volume XIII

7-NB-951

Muskogee, Indian Territory, August 22, 1905.

Delilah Jacob,
  Bethel, Indian Territory.

Dear Madam:

Receipt is hereby acknowledged f the application for the enrollment of your infant child James Bathest which has been corrected by having the date of acknowledgment by Wesley Baker and Charley Noah of their joint affidavit inserted by the Notary Public before whom the same was acknowledged.

Respectfully,

Commissioner.

---

**BIRTH AFFIDAVIT.**   7 - NB - 951

### DEPARTMENT OF THE INTERIOR.
### COMMISSION TO THE FIVE CIVILIZED TRIBES.

---

**IN RE APPLICATION FOR ENROLLMENT,** as a citizen of the    Choctaw    Nation, of James Bathest   , born on the $3^d$   day of June   , 1903

Name of Father: Pitchlynn Bathest dec!        a citizen of the   Choctaw   Nation.
Name of Mother: Delilah Jacob  Roll 2033     a citizen of the   Choctaw   Nation.

Postoffice   Bethel Ind Ter

---

**AFFIDAVIT OF MOTHER.**

UNITED STATES OF AMERICA, Indian Territory, }
  Central           DISTRICT.                }

I, Delilah Jacob   , on oath state that I am   17   years of age and a citizen by blood   , of the   Choctaw   Nation; that I ~~am~~ *was* the lawful wife of   Pitchlynn Bathest dec$^d$   , who ~~is~~ *was* a citizen, by blood   of the   Choctaw   Nation; that a   male   child was born to me on   3rd   day of   June   , 1903; that said child has been named   James Bathest   , and was living March 4, 1905.

her<br>
Delilah x Jacob<br>
mark

289

# Applications for Enrollment of Choctaw Newborn
## Act of 1905   Volume XIII

Witnesses To Mark:
- Almond F. Carterby  PO Bethel IT
- Allen Willis         "  Bethel IT

Subscribed and sworn to before me this  3  day of   Aug   , 1905

J H Matthews
Notary Public.

---

**AFFIDAVIT OF ATTENDING PHYSICIAN OR MID-WIFE.**

UNITED STATES OF AMERICA, Indian Territory, }
Central            DISTRICT. }

*we are acquainted with*

We, Wesley Baker and Charley Noah , on oath state that ~~I attended on~~ Mrs. Delilah Jacob *who was*, wife of   Pitchlynn Bathest dec$^d$ *and that* on or *about* the 3rd day of  June  , 1903; that there was born to her on said date a male child; that said child was living March 4, 1905, and is said to have been named James Bathest *and that we are not related to the applicant nor interested in the case*

Charley Noah (his mark)
Witnesses To Mark:              Wesley Baker (mark)
- Tracy Matthews Bethel IT
- (Name Illegible) Bethel I.T.

Subscribed and sworn to before me this  3  day of   Aug   , 1905

J H Matthews
Notary Public.

---

**BIRTH AFFIDAVIT.**

## DEPARTMENT OF THE INTERIOR.
## COMMISSION TO THE FIVE CIVILIZED TRIBES.

IN RE APPLICATION FOR ENROLLMENT, as a citizen of the   Choctaw   Nation, of  James Bathest   , born on the 3rd  day of  June  , 1903

Name of Father: Pitchlynn Battiest[sic]    a citizen of the  Choctaw  Nation.
Name of Mother: Delilah Jacob              a citizen of the  Choctaw  Nation.

Postoffice   Bethel Ind Ter

# Applications for Enrollment of Choctaw Newborn
# Act of 1905 Volume XIII

## AFFIDAVIT OF MOTHER.

UNITED STATES OF AMERICA, Indian Territory, }
Central  DISTRICT.

I, Delilah Jacob, on oath state that I am 17 years of age and a citizen by blood, of the Choctaw Nation; that I ~~am~~ *was* the lawful wife of Pitchlynn Bathest deceased, who ~~is~~ *was* a citizen, by blood of the Choctaw Nation; that a male child was born to me on 3rd day of June, 1903; that said child has been named James Bathest, and was living March 4, 1905. *and that no one was present at the birth of said child*

                              her
                         Delilah x Jacob
                            mark

Witnesses To Mark:
{ Vester W Rose
{ Robert Anderson

Subscribed and sworn to before me this 5th day of April, 1905

                        Wirt Franklin
                        Notary Public.

## AFFIDAVIT OF ATTENDING PHYSICIAN OR MID-WIFE.

UNITED STATES OF AMERICA, Indian Territory, }
Central  DISTRICT.

*was acquainted with*

I, Wesley Baker, ~~a~~ ..................., on oath state that I ~~attended on~~ Mrs. Delilah Jacob *who was* wife of Pitchlynn Battiest deceased on the 3rd day of June, 1903; that there was born to her on said date a male child; that said child was living March 4, 1905, and is said to have been named James Battiest

                        his
                    Wesley x Baker

Witnesses To Mark:           mark
{ Vester W Rose
{ Robert Anderson

Subscribed and sworn to before me this 5th day of April, 1905

                        Wirt Franklin
                        Notary Public.

## Applications for Enrollment of Choctaw Newborn
## Act of 1905  Volume XIII

<u>Choc New Born 952</u>
    Balleid[sic] Carterby  b. 11-2-02
    Dora Carterby  b. 12-9-04

---

7-NB-952

Muskogee, Indian Territory, June 1, 1905.

Siglow[sic] Carterby,
    Bethel, Indian Territory.

Dear Sir:

    Referring to the application for the enrollment of your infant child, Balleid[sic] Carterby, born November 2, 1902, it is noted from the affidavits heretofore filed in this office that you were the only one in attendance upon your wife at the time of the birth of the applicant.

    In this event it will be necessary that the affidavits of two persons, who are disinterested and not related to the applicant, who have actual knowledge of the facts that the child was born, the date of birth; that he was living March 4, 1905, and that Tullis Carterby is his mother be filed in this office.

    The affidavit of Simeon Noah to these facts has been filed. It will, therefore, be necessary that you secure a simular[sic] affidavit of another person.

    This matter should receive your immediate attention as no further action can be taken relative to the enrollment of your child until the Commission has been furnished with this affidavit.

                          Respectfully,

                              Chairman.

## Applications for Enrollment of Choctaw Newborn
## Act of 1905   Volume XIII

Substitute.

7-NB-952.

Muskogee, Indian Territory, June 8, 1905.

Siglon Carterby,
    Bethel, Indian Territory.

Dear Sir:

    Referring to the application for the enrollment of your infant child, Dora Carterby, born December 9, 1904, it is noted that you were the only one in attendance upon your wife at the time of the birth of the applicant.

    In this event it will be necessary that the affidavits of two persons who are disinterested and not related to the applicant, who have actual knowledge of the facts; that the child was born, the date of her birth, that she was living on March 4, 1905, and that Tillis[sic] Carterby is her mother, be filed in this office.

    The affidavit of Simeon Noah to these facts has been filed. It will therefore be necessary that you secure a similar affidavit from another person.

    This matter should receive your immediate attention as no further action can be taken relative to the enrollment of this child, until the Commission has been furnished with this affidavit.

                        Respectfully,

                                                Chairman.

7 NB 952

Muskogee, Indian Territory, June 16, 1905.

Siglon Carterby,
    Bethel, Indian Territory.

Dear Sir:

    Receipt is hereby acknowledged of the affidavit of Joel Battiest to the birth of Dora Carterby, daughter of Siglon and Tellis Carterby, December 9, 1904; also affidavit of Colbert Battiest to the birth of Ballard Carterby, son of Siglon and Tellis Carterby, November 2, 1902, and the same have been filed with our records in the matter of the enrollment of said children.

                        Respectfully,

                                                Chairman.

## Applications for Enrollment of Choctaw Newborn
## Act of 1905 Volume XIII

7-NB-952

Muskogee, Indian Territory, July 12, 1905.

Siglon Cartubby[sic],
    Bethel, Indian Territory.

Dear Sir:

    Receipt is hereby acknowledged of your letter of July 1, 1905, asking to be notified when the enrollment of your children Ballard and Dora Cartubby is approved by the Secretary of the Interior.

    In reply to your letter you are advised that you will be notified when the enrollment of your children Balleid[sic] and Dora Carterby has been approved by the Secretary of the Interior.

                  Respectfully,

                                      Commissioner.

*(The affidavit below typed as given.)*

                    United States of America
                    Central District Indian Territory

Joel Battiest on oath states that    is   years of age and a citizen by blood of the Choctaw Nation and no relation to Dora Carterby who was born Dec 9, 1904 I visited Siglon Carterby and Tellis Carterby father and mother of the child on Dec 10 and the child was born then and was named Dora Carterby and was still living March 4 1905

Subscribed and sworn to before me this the 8 day of June 1905

                                  Joel Battiest

                                  *(Name Illegible)*
                                      Notary Public

My Commission expires Dec 4, 1906

## Applications for Enrollment of Choctaw Newborn
## Act of 1905  Volume XIII

United States of America, )
)
Indian Territory, ) ss.
)
Central District. )

I, Simeon Noah, Indian Territory, on oath state that I am thirty-four years of age and a citizen by blood of the Choctaw Nation; that I am personally acquainted with Tillis Carterby, wife of Siglon Carterby; that I have known said parties for about twenty-five years; that said parties have lived about three miles from where I have lived near Bethel, Indian Territory, for about twenty years; that there was born to the said Tillis Carterby on or about the 9th day of December, 1904, a female child; that said child is now living and is said to have been named Dora Carterby.

Simeon Noah

Subscribed and sworn to before me this 5th day of April, 1905.

Wirt Franklin
Notary Public.

BIRTH AFFIDAVIT.

### DEPARTMENT OF THE INTERIOR.
### COMMISSION TO THE FIVE CIVILIZED TRIBES.

**IN RE APPLICATION FOR ENROLLMENT**, as a citizen of the Choctaw Nation, of Dora Carterby, born on the 9th day of December, 1904

Name of Father: Siglon Carterby  a citizen of the Choctaw Nation.
Name of Mother: Tillis Carterby  a citizen of the Choctaw Nation.

Postoffice  Bethel, Ind. Ter.

### AFFIDAVIT OF MOTHER.

UNITED STATES OF AMERICA, Indian Territory,
Central  DISTRICT.

I, Tillis Carterby, on oath state that I am about 34 years of age and a citizen by blood, of the Choctaw Nation; that I am the lawful wife of Siglon Carterby, who is a citizen, by blood of the Choctaw Nation; that a female child was born to me on 9th day of December, 1904; that said child has been named Dora Carterby, and was living March 4, 1905. *and that no physician or mid wife attended me at the birth of said child*

## Applications for Enrollment of Choctaw Newborn
## Act of 1905   Volume XIII

                                  her
                              Tillis x Carterby

Witnesses To Mark:                      mark
{ Robert Anderson
  Vester W Rose

    Subscribed and sworn to before me this  5th   day of     April        , 1905

                                      Wirt Franklin
                                      Notary Public.

---

**AFFIDAVIT OF ATTENDING PHYSICIAN OR MID-WIFE.**

UNITED STATES OF AMERICA, Indian Territory, }
   Central                  DISTRICT.

    I,   Siglon Carterby   , ~~a~~ _____, on oath state that I attended on Mrs.   Tillis Carterby   my , wife ~~of~~ _____ on the 9th   day of December  , 1904; that there was born to her on said date a   female   child; that said child was living March 4, 1905, and ~~is said to have~~ has been named   Dora Carterby and that no one else was present at the birth of said child

                                     Siglon Carterby

Witnesses To Mark:

{

    Subscribed and sworn to before me this  5th   day of    April        , 1905

                                      Wirt Franklin
                                      Notary Public.

---

*(The affidavit below typed as given.)*

                        United States of America
                      Central District Indian Terr

    Colbert Battiest on oath states that he is 29 years of age and a citizen by blood of the Choctaw Nation and no relation to Ballard Carterby who was born on the 2 of November, 1902 I visited Siglon Carterby and Tillis Carterby on the 3 day of November and their had bin a child born to them had bin named Ballard Carterby and was living on March the 4 1905 and Tillis Carterby was the mother of Ballard Carterby

Subscribed and sworn to before me this the 8 day of June 1905

## Applications for Enrollment of Choctaw Newborn
## Act of 1905 Volume XIII

Colbert Battiest

*(Name Illegible)*
Notary Public

My Commission expires Dec 4 1906

United States of America, )
)
Indian Territory, ) ss.
)
Central District. )

I, Simeon Noah, Indian Territory, on oath state that I am thirty-four years of age and a citizen by blood of the Choctaw Nation; that I am personally acquainted with Tillis Carterby, wife of Siglon Carterby; that I have known said parties for about twenty-five years; that said parties have lived about three miles from where I have lived near Bethel, Indian Territory, for about twenty years; that there was born to the said Tillis Carterby on or about November 2, 1902, a male child; that said child is now living and is said to have been named Balleid[sic] Carterby.

Simeon Noah

Subscribed and sworn to before me this 5th day of April, 1905.

Wirt Franklin
Notary Public.

BIRTH AFFIDAVIT.

### DEPARTMENT OF THE INTERIOR.
### COMMISSION TO THE FIVE CIVILIZED TRIBES.

**IN RE APPLICATION FOR ENROLLMENT,** as a citizen of the Choctaw Nation, of Balleid Carterby , born on the 2nd day of November , 1902

Name of Father: Siglon Carterby    a citizen of the Choctaw Nation.
Name of Mother: Tillis Carterby    a citizen of the Choctaw Nation.

Postoffice    Bethel, Ind. Ter.

# Applications for Enrollment of Choctaw Newborn
## Act of 1905   Volume XIII

### AFFIDAVIT OF MOTHER.

UNITED STATES OF AMERICA, Indian Territory, }
Central        DISTRICT.

I, Tillis Carterby, on oath state that I am about 34 years of age and a citizen by blood, of the Choctaw Nation; that I am the lawful wife of Siglon Carterby, who is a citizen, by blood of the Choctaw Nation; that a male child was born to me on 2nd day of November, 1902; that said child has been named Balleid Carterby, and was living March 4, 1905. and that no physician or mid-wife attended me at the birth of said child

           her
          Tillis x Carterby
Witnesses To Mark:      mark
{ Robert Anderson
  Vester W Rose

Subscribed and sworn to before me this 5th day of April, 1905

          Wirt Franklin
           Notary Public.

---

### AFFIDAVIT OF ATTENDING PHYSICIAN OR MID-WIFE.

UNITED STATES OF AMERICA, Indian Territory, }
Central        DISTRICT.

I, Siglon Carterby, a ~~_____~~, on oath state that I attended on Mrs. Tillis Carterby my, wife ~~of~~ _____ on the 2nd day of November, 1902; that there was born to her on said date a male child; that said child was living March 4, 1905, and ~~is said to have~~ has been named Balleid Carterby and that no one else was present at the birth of said child

          Siglon Carterby
Witnesses To Mark:
{

Subscribed and sworn to before me this 5th day of April, 1905

          Wirt Franklin
           Notary Public.

# Applications for Enrollment of Choctaw Newborn
# Act of 1905 Volume XIII

Choc New Born 953
    Carlo Wallace b. 9-20-05

7-NB-953

Muskogee, Indian Territory, June 1, 1905.

Loston Wallace,
    Bethel, Indian Territory.

Dear Sir:

    Referring to the application for the enrollment of your infant child, Carlo Wallace, born February 20, 1905, it is noted from the affidavits heretofore filed in this office that you were the only one in attendance upon your wife at the time of the birth of the applicant.

    In this event it will be necessary that the affidavits of two persons, who are disinterested and not related to the applicant, who have actual knowledge of the facts that the child was born, the date of his birth; that he was living on March 4, 1905, and that Silean Wallace is his mother be filed in this office.

    The affidavit of Siglon Carterby to these facts has been filed. It will, therefore, be necessary that you secure a similar affidavit from another person.

    This matter should receive your immediate attention as no further action can be taken relative to the enrollment of your child until the Commission has been furnished with this affidavit.

                    Respectfully,

                    Chairman.

7-NB-953

Muskogee, Indian Territory, July 5, 1905.

Loston Wallace,
    Bethel, Indian Territory.

Dear Sir:

    Receipt is hereby acknowledged of the affidavit of Bazel Bakan to the birth of Carlo Wallace, son of Loston and Gilan[sic] Wallace, February 20, 1905, and the same has been filed with the records of this office in the matter of the enrollment of said child.

# Applications for Enrollment of Choctaw Newborn
## Act of 1905    Volume XIII

Respectfully,

Commissioner.

$W^mO.B.$

COMMISSIONERS:
TAMS BIXBY,
THOMAS B. NEEDLES,
C.R. BRECKINBRIDGE.

WM. O. BEALL
Secretary

**DEPARTMENT OF THE INTERIOR,**
**COMMISSIONER TO THE FIVE CIVILIZED TRIBES.**

REFER IN REPLY TO THE FOLLOWING:

7-NB-953

ADDRESS ONLY THE
COMMISSION TO THE FIVE CIVILIZED TRIBES.

Muskogee, Indian Territory, June 1, 1905.

Loston Wallace,
    Bethel, Indian Territory.

Dear Sir:

    Referring to the application for the enrollment of your infant child, Carlo Wallace, born February 20, 1905, it is noted from the affidavits heretofore filed in this office that you were the only one in attendance upon your wife at the time of the birth of the applicant.

    In this event it will be necessary that the affidavits of two persons, who are disinterested and not related to the applicant, who have actual knowledge of the facts that the child was born, the date of his birth; that he was living on March 4, 1905, and that Silean Wallace is his mother be filed in this office.

    The affidavit of Siglon Carterby to these facts has been filed. It will, therefore, be necessary that you secure a similar affidavit from another person.

    This matter should receive your immediate attention as no further action can be taken relative to the enrollment of your child until the Commission has been furnished with this affidavit.

                  Respectfully,
                  T.B. Needles
                  Commissioner in Charge.

## Applications for Enrollment of Choctaw Newborn
## Act of 1905   Volume XIII

*(The affidavit below typed as given.)*

    Came before me a Notary Public this 26 day of June Bazel Baken and testify that he is acquinted with Silan Wallace and states ~~that~~ on oath that Carlo Wallas was borned[sic] to her on 20 day of Feb 1905 and that he was living March the 4=1905 and is living at this time  and he alsow testifies that Silan Wallace is the wife of Loston Wallace

Witness ⎫  
to mark ⎭   John Noah  Noah IT  
        Tracy Matthews  Bethel I.T.

            his  
Bazel x Baken  
          mark

    Subscribed and sworn to before me this 26 day of June 1905

                      J H Matthews  
                                        Notary Public

My Commission expires  
    Feb 13=1909

---

United States of America,  )  
                              )  
Indian Territory,            )  ss.  
                              )  
Central District.           )

    I, Siglon Carterby, on lath state that I am thirty-three years of age and a citizen by blood of the Choctaw Nation; that I am personally acquainted with Silean Wallace, wife of Loston Wallace, that I have known said parties since their birth; that on the 20th day of February, 1905, there was born to the said Silean Wallace a male child; that said child is now living and is said to have been named Carlo Wallace; and that at the time of the birth of the said child said parties were living and do now live about one mile from me near Bethel, Indian Territory.

                                            Siglon Carterby

Subscribed and sworn to before me this 5th day of April, 1905.

                                          Wirt Franklin  
                                              Notary Public.

# Applications for Enrollment of Choctaw Newborn
## Act of 1905   Volume XIII

**BIRTH AFFIDAVIT.**

### DEPARTMENT OF THE INTERIOR.
### COMMISSION TO THE FIVE CIVILIZED TRIBES.

IN RE APPLICATION FOR ENROLLMENT, as a citizen of the Choctaw Nation, of Carlo Wallace, born on the 20th day of February, 1905

Name of Father: Loston Wallace       a citizen of the Choctaw Nation.
Name of Mother: Silean Wallace       a citizen of the Choctaw Nation.

Postoffice   Bethel, Ind. Ter.

**AFFIDAVIT OF MOTHER.**

UNITED STATES OF AMERICA, Indian Territory,
Central                DISTRICT.

I, Silean Wallace, on oath state that I am 17 years of age and a citizen by blood, of the Choctaw Nation; that I am the lawful wife of Loston Wallace, who is a citizen, by blood of the Choctaw Nation; that a male child was born to me on 20th day of February, 1905; that said child has been named Carlo Wallace, and was living March 4, 1905. *and that no physician or midwife attended me at the birth of said child*

                        her
                 Silean x Wallace
Witnesses To Mark:    mark
  { Robert Anderson
  { Vester W Rose

Subscribed and sworn to before me this 5th day of April, 1905

                 Wirt Franklin
                    Notary Public.

**AFFIDAVIT OF ATTENDING PHYSICIAN OR MID-WIFE.**

UNITED STATES OF AMERICA, Indian Territory,
Central                DISTRICT.

I, Loston Wallace, a ~~~~~, on oath state that I attended on Mrs. Silean Wallace, ~~wife of~~ *my wife* on the 20th day of February, 1905; that there was born to her on said date a male child; that said child was living March 4, 1905, and ~~is said to have~~ *has* been named Carlo Wallace *and that no one else was present when said child was born*

## Applications for Enrollment of Choctaw Newborn
## Act of 1905   Volume XIII

Loston Wallace

Witnesses To Mark:
{

Subscribed and sworn to before me this 5$^{th}$ day of April    , 1905

Wirt Franklin
Notary Public.

---

Choc New Born 954
    Andrew Battiest   b. 8-17-04

7--NB--954

Muskogee, Indian Territory, June 2, 1905.

Wade Battiest,
    Bethel, Indian Territory.

Dear Sir:

    Referring to the application for the enrollment of your infant child, Andrew Battiest, born August 17, 1904, it is noted from the affidavits heretofore filed in this office that you were the only one in attendance upon your wife at the time of the birth of the applicant.

    In this event it will be necessary that the affidavits of two persons, who are disinterested and not related to the applicant, who have actual knowledge of the facts that the child was born, the date of his birth; that he was living on March 4, 1905, and that Siney Battiest is his mother be filed in this office.

    The affidavit of Loston Wallace to these facts has been filed. It will, therefore, be necessary that you secure ahsimular[sic] affidavit from another person.

    This matter should receive your immediate attention as no further action can be taken relative to the enrollment of your child until the Commission has been furnished with this affidavit.

    Respectfully,

[sic]

# Applications for Enrollment of Choctaw Newborn
## Act of 1905 Volume XIII

7 NB 954

Muskogee, Indian Territory, June 19, 1905.

Wade Battiest,
 Bethel, Indian Territory.

Dear Sir:

Receipt is hereby acknowledged of the affidavit of Williamson Noahubi to the birth of Andrew Battiest, son of Wade and Siney Battiest, August 17, 1904, and the same has been filed with our records in the matter of the enrollment of said child.

Respectfully,

Chairman.

---

United States of America
 Indian Territory
Central District

I Williamson Noahaby[sic] on oath state that I am 37 years of age and a citizen by blood of the Choctaw Nation that my post office address is Bethel, Ind. Ter. that I am not related to the applicant who is a citizen by; that I am personally acquainted with Siney Battiest wife of Wade Battiest, who is a citizen by, and that a male child was born to Siney Battiest on the 17$^{th}$ day of August 1904 and that said male child has been named Andrew Datticst and the said Andrew Battiest was living on the 4$^{th}$ day of March 1905, and is now living, and that I have personal knowledge that Siney Battiest is the mother of said Andrew Battiest

Williamson Noahubi

Subscribed and sworn to before me this 12$^{th}$ day of June 1905

W.H. McKinney
Notary Public

My Commission expires
 March 30, 1909

DEPARTMENT OF THE INTERIOR,
Commission to the Five Civilized Tribes.
**FILED**
APR -8 1905

*Tams Bixby* CHAIRMAN.

## Applications for Enrollment of Choctaw Newborn
## Act of 1905   Volume XIII

United States of America,   )
                            )
Indian Territory,           )   ss.
                            )
Central District.           )

I, Loston Wallace, on oath state that I am twenty-three years of age and a citizen by blood of the Choctaw Nation; that I am personally acquainted with Siney Battiest, wife of Wade Battiest; that there was born to the said Siney Battiest on the 17th day of August, 1904, a male child; that said child has been named Andrew Battiest, and that I was present when said child was born.

Loston Wallace

Subscribed and sworn to before me this 5th day of April, 1905.

Wirt Franklin<br>Notary Public.

---

**BIRTH AFFIDAVIT.**

### DEPARTMENT OF THE INTERIOR.
### COMMISSION TO THE FIVE CIVILIZED TRIBES.

---

**IN RE APPLICATION FOR ENROLLMENT**, as a citizen of the   Choctaw   Nation, of Andrew Battiest   , born on the 17th   day of August   , 1904

Name of Father: Wade Battiest          a citizen of the   Choctaw   Nation.
Name of Mother: Siney Battiest         a citizen of the   Choctaw   Nation.

Postoffice   Bethel, Ind. Ter.

---

AFFIDAVIT OF MOTHER.

UNITED STATES OF AMERICA, Indian Territory, }
       Central                DISTRICT.      }

I,   Siney Battiest   , on oath state that I am   35   years of age and a citizen by blood   , of the   Choctaw   Nation; that I am the lawful wife of   Wade Battiest   , who is a citizen, by blood   of the   Choctaw   Nation; that a   male   child was born to me on   17th   day of   August   , 1904; that said child has been named Andrew Battiest   , and was living March 4, 1905.

her<br>Siney x Battiest<br>mark

Witnesses To Mark:
  { Robert Anderson
  { Vester W Rose

# Applications for Enrollment of Choctaw Newborn
## Act of 1905   Volume XIII

Subscribed and sworn to before me this   5th day of    April    , 1905

                          Wirt Franklin
                          Notary Public.

### AFFIDAVIT OF ATTENDING PHYSICIAN OR MID-WIFE.

UNITED STATES OF AMERICA, Indian Territory, }
   Central                DISTRICT. }

    I,   Wade Battiest   , ~~a~~ ................., on oath state that I attended on Mrs.   Siney Battiest   , ~~wife of~~   *my wife*   on the 17th   day of   August   , 1904; that there was born to her on said date a    male    child; that said child was living March 4, 1905, and is said to have been named   Andrew Battiest

                             her
                        Wade x  Battiest
Witnesses To Mark:           mark
   { Robert Anderson
   { Vester W Rose
    Subscribed and sworn to before me this   5th day of    April    , 1905

                         Wirt Franklin
                         Notary Public.

---

<u>Choc New Born 955</u>
       Amanda Haiakanubbi[sic]   b. 11-23-04

### NEW-BORN AFFIDAVIT.

         Number.............

## ...Choctaw Enrolling Commission...

    IN THE MATTER OF THE APPLICATION FOR ENROLLMENT, as a citizen of the Choctaw    Nation, of    Amanda Haiakanubbe

born on the   23rd   day of   Nov    190 4

Name of father   Wellington Haiakanubbe          a citizen of    Choctaw
Nation final enrollment No.   3328

# Applications for Enrollment of Choctaw Newborn
## Act of 1905    Volume XIII

Name of mother    Mary Haiakanubbe    a citizen of    Choctaw Nation final enrollment No.    1075

Postoffice    Idabel I T

### AFFIDAVIT OF MOTHER.

UNITED STATES OF AMERICA
INDIAN TERRITORY
Central    DISTRICT

I    Mary Haiakanubbee    , on oath state that I am 20 years of age and a citizen by blood of the Choctaw Nation, and as such have been placed upon the final roll of the Choctaw Nation, by the Honorable Secretary of the Interior my final enrollment number being    1075 ; that I am the lawful wife of    Wellington Haiakanubbee    , who is a citizen of the    Choctaw    Nation, and as such has been placed upon the final roll of said Nation by the Honorable Secretary of the Interior, his final enrollment number being    3328    and that a    female    child was born to me on the    23$^{rd}$    day of    Nov    190 4; that said child has been named    Amanda Haiakanubbee    , and is now living.

Mary Haiakonabe[sic]

Witnesseth.
Must be two ⎫  Wilburn Kaniatobe
Witnesses who ⎬
are Citizens. ⎭  Levi Stewart

Subscribed and sworn to before me this    21    day of    Jan    190 5

W.A. Shoney
Notary Public.

My commission expires:    Jan 10, 1909

## AFFIDAVIT OF ATTENDING PHYSICIAN OR MIDWIFE

UNITED STATES OF AMERICA
INDIAN TERRITORY
Central    DISTRICT

I,    Louisian[sic] Haiakonubbe    a    Midwife on oath state that I attended on Mrs. Mary Haiakonubbe    wife of    Wellington Haiakonubbe on the    23$^{rd}$    day of    Nov    , 190 4, that there was born to her on said date a    female child, that said child is now living, and is said to have been named    Amanda Haiakonubbe

her
Louisan Haiakonubbee    x
mark

## Applications for Enrollment of Choctaw Newborn
## Act of 1905 Volume XIII

Subscribed and sworn to before me this, the 21 day of Jan 190 5

W.A. Shoney  Notary Public.

**WITNESSETH:**
Must be two witnesses who are citizens
{ Wilburn Kaniatobe
Levi Stewart

We hereby certify that we are well acquainted with Louisian[sic] Haiakonubbe a Midwife and know her to be reputable and of good standing in the community.

Levi Stewart  _____

W.S. Ward  _____

**BIRTH AFFIDAVIT.**

### DEPARTMENT OF THE INTERIOR.
### COMMISSION TO THE FIVE CIVILIZED TRIBES.

**IN RE APPLICATION FOR ENROLLMENT,** as a citizen of the Choctaw Nation, of Amanda Haiakonubbee , born on the 23 day of November , 1904

Name of Father: Wellington Haiakonubbee  a citizen of the Choctaw Nation.
Name of Mother: Mary Haiakonubbee  a citizen of the Choctaw Nation.

Postoffice  Idabel, Ind. Ter.

**AFFIDAVIT OF MOTHER.**

**UNITED STATES OF AMERICA, Indian Territory,**
Central  **DISTRICT.**

I, Mary Haiakonubbee , on oath state that I am 20 years of age and a citizen by blood , of the Choctaw Nation; that I am the lawful wife of Wellington Haiakonubbee , who is a citizen, by blood of the Choctaw Nation; that a female child was born to me on 23rd day of November , 1904; that said child has been named Amanda Haiakonubbee , and was living March 4, 1905.

Mary Haiakonubbee

Witnesses To Mark:
{

# Applications for Enrollment of Choctaw Newborn
# Act of 1905 Volume XIII

Subscribed and sworn to before me this 10th day of April, 1905

Wirt Franklin
Notary Public.

### AFFIDAVIT OF ATTENDING PHYSICIAN OR MID-WIFE.

UNITED STATES OF AMERICA, Indian Territory,
Central DISTRICT.

I, Louisiana Haiakonubbee, a mid-wife, on oath state that I attended on Mrs. Mary Haiakonubbee, wife of Wellington Haiakonubbee on the 23rd day of November, 1904; that there was born to her on said date a female child; that said child was living March 4, 1905, and is said to have been named Amanda Haiakonubbee

                                            her
                          Louisiana x Haiakonubbee
Witnesses To Mark:          mark
   { Robert Anderson
     Vester W Rose

Subscribed and sworn to before me this 10th day of April, 1905

Wirt Franklin
Notary Public.

---

Choc New Born 956
    Louis Stephen Ontaiyabi[sic]  b. 10-24-02

BIRTH AFFIDAVIT.
### DEPARTMENT OF THE INTERIOR.
## COMMISSION TO THE FIVE CIVILIZED TRIBES.

IN RE APPLICATION FOR ENROLLMENT, as a citizen of the Choctaw Nation, of Louis Stephen Ontahyubbe, born on the 24rd[sic] day of October, 1902

Name of Father: Stephen Ontahyubbe    a citizen of the Choctaw Nation.
Name of Mother: Juisy Cooper          a citizen of the Choctaw Nation.

Postoffice   Eagletown, Ind. Ter.

# Applications for Enrollment of Choctaw Newborn
# Act of 1905  Volume XIII

### AFFIDAVIT OF MOTHER.

UNITED STATES OF AMERICA, Indian Territory, }
Central       DISTRICT.

    I, Juicy Cooper, on oath state that I am 34 years of age and a citizen by blood, of the Choctaw Nation; that I am ~~not~~ the lawful wife of Stephen Ontahyubbe, who is a citizen, by blood of the Choctaw Nation; that a male child was born to me on 24th day of October, 1902; that said child has been named Louis Stephen Ontahyubbe, and was living March 4, 1905.

                                               her
                                    Juicy x Cooper
Witnesses To Mark:              mark
{ Robert Anderson
  Vester W Rose

    Subscribed and sworn to before me this 10th day of April, 1905

                                    Wirt Franklin
                                    Notary Public.

---

### AFFIDAVIT OF ATTENDING PHYSICIAN OR MID-WIFE.

UNITED STATES OF AMERICA, Indian Territory, }
Central       DISTRICT.

    I, Susan Cooper, a mid-wife, on oath state that I attended on Mrs. Juicy Cooper ~~not~~, wife of Stephen Ontahyubbe on the 24th day of October, 1902; that there was born to her on said date a male child; that said child was living March 4, 1905, and is said to have been named Louis Stephen Ontahyubbe

                                               her
                                    Susan x Cooper
Witnesses To Mark:              mark
{ Robert Anderson
  Vester W Rose

    Subscribed and sworn to before me this 10th day of April, 1905

                                    Wirt Franklin
                                    Notary Public.

## Applications for Enrollment of Choctaw Newborn
## Act of 1905 Volume XIII

Choc New Born 957
   Laura Washington  b. 8-24-04

**BIRTH AFFIDAVIT.**

DEPARTMENT OF THE INTERIOR.
## COMMISSION TO THE FIVE CIVILIZED TRIBES.

IN RE APPLICATION FOR ENROLLMENT, as a citizen of the Choctaw Nation, of Laura Washington , born on the 24th day of August , 1904

Name of Father: George L. Washington   a citizen of the Choctaw Nation.
Name of Mother: Sally Washington   a citizen of the Choctaw Nation.

Postoffice   Garvin, - Ind. Ter.

**AFFIDAVIT OF MOTHER.**

UNITED STATES OF AMERICA, Indian Territory, }
   Central           DISTRICT.

I, Sally Washington , on oath state that I am 25 years of age and a citizen by blood , of the Choctaw Nation; that I am the lawful wife of George L. Washington , who is a citizen, by blood of the Choctaw Nation; that a female child was born to me on 24th day of August , 1904; that said child has been named Laura Washington , and was living March 4, 1905.

                                   her
Witnesses To Mark:          Sally x Washington
   { Robert Anderson              mark
   { Vester Rose

Subscribed and sworn to before me this 10th day of April , 1905

                        Wirt Franklin
                        Notary Public.

**AFFIDAVIT OF ATTENDING PHYSICIAN OR MID-WIFE.**

UNITED STATES OF AMERICA, Indian Territory, }
   Central           DISTRICT.

I, Lily Taylor , a mid-wife , on oath state that I attended on Mrs. Sally Washington , wife of George L Washington on the 24th day of

311

# Applications for Enrollment of Choctaw Newborn
## Act of 1905  Volume XIII

August  , 1904; that there was born to her on said date a   female   child; that said child was living March 4, 1905, and is said to have been named  Laura Washington

             her
         Lily  x  Taylor
Witnesses To Mark:      mark
 { Robert Anderson
  Vester Rose

  Subscribed and sworn to before me this  10th  day of  April  , 1905

          Wirt Franklin
          Notary Public.

---

## AFFIDAVIT OF ATTENDING PHYSICIAN OR MIDWIFE

UNITED STATES OF AMERICA
INDIAN TERRITORY
 Central   DISTRICT

  I,  Silvia Harley  a   midwife  on oath state that I attended on Mrs.  Sally Washington  wife of  George L Washington  on the  24th  day of  August , 190 4, that there was born to her on said date a   female  child, that said child is now living, and is said to have been named  Laura Washington

         her
       Silvia  x  Harley   M.D.
WITNESSETH:      mark

Must be two witnesses { John A Garland
who are citizens and
know the child.    Allen Watson

   Subscribed and sworn to before me this, the   21$^{st}$   day of  Feb    190 5

       W.A. Shoney  Notary Public.

 We hereby certify that we are well acquainted with   Silvia Harley   a   midwife   and know   her   to be reputable and of good standing in the community.

      { John A Garland
       Allen Watson

## Applications for Enrollment of Choctaw Newborn
## Act of 1905   Volume XIII

**NEW-BORN AFFIDAVIT.**

Number............

### ...Choctaw Enrolling Commission...

IN THE MATTER OF THE APPLICATION FOR ENROLLMENT, as a citizen of the Choctaw Nation, of Laura Washington born on the 24 day of August 190 4

Name of father   George L Washington     a citizen of   Choctaw Nation final enrollment No.   1585
Name of mother   Sally Washington     a citizen of   Choctaw Nation final enrollment No.   1571

Postoffice   Garvin, I.T.

### AFFIDAVIT OF MOTHER.

UNITED STATES OF AMERICA
INDIAN TERRITORY
Central   DISTRICT

I   Sally Washington                    , on oath state that I am 25   years of age and a citizen by   blood   of the   Choctaw   Nation, and as such have been placed upon the final roll of the   Choctaw   Nation, by the Honorable Secretary of the Interior my final enrollment number being   1571 ; that I am the lawful wife of   George L Washington   , who is a citizen of the   Choctaw   Nation, and as such has been placed upon the final roll of said Nation by the Honorable Secretary of the Interior, his final enrollment number being   1585   and that a   female   child was born to me on the   24   day of   August   190 4; that said child has been named   Laura Washington   , and is now living.

Sally x Washington
mark

Witnesseth.
Must be two Witnesses who are Citizens.   John A Garland
Allen Watson

Subscribed and sworn to before me this   21st   day of   Feb   190 5

W.A. Shoney
Notary Public.

My commission expires:   Jan 10 1909

Applications for Enrollment of Choctaw Newborn
Act of 1905   Volume XIII

Choc New Born 958
     Orren Farver Denson  b. 5-20-03

# NEW BORN AFFIDAVIT

No ........

## CHOCTAW ENROLLING COMMISSION

IN THE MATTER OF THE APPLICATION FOR ENROLLMENT as a citizen of the Choctaw Nation, of Orren F. Denson born on the 20$^{th}$ day of May 190 3

Name of father  Richard C. Denson   a citizen of   Choctaw   Nation, final enrollment No. 603
Name of mother  Lula Denson   a citizen of   Choctaw   Nation, final enrollment No. 13577

Idabel I.T.                    Postoffice.

### AFFIDAVIT OF MOTHER

UNITED STATES OF AMERICA
   INDIAN TERRITORY
DISTRICT   Central

I   Lula Denson   , on oath state that I am  20  years of age and a citizen by  blood  of the  Choctaw  Nation, and as such have been placed upon the final roll of the  Choctaw  Nation, by the Honorable Secretary of the Interior my final enrollment number being  13577  ; that I am the lawful wife of  Richard C Denson  , who is a citizen of the  Choctaw  Nation, and as such has been placed upon the final roll of said Nation by the Honorable Secretary of the Interior, his final enrollment number being  603  and that a  male  child was born to me on the  20$^{th}$  day of  May  190 3 ; that said child has been named  Orren F Denson  , and is now living.

WITNESSETH:                    Lula Denson
  Must be two witnesses ⎰ Henry C Stanford
  who are citizens      ⎱ John R White

Subscribed and sworn to before me this, the  6$^{th}$  day of  Feb  , 190 5

                    W A Shoney
                         Notary Public.

My Commission Expires:  Jan 10 1909

**Applications for Enrollment of Choctaw Newborn
Act of 1905   Volume XIII**

*Affidavit of Attending Physician or Midwife*

UNITED STATES OF AMERICA,  
  INDIAN TERRITORY,  
Central    DISTRICT

I, C A Denson a Physician on oath state that I attended on Mrs. Lula Denson wife of Richard C Denson on the $20^{th}$ day of May, 190 3, that there was born to her on said date a male child, that said child is now living, and is said to have been named Orren F Denson

                    C A Denson    M. D.

Subscribed and sworn to before me this the $6^{th}$ day of Feb 1905

                    W.A. Shoney  
                        Notary Public.

WITNESSETH:  
Must be two witnesses who are citizens and know the child.  {  Henry C. Stanford  
                John R White

We hereby certify that we are well acquainted with ................................
a ........................ and know ........................ to be reputable and of good standing in the community.

          Must be two citizen witnesses. { Henry C Stanford  
                                John R White

BIRTH AFFIDAVIT.

**DEPARTMENT OF THE INTERIOR.
COMMISSION TO THE FIVE CIVILIZED TRIBES.**

IN RE APPLICATION FOR ENROLLMENT, as a citizen of the Choctaw Nation, of Orren Farver Denson, born on the 20th day of May, 1903

Name of Father: Richard C Denson    a citizen of the Choctaw Nation.  
Name of Mother: Lula Denson    a citizen of the Choctaw Nation.

              Postoffice    Idabel, Ind. Ter.

# Applications for Enrollment of Choctaw Newborn
## Act of 1905  Volume XIII

**AFFIDAVIT OF MOTHER.**

UNITED STATES OF AMERICA, Indian Territory, } Central DISTRICT.

I, Lula Denson, on oath state that I am 21 years of age and a citizen by blood, of the Choctaw Nation; that I am the lawful wife of Richard C Denson, who is a citizen, by marriage of the Choctaw Nation; that a male child was born to me on 20th day of May, 1903; that said child has been named Orren Farver Denson, and was living March 4, 1905.

Lula Denson

Witnesses To Mark:

Subscribed and sworn to before me this 11th day of April, 1905

Wirt Franklin
Notary Public.

---

**AFFIDAVIT OF ATTENDING PHYSICIAN OR MID-WIFE.**

UNITED STATES OF AMERICA, Indian Territory, } Central DISTRICT.

I, Caledonia Adams, a mid-wife, on oath state that I attended on Mrs. Lula Denson, wife of Richard C Denson on the 20th day of May, 1903; that there was born to her on said date a male child; that said child was living March 4, 1905, and is said to have been named Orren Farver Denson

Caledonia x Adams (her mark)

Witnesses To Mark:
{ Robert Anderson
{ Vester W Rose

Subscribed and sworn to before me this 11th day of April, 1905

Wirt Franklin
Notary Public.

## Applications for Enrollment of Choctaw Newborn
## Act of 1905 Volume XIII

Choc New Born 959
    Arthur Alexander b. 7-30-03

7--NB--959

Muskogee, Indian Territory, June 1, 1905.

Henry Alexander,
    Janis, Indian Territory.

Dear Sir:

    Referring to the application for the enrollment of your infant child, Arthur Alexander, born July 30, 1903, it is noted from the affidavits heretofore filed in this office that you were the only one in attendance upon your wife at the time of the birth of this applicant.

    In this event it will be necessary that the affidavits of two persons, who are disinterested and not related to the applicant, who have actual knowledge of the facts that the child was born, the date of birth; that he was living March 4, 1905, and that Eliza Alexander is his mother be filed in this office.

    The affidavit of Simeon Byington to these facts has been filed. It will, therefore, be necessary that you secure a simular[sic] affidavit from another person.

    This matter should receive your immediate attention as no further action can be taken relative to the enrollment of our child until the Commission has been furnished with this affidavit.

                   Respectfully,

                   Chairman.

7-NB-959

Muskogee, Indian Territory, July 28, 1905.

Henry Alexander,
    Janis, Indian Territory.

Dear Sir:

    Receipt is hereby acknowledged of the affidavit of Johnson William to the birth of Arthur Alexander, son of Henry and Eliza Alexander, July 30, 1903, and the same have been filed with the records of this office in the matter of the enrollment of said child.

Applications for Enrollment of Choctaw Newborn
Act of 1905   Volume XIII

Respectfully,

Commissioner.

# NEW BORN AFFIDAVIT

No ........

## CHOCTAW ENROLLING COMMISSION

IN THE MATTER OF THE APPLICATION FOR ENROLLMENT as a citizen of the Choctaw Nation, of   Arthur Alexander   born on the 30$^{th}$ day of July   190 3

Name of father   Henry Alexander   a citizen of   Choctaw   Nation, final enrollment No. 3159
Name of mother   Eliza Tushka   a citizen of   Choctaw   Nation, final enrollment No. 2526

Janis I.T.   Postoffice.

### AFFIDAVIT OF MOTHER

UNITED STATES OF AMERICA  
   INDIAN TERRITORY  
DISTRICT   Central

I   Eliza Tushka   , on oath state that I am   29   years of age and a citizen by   blood   of the   Choctaw   Nation, and as such have been placed upon the final roll of the   Choctaw   Nation, by the Honorable Secretary of the Interior my final enrollment number being   2526   ; that I am the lawful wife of   Henry Alexander   , who is a citizen of the   Choctaw   Nation, and as such has been placed upon the final roll of said Nation by the Honorable Secretary of the Interior, his final enrollment number being   3159   and that a   male   child was born to me on the   30$^{th}$   day of   July   190 3; that said child has been named   Arthur Alexander   , and is now living.

WITNESSETH:                                     Eliza Tushka
 Must be two witnesses ⎰ Simeon Byington
 who are citizens       ⎱ Julius Jefferson

318

## Applications for Enrollment of Choctaw Newborn
## Act of 1905   Volume XIII

Subscribed and sworn to before me this, the 16 day of Feb, 190 5

W.A. Shoney
Notary Public.

My Commission Expires: Jan 10 1909

### *Affidavit of Attending Physician or Midwife*

UNITED STATES OF AMERICA,
INDIAN TERRITORY,
Central DISTRICT

I, Henry Alexander a attendant on oath state that I attended on Mrs. Eliza Tushka wife of Henry Alexander on the 30<sup>th</sup> day of July, 190 3, that there was born to her on said date a male child, that said child is now living, and is said to have been named Arthur Alexander

Henry Alexander ~~M.D.~~

Subscribed and sworn to before me this the 16 day of Feb 1905

W.A. Shoney
Notary Public.

WITNESSETH:
Must be two witnesses who are citizens and know the child. { Simeon Byington
Julius Jefferson

We hereby certify that we are well acquainted with Henry Alexander a attendant and know him to be reputable and of good standing in the community.

Must be two citizen witnesses. { Simeon Byington
Julius Jefferson

UNITED STATES OF AMERICA,
INDIAN TERRITORY,
CENTRAL JUDICIAL DISTRICT.

Jonson[sic] Williams[sic], a citizen of the Choctaw Nation, and residing at or near Janis, Indian Territory, being first duly sworn upon his oath, deposes and says as follows:- That he is well acquainted with Henry Alexander, and Eliza Alexander, father and mother of Arthur Alexander, and that said Arthur Alexander, was born July 30th, 1903, and that he was still living on March 4th, 1905., and that said child is still alive,

## Applications for Enrollment of Choctaw Newborn
## Act of 1905   Volume XIII

and was born to the said Eliza and Henry Alexander, on July 30t..., 1903, at or near Janis, Indian Territory.

Johnson William

Subscribed and sworn to before me this the undersigned authority, within and for the District and Territory aforesaid, this   22   day of July, A.D. 1905.

(Name Illegible)<br>Notary Public.

My commission expires   Feb 28   1909

---

United States of America,   )
                             )
Indian Territory,            )   ss.
                             )
Central District.            )

    I, Simeon Byington, on oath state that I am twenty-two years of age and a citizen by blood of the Choctaw Nation; that my post office address is Goodwater, Indian Territory; that I am personally acquainted with Eliza Alexander, wife of Henry Alexander, and have known said parties for many years; that for the last nine years I have lived withing[sic] six miles of where said parties have lived and know of my own knowledge that on or about the 30th day of July, 1903, there was born to the said Eliza Alexander a male child; that said child has been named Arthur Alexander, and is now living.

Simeon Byington

Subscribed and sworn to before me this 10th day of April, 1905.

Wirt Franklin<br>Notary Public.

---

**BIRTH AFFIDAVIT.**

DEPARTMENT OF THE INTERIOR.<br>COMMISSION TO THE FIVE CIVILIZED TRIBES.

---

**IN RE APPLICATION FOR ENROLLMENT,** as a citizen of the   Choctaw   Nation, of Arthur Alexander   , born on the 30th   day of   July   , 1903

Name of Father: Henry Alexander     a citizen of the   Choctaw   Nation.
Name of Mother: Eliza Alexander     a citizen of the   Choctaw   Nation.

Postoffice   Janis, Ind. Ter.

# Applications for Enrollment of Choctaw Newborn
# Act of 1905 Volume XIII

**AFFIDAVIT OF MOTHER.**

UNITED STATES OF AMERICA, Indian Territory,
Central DISTRICT.

I, Eliza Alexander, on oath state that I am about 25 years of age and a citizen by blood, of the Choctaw Nation; that I am the lawful wife of Henry Alexander, who is a citizen, by blood of the Choctaw Nation; that a male child was born to me on 30th day of July, 1903; that said child has been named Arthur Alexander, and was living March 4, 1905. *and that no physician or midwife attended me at the birth of said child*

Eliza Alexander

Witnesses To Mark:
{

Subscribed and sworn to before me this 10th day of April, 1905

Wirt Franklin
Notary Public.

**AFFIDAVIT OF ATTENDING PHYSICIAN OR MID-WIFE.**

UNITED STATES OF AMERICA, Indian Territory,
Central DISTRICT.

I, Henry Alexander, ~~a~~ ................, on oath state that I attended on Mrs. Eliza Alexander, ~~wife of~~ *my wife* on the 30th day of July, 1903; that there was born to her on said date a male child; that said child was living March 4, 1905, and ~~is said to have~~ *has* been named Arthur Alexander *and that no one else was present when said child was born*

Henry Alexander

Witnesses To Mark:
{

Subscribed and sworn to before me this 10th day of April, 1905

Wirt Franklin
Notary Public.

# Applications for Enrollment of Choctaw Newborn
## Act of 1905   Volume XIII

Choc New Born 960
    Silman Thompson  b. 8-29-04

---

7-NB-960

Muskogee, Indian Territory, June 1, 1905.

Wincey Thompson,
    Goodwater, Indian Territory.

Dear Madam:

    Referring to the application for the enrollment of your infant child, Silman Thompson, born August 29, 1904, it is noted from the affidavits heretofore filed in this office that you were not attended by a physician or midwife at the time of the birth of the applicant.

    In this event it will be necessary that the affidavits of two persons, who are disinterested and not related to the applicant, who have actual knowledge of the facts that the child was born, the date of birth; that he was living March 4, 1905, and that you are his mother be filed in this office.

    The affidavit of Kitsy Wilson to these facts has been filed. It will, therefore, be necessary that you secure a simular[sic] affidavit form another person.

    This matter should receive your immediate attention as no further action can be taken relative to the enrollment of your child until the Commission has been furnished with this affidavit.

                    Respectfully,

                    Chairman.

---

*(The affidavit below typed as given.)*

W. J. WHITEMAN.

## WHITEMAN MERCANTILE CO.,
### DEALERS IN
## GENERAL MERCHANDISE

GOODWATER, I. T., _____ 1905

To the, Commission to the five civilized tribes,
    Muskogee, Ind. Ter.
    7-NB-960.

---

## Applications for Enrollment of Choctaw Newborn
## Act of 1905 Volume XIII

I, Sarah Brown on oath states that ~~she is~~ *I am* 50 years old, a citizen by blood of the Choctaw Nation, ~~her~~ *my* Post Office address is Janis I.T. that ~~she is~~ *I am* personaly acquainted with and not in any way related to Wincey Thompson.
I know that on August the ~~29~~ 29th, 1904.there was bore to Wincy Thompson, a male child, said child has been named Silman.Thompson, and was living on the 4th, day of March 1905. and is living on this day the 3rd, of July, 05.
I farther know that said Wincy Thompson is a Choctaw by blood,

                                  Sarah Brown

Subscribed and sworn to before me this 3$^{rd}$ day of July 1905.

                                  M J Whiteman
                                  Notary Public.

---

United States of America, )
                              )
Indian Territory,         ) ss.
                              )
Central District.        )

    I, Kitsy Wilson, on oath state that I am about eighteen years of age and a citizen by blood of the Choctaw Nation; that I am personally acquainted with Wincey Thompson and have known her all my life; that I know of my own knowledge that on or about the 29th day of August, 1904, there was born to the said Wincey Thompson a male child, that said child is now living and is said to have been named Silman Thompson; and that it is generally understood in the neighborhood where we reside that the father of the said child is Joe Thompson.                                   her

                                  Kitsy x Wilson
                                  mark

Subscribed and sworn to before me this 10th day of April, 1905.

                                  Wirt Franklin
                                  Notary Public.

Witnesses to mark.
    Robert Anderson
    Vester W Rose

Applications for Enrollment of Choctaw Newborn
Act of 1905   Volume XIII

# NEW BORN AFFIDAVIT

No _____

## CHOCTAW ENROLLING COMMISSION

IN THE MATTER OF THE APPLICATION FOR ENROLLMENT as a citizen of the Choctaw Nation, of  Silman Thompson  born on the 29$^{th}$ day of  August  190 4

Name of father  Joe Thompson   a citizen of  Choctaw  Nation, final enrollment No............
Name of mother  Winsie Jefferson   a citizen of  Choctaw  Nation, final enrollment No............

Goodwater I.T.   Postoffice.

### AFFIDAVIT OF MOTHER

UNITED STATES OF AMERICA  
    INDIAN TERRITORY  
DISTRICT   Central

I  Winsie Thompson  , on oath state that I am  30  years of age and a citizen by  blood  of the  Choctaw  Nation, and as such have been placed upon the final roll of the  Choctaw  Nation, by the Honorable Secretary of the Interior my final enrollment number being _____; that I am the lawful wife of ——————— , who is a citizen of the _____ Nation, and as such has been placed upon the final roll of said Nation by the Honorable Secretary of the Interior, his final enrollment number being _____ and that a  male  child was born to me on the  29  day of August  190 4; that said child has been named  Silman Thompson  , and is now living.

WITNESSETH:   Wincey Thompson
Must be two witnesses  { Louis Dyer
who are citizens        { Arlington King

Subscribed and sworn to before me this, the  14$^{th}$  day of  March  , 190 5

W.A. Shoney  
    Notary Public.

My Commission Expires:

# Applications for Enrollment of Choctaw Newborn
## Act of 1905   Volume XIII

**BIRTH AFFIDAVIT.**

## DEPARTMENT OF THE INTERIOR.
## COMMISSION TO THE FIVE CIVILIZED TRIBES.

IN RE APPLICATION FOR ENROLLMENT, as a citizen of the Choctaw Nation, of Silman Thompson, born on the 29th day of August, 1904

Name of Father: Joe Thompson    a citizen of the Choctaw Nation.
Name of Mother: Wincey Thompson    a citizen of the Choctaw Nation.

Postoffice    Goodwater, Ind. Ter.

**AFFIDAVIT OF MOTHER.**

UNITED STATES OF AMERICA, Indian Territory, }
Central    DISTRICT.

I, Wincey Thompson, on oath state that I am 35 years of age and a citizen by blood, of the Choctaw Nation; that I am *not* the lawful wife of Joe Thompson, who is a citizen, by blood of the Choctaw Nation; that a male child was born to me on 29th day of August, 1904; that said child has been named Silman Thompson, and was living March 4, 1905. *and that no one was with me when said child was born*

                 Wincey Thompson

Witnesses To Mark:
{

Subscribed and sworn to before me this 10th day of April, 1905

                 Wirt Franklin
                     Notary Public.

# Index

ADAMS
  Caledonia...............................97,98,316
  Call ...........................................96,100
ALEXANDER
  Arthur ...............317,318,319,320,321
  D S............................................... 24
  Eliza.......................317,319,320,321
  Henry ................317,318,319,320,321
ALLEN
  Charley . 164,165,166,167,168,169,170
  Cora E .......... 164,166,167,168,169,170
  Forest Claud ............................169,170
  Forrect C......................................... 166
  Forrest C ................... 164,165,167,168
  Forrest E ................................166,168
  Nicey .....................................107,108
ANDERSON
  C H .................................115,116,148
  C J................................................. 148
  Colbert............................................. 26
  Crawford J ...............................147,148
  H D ...........................................115,116
  Jane............................................26,27
  John ................................................ 31
  Leviney ....................................153,154
  Maggie............................................ 26
  Robert .......... 2,3,26,27,30,32,38,40,41,
  42,47,48,58,60,64,67,68,69,71,72,73,
  77,79,80,81,82,83,85,86,99,106,107,
  111,112,119,125,126,133,136,137,138
  ,145,146,174,175,176,180,181,192,
  194,202,204,205,206,208,209,210,214
  ,219,224,226,227,228,230,231,232,
  237,238,241,242,245,246,249,250,251
  ,252,253,255,261,262,263,267,268,
  271,287,291,296,298,302,305,306,309
  ,310,311,312,316,323
ANGELL, W H ................................... 167
AUSTIN, Susan .............................65,66
BACON
  Jefferson ..................................153,154
  Melviney ........................................ 153
  Melvinie ..................................153,154
  Oscar Lee .................................153,154
BAKAN, Bazel ...........................299,301
BAKER
  Isham ............................................ 287

Judy ..............................................82,83
Lorena...........................................286,287
Lyman............................................... 229
Minnie ............................................... 287
Nancy ............................................... 205
Nantie ................................................. 83
Silas ..............................................82,83
Wesley ............ 82,83,288,289,290,291
BALDWIN, Jno D .......................150,151
BARNETT, William ........................... 40
BARNEY, Joseph .......................106,108
BATHEST
  Allington .........................268,270,271
  Austin ............................268,270,271
  Delilah .......................................... 288
  James ....................... 288,289,290,291
  Melwissie .............................270,271
  Pitchlynn ...................288,289,290,291
BATTIEST
  Allington ........................................ 269
  Andrew ......................303,304,305,306
  Austin ............................................ 269
  Colbert ............... 178,179,183,296,297
  James ............................................. 291
  Joel .........................................293,294
  Melwissie ....................................... 269
  Pitchlynn ................................290,291
  Siney ................................304,305,306
  Wade.........................303,304,305,306
BEALL, Wm O ......................274,275,285
BEE, William ....................................... 9
BELL, M D................................160,161
BENJAMIN, Narsie............................. 3
BENTON
  Ellen .......................................151,152
  Lewis ......................................151,152
BILLY, Tushka.................................. 189
BIXBY, Tams.... 84,124,133,134,137,142,
174,239,269,273,277,279,304
BOBO, Lacey P ...........................56,273
BOHANAN
  Amy ............................................70,71
  Ethel .......................................256,257
  James ............................................ 265
  Jesse................................70,71,72,73
  Jonas ................. 264,265,266,267,268
  Lartin S .......................................... 257

# Index

Lucinda ..................... 264,265,266,267
Sallie Ann ........................................ 256
Sally Ann ......................................... 257
Somlin ................................ 69,70,71,72
Sophia ................................... 70,71,72
Sophie ............................................... 71
Willis ......................... 264,265,266,267
BOHANON, Sally Ann ..................... 257
BOLAND, James ............................... 158
BOND
   Byington ............ 131,133,136,176,177,
   178,179,180,182,183
   Dixie .............................. 176,180,181
   Liksi ........................................ 178,183
   Lixie ................................................ 177
   Sam ............. 176,177,178,179,180,181,
   182,183
BOWER, James ..................... 138,141,162
BOWERS, C H ................................... 215
BOZARTH, Chas ......................... 284,285
BREAKER
   J J ............... 155,156,157,158
   J J, MD ......................................... 157
BREWER
   Agnes ............................................. 200
   Ellis ................................................ 200
BROWN
   Eastman ......................................... 191
   Louisa ............................................ 191
   Nancy ........................................... 5,6
   Sarah ............................................. 323
BUTLER
   Amanda ....................................... 24,25
   Lemon .................................... 213,216
BYINGTON
   Maimie ........................................... 63
   Moody ........................................ 62,63
   Simeon ........ 33,35,36,317,318,319,320
   Simmon ..................................... 62,63
   Zona ............................................ 62,63
CALDWELL, Willie ..................... 244,245
CARNEY
   Mary ............................. 173,174,175
   Payson ...................... 172,173,174,175
   Timothy .................... 172,173,174,175
CARTERBY
   Almon ....................... 177,178,182,183

Almon F ............................................ 184
Almond F .......................................... 290
Ballard .............................................. 296
Balleid ..................... 292,294,297,298
Dora .................... 292,293,294,295,296
Siglon ......... 293,294,295,296,297,298,
299,300,301
Siglow ............................................. 292
Tellis ........................................ 293,294
Tillis ................... 293,295,296,297,298
Tullis ............................................... 292
CARTUBBY
   Ballard ........................................... 294
   Dora ............................................... 294
   Siglon ............................................ 294
CEPHUS, Wilbon ....................... 232,233
CHADWICK
   Ira B ........................................... 22,23
   Ira B, MD ....................................... 23
CHASTAIN, J D ................................ 7,8
CLAY
   Abner H ....... 112,113,114,115,116,117
   Abner H, Jr ..................................... 115
   Andrew ......................................... 4,5,6
   Betsy .............................................. 249
   Catherine ....................................... 248
   Henry ............................................. 4,5
   Louisa .......................................... 4,5,6
   Mary Lyda ... 112,113,114,115,116,117
   Mattie ................. 112,113,114,116,117
   Mattie E ................................... 113,115
   Mattie Lurena ................................ 115
   Myrtle Eugenia ............................. 115
   Patsey ............................................ 248
   Phoebe ......................................... 4,5,6
COCHNAUER
   David W ............................ 155,156,157
   Don W ...................... 154,155,156,157
   Rhoda ................................ 155,156,157
COGSWELL, Johnson ................. 220,223
COLBERT
   Levi ....... 184,185,186,187,188,189,190
   Louina ...................... 185,186,187,189
   Luena ............................................. 186
   Lylie ........................................ 225,226
   Sampson ............ 184,185,186,187,188,
189,190

# Index

Simpson ................................. 225,226
Timesy .................................. 225,226
Winnie ...................... 185,188,189,190
COLLINS, Annie ......................... 55,57
COLUMBUS, Nicholas ......... 198,199,201
COMPTON
   Amanda ................................ 160,161
   Betty ..................................... 158,160
   E W ................................. 158,159,160
   Elisebeth .......................... 158,159,160
   Elizabeth .................................... 158
   Emma ................................... 160,161
   Sarah ............................... 158,159,160
   Sarah H ....................................... 159
COOPER
   Juicy ............................................ 310
   Juisy ............................................ 309
   Susan ........................................... 310
COSTILOW
   Elijah ........................................ 24,25
   J W ............................................... 25
   Jennie ....................................... 24,25
   Lula Bell ................................... 24,25
COVINGTON, W P .................... 56,273
COXWELL, Johnson .................. 222,235
CRANFILL
   L J .................................................. 16
   L J, MD .......................................... 19
CRUTCHFIELD, Gertrude ............. 12,13
DANEY, Solomon .......................... 154
DAVIS
   Caroline ........................... 138,139,140
   Julia ........................................ 171,172
   Minnie ......................................... 7,8,9
   W A .............................................. 172
DENISON
   B L ................................................. 61
   B L, MD ........................................ 61
DENNEY, E A ................................... 23
DENSON
   C A ............................................... 315
   C A, MD ...................................... 315
   Lula ................... 114,115,314,315,316
   Mattie A ................................ 113,117
   Orren F .................................. 314,315
   Orren Farver ..................... 314,315,316
   Richard C ......... 97,114,115,212,314, 315,316
DICKERSON, John ................... 65,66,67
DIFENDAFER, Chas T ............. 4,5,6,276
DWIGHT, Edward ......................... 45,46
DYER
   Joel .......................... 213,214,215,216
   Louis .................... 37,38,39,40,41,324
   Maggie .................................. 37,38,40
   Maggie Harley ........................... 39,40
   Mary ....................... 213,214,215,216
   Minnie ............... 212,213,214,215,216
   Winston .............................. 37,38,39,40
EDWARDS
   Louisa ............................................ 32
   Morton ......................................... 269
   Silway ........................................ 31,32
ELLIOTT, Abbott ................. 141,142,143
ELLIS
   Ada B ................................. 138,140,141
   Ada Byron .............................. 139,140
   John Thomas .......................... 139,140
   Thomas J ......................... 138,140,141
   William Leo .............. 138,139,140,141
FANNIN, E J ............................... 276,277
FOBB
   Acy ....................................... 145,146
   Eastman ....................................... 236
   Eliza ..................................... 145,146
   Sally ............................................ 236
   Simeon .................................. 145,146
FOLSOM
   Dora Eunice ........................... 16,17,18
   Dora Unice ................................... 16
   A E ................................... 13,14,169
   Junier Wade ....................... 16,17,18,19
   Maude A ........................... 16,17,18,19
   Wade ................................ 16,17,18,19
FORBIT, Singlin .............. 68,194,195,196
FORD
   Annie ....................... 272,276,277,280
   Hetty ........................................... 276
FORT, Brooks ................... 11,12,167,170
FRANKLIN, Wirt .... 1,2,3,26,27,30,31,32, 36,37,38,40,42,43,44,47,48,51,58,59,60, 61,64,67,68,69,71,72,73,76,77,79,80,81, 82,83,86,90,92,93,94,95,98,99,103,105, 106,107,111,112,117,118,119,122,123,

# Index

125,126,130,133,136,137,138,139,140,
145,146,174,175,176,180,181,187,192,
193,194,195,196,197,201,202,203,204,
205,206,208,209,210,214,215,216,219,
223,224,225,226,227,228,230,231,232,
236,237,238,240,241,242,246,249,251,
252,253,254,255,256,257,258,260,261,
262,263,264,266,267,268,270,271,287,
288,291,295,296,297,298,301,302,303,
305,306,309,310,312,316,320,321,323,
325
FRAZIER, Viney............................................ 60
FREY, E W.................................. 155,156,157
FRY, Fannie .................................................. 286
GABLE, Albert.......................................213,215
GARDNER
    Basil L ....................................................162,163
    D H ........................................................... 157
    Daniel H .................................................. 157
    Jeff........................................143,144,215,216
    Mary A ....................................................162,163
    Scott........................................................ 143
GARLAND, John A ...................................312,313
GARRISON
    Effie M .....................................................89,90
    Lafayette O .............................................89,90
    Sarah E T .................................................89,90
GATES, J L ..................................................... 277
GIBBS
    Fred...........................................................91,92
    Lizzie .................................................91,92,93,94
    Ollie Lee .................................................91,92
GIBSON, Stephen ............................................ 199
GIPSON, Stephen....................................198,199
GOING
    Abner ..............................84,85,86,87,88,89
    Elyara ....................................................... 208
    Gibson ................................84,85,86,87,88,89,208
    Osborne ...............................................87,88,207
    Peter.................................................1,87,88,207
    Robinson.................................206,207,208,209
    Selseniey............................................... 208
    Silsainey .............................................206,207
    Silseiney ..............................................208,209
    Sophia ...................................85,86,87,88,89
    Vinson ..........1,87,88,206,207,208,209
GOODMAN
    Ida ..............................................................171,172
    Ida I .......................................................... 171
    Joe W .......................................................171,172
    Lora .................................................170,171,172
GRAVES
    Dr William................................................ 14
    Will............................................................ 14
    William ................................................... 10,15
    William DO ............................................ 14
HAIAKANUBBE
    Amanda ................................................... 306
    Mary ........................................................ 307
    Wellington .............................................. 306
HAIAKANUBBEE
    Amanda ................................................... 307
    Mary ........................................................ 307
    Wellington .............................................. 307
HAIAKANUBBI, Amanda................ 306
HAIAKONABE, Mary..................... 307
HAIAKONUBBE
    Amanda ................................................... 307
    Louisan ................................................... 307
    Louisian .............................................307,308
    Mary ........................................................ 307
    Willington................................................ 307
HAIAKONUBBEE
    Amanda ...............................................308,309
    Louisiana ................................................ 309
    Mary ....................................................308,309
    Wellington .........................................308,309
HAISKONABBE, Willington ..56,57,102,
104,217,218
HALL, Nellie................................................66,67
HARLEY
    Silvia........................................................ 312
    Sissie........................................................ 64
HARRIS
    Abel ......................................................... 285
    Amelia .....................................10,11,12,13,14,15
    Annie ....272,273,275,276,278,279,286
    Annie L .................................................285,286
    Bessie L .................................................. 286
    Charlie .................................................... 286
    Clifford ........271,272,273,274,275,276,
278,279,280,281,282,283,284,285,286
    Elizabeth ................................................. 285
    Everett J .................................................. 285

# Index

Henry .................................... 285
Henry C ................................. 286
J E ............................................. 35
J H Rayburn ........................ 10,11
Jack L .................. 10,11,12,13,14,15
Jack L, Jr ............................. 13,14
James ..................................... 285
John H R ........................... 11,12,13
Maggie E ................................ 286
Mattie M ................................ 286
Nancy .................................... 208
Nettie Ella ............................. 286
Ruthie .................................... 285
Sarah ..................................... 286
Thomas .................................. 285
W A ............................... 276,277,280
Walter C ...................... 39,40,41,286
William ....... 272,273,274,275,276,278, 279,281,282,283,284,285,286
Wm ........................................ 283
Zado ...................................... 285
HARRISON, Robert S ............ 211,212
HERNDON
  Emma J ............................. 59,60
  Leo .................................... 59,60
  Sidney J ............................. 59,60
HICKS
  Adam .... 130,131,132,133,136,137,138
  Cephus ...... 130,131,132,133,134,135, 136,137,138,178,182,183,184,269
  Hephus ................................ 177
  Lincey ....... 131,132,133,134,135,136, 137,138
  Mary ........ 130,131,132,133,134,135
HIGHTOWER, A M ..................... 19
HOFFMAN, A M ...................... 100
HOLMES, Mimy .................. 232,233
HOLT, Annie .......................... 286
HOMER, Sol J ......................... 168
HORNER, Byington ................. 189
HOTINLOBBE, Joe ................ 46,47
HOTINLUBBEE, Joe ................. 42
HOTUBBEE, Selina ................. 146
HUDSON
  Roar .................................. 143
  Roosevelt Easton ...... 258,259,260,261
  Rosevelt Easton .................. 259
  Rufus ................... 258,259,260,261
  Sallie ................. 255,258,259,260,261
HULSEY, Wm J ....................... 7,8
HYDSON, Roar ....................... 142
IMPALUMBE, Louina ................ 85
IMPALUMBI, Louina ................ 89
IMPSON, T J ......................... 158
INGE, C M .............................. 18
ISTIATUBBEE ........................ 200
JACKMAN, F M ....................... 18
JACKSON
  F M ..................................... 16
  Minnie ................................. 54
  Nicholas .......................... 244,245
JACOB
  Delilah ................... 289,290,291
  Jonas .................. 243,244,245,246
  Rhoda ................... 244,245,246
  Simeon ........... 146,243,244,245,246
  Sophie ................. 243,244,245,246
JACOBS, Delilah .................... 288
JAMES
  Agnes ................................. 257
  Allen W .......................... 264,266
  Patterson ..................... 147,148,149
  Sallie ........................... 147,148,149
  Sarah ........................... 147,148,149
  Sela ........................... 45,46,47,48
JEFFERSON
  Adaline ...................... 250,251,252
  Adeline ......................... 252,253
  Agnes ......... 198,199,200,201,202,203
  Allson Perry ........................ 198
  Austin ........ 198,199,200,201,202,203
  Berry .............. 198,201,202,203
  Cain .................................. 79,80
  Daniel ..................... 220,221,223
  Edson .................. 80,81,82,188
  Eliza ................................ 79,81,82
  Ella ............................ 231,232,233
  Ellis ........................... 231,232,233
  Emiline ....................... 251,252,253
  Euson ................................. 185
  Foster ............................ 252,253
  Helen ............................. 251,252
  Hickson .......................... 252,253
  Juliua ................................ 318

# Index

Julius............................................. 319
Lizzie.................................231,232,233
Perry..................197,198,199,200,201
Samuel.........................239,240,251,252
Sealy..........................................80,81,82
Winsie......................................... 324
JOHN
   Lena..........................................78,79
   Museton....................................78,79
   Rayson...............................239,240,243
   Semah............................................ 78
   Semiah....................................77,78,79
   Simih.............................................. 78
   Susan............................................ 230
JOHNSON
   Elsie........................................101,102
   Joseph........................................... 259
   Lucy Ann.................. 101,103,120,121
   Norman Joseph.......................261,262
   O L................................4,5,6,275,276
   Sinsie J...................................254,261,262
   Wilmon...................................173,189
   Wilmon J..................258,260,261,262
JONES
   Artie Ann..................................... 250
   B W...........................................60,61
   Carl...........................................60,61
   Clyde....................................65,66,67
   Eizar.............................................. 51
   Hannah.................................65,66,67
   Ida..........................................250,251
   Isaac.............................................. 250
   Jimmie......................................27,29
   Josephine..................................60,61
   Logan........................................... 208
   Nancy........................................... 208
JONSON, Wilmon............................ 173
JULIUS, W A...................................... 25
JUZAN
   Eddie....................................124,125
   Hattie.................. 123,124,126,127,128
   Jackaway ...........................124,128
   Philiston...............................126,127
   Philliston......... 123,124,125,126,128
   Sattie....................................124,125,128
   Sudie....................................126,127
   Suttie............................................ 127

KANIATOBE
   Ellen............................................. 219
   Gibson......... 100,101,102,103,104,105
   Johnson........................44,45,46,47,48
   Rhoda..............................217,218,219
   Rosa.................................217,218,219
   Sally............................................... 48
   Sam..............................44,45,46,47,48
   Sely...................101,102,103,104,105
   Sily............................................... 100
   Susan......... 100,101,102,103,104,105
   Wilburn............. 102,104,217,218,219, 307,308
KANIATUBBEE
   Gibson....................................217,218
   Helen............................................ 218
KELSEY, Dana M............................ 283
KIATOBE, Gibson............................ 101
KING
   Arlington....................35,62,63,64,324
   Mary.............................................. 79
   Smallwood..........................62,63,64
   Zona.........................................62,64
KINIATOBE
   Gibson.......................................... 103
   Sely............................................... 103
   Susan............................................ 103
KIRBY, Ed....................................39,40,41
KUNIATUBBEE, Sally....................... 42
LEFLORE
   James.......................................65,66
   Jeff............................................31,32
   Salina............................................. 65
   Watson......................................31,32
LESTER, C L........................87,207,266
LEWIS
   Annie Belle..............................92,94
   David.........................................93,94
   Davis.............................................. 92
   Harmon.........................................1,2
   Jamison.........................189,265,266
   Lena.......................................92,93,94
   Littie..........................................1,2,3
   Mabel......................................92,93
   Simmon....................................1,2,3
   Thurman..................................1,2,3
LLOD, Louisa.................................. 191

# Index

LONG
  Dr Leroy .................................. 12,170
  Leroy ........ 10,11,164,166,167,168,170
  Leroy, MD ............................... 11,170
  W B ............................................... 90
LUCAS, Thomas L ............................. 229
LUNSFORD, T B .............................. 279
LYON, W T ............................. 113,116,117
MCAFEE
  Elsie ........................................ 42,43,44
  Frank ...................................... 42,43,44
  Sena ....................................... 42,43,44
MCCLURE
  Ellen ................... 234,235,236,237,238
  Racie ......................................... 234,235
  Racy ....................... 234,236,237,238
  Reuben ......... 222,234,235,236,237,238
  Stephen ........................................ 235
MCCOY
  Annie ....................................... 207,209
  Easton ...................................... 185,188
  Hilbon N ..................................... 74,75
  Holman ..................................... 254,255
  Wickens .......................................... 89
MCCURTAIN, Hon Green ................... 53
MCFARLAND, J B ........................... 49,50
MCKINNEY
  Eliza ............................ 27,28,29,30,31
  Elliot ......................................... 27,28
  Elliott .................................... 27,30,31
  John ........................... 27,28,29,30,31
  W H .......... 71,75,88,89,134,136,174, 178,179,188,189,190,259,269,304
  William H ....................................... 78
MCLURE, Reuben ............................ 222
MAMBI, Ellen .................................. 227
MANNING, F ............................. 12,13,14
MANSFIELD, MCMURRAY &
  CORNISH ..................................... 274
MARSHALL, John ............................. 100
MATTHEWS
  J H ........ 133,182,184,199,202,239,242, 243,288,290,301
  Joseph H ......................................... 182
  Tracy ........................................ 290,301
MAYTOBE
  Benson ........................ 56,57,107,108

Casey ............................................ 109,111
Elina ............................................. 107,108
Frances ............................................ 107
Francis ....................................... 107,108,111
Lina ............................................... 106,107
Nancy ............................................... 111
Rayburn ............................................ 111
Samaie ........................................ 106,107
Semie ........................................... 107,108
MAYTUBBY
  Elina ............................................... 108
  Francis ............................................ 110
  Kizzie ........................................ 109,110
  Nancy ........................................ 109,110
  Raybin ........................................ 109,110
MERRY, G G .............................. 102,103
MIASHINTUBBEE, Mary ................. 204
MILLER, D S ..................................... 25
MOORE
  E A ........................................ 138,139,141
  Frances ................................... 220,223,224
  Francis .............................. 220,221,222,223
  John ............ 220,221,222,223,224,225
  Salena ........................................ 221,222
  Selena .............................................. 223
  Selina ......................................... 220,221
  Silena ......................................... 220,224
MORGAN, William K ................. 151,152
MORRIS
  Esais .......................................... 242,243
  S E ............................................... 49,50
MORRISON
  Eleas ............................................... 232
  Eleyis .............................................. 233
  Eleysis ............................................. 232
  Lizzie .............................................. 233
NARLETT
  Ada ................................................. 74
  Adam ............................ 73,74,75,76,77
  Emma ........................... 73,74,75,76,77
  Grincy .......................... 73,74,75,76,77
NEEDLES
  T B ....................... 70,73,198,239,300
NOAH
  Charley ..................................... 288,289,290
  John ............ 131,132,133,134,136,301
  S B .......................................... 239,240,242

# Index

Simeon..........268,270,292,293,295,297
NOAHABI, Lixie................................ 177
NOAHABY, Williamson................... 304
NOAHOBI, Liksi ....177,178,179,181,182
NOAHUBI, Williamson..................... 304
NOLEN, Thomas, Jr.................74,75,190
NORLETT, Grincy................................ 73
NORRIEL, W H.................................. 172
O'DONBY, W J..............................163,164
OKLAHAMBI
    Mary.....................................33,34,35,36
    Rayson...........................................34,35
    Reason............................................33,36
ONTAHYUBBE
    Louis Stephen................................ 310
    Stephen........................................... 310
ONTAIYABI
    Louis Stephen................................ 309
    Stephen........................................... 309
PARK, R A............................................ 23
PARKER, Dixon............................211,212
PATTERSON, W R................................ 9
PERRY
    Cornealia C....................................... 23
    Cornelia C....................................22,23
    Elmer................................................ 22
    Ola Edith........................19,20,21,22,23
    Thomas............................................. 22
    Thomas Elmer...............19,20,21,22,23
    Thomas L.......................................... 20
PITCHLYNN, Edward E..................... 14
PLUMBBI, Louina. 80,82,86,173,174,262
PLUMMER
    Laura B.......................149,150,151,152
    M S.................................................. 151
    Mary A.......................149,150,151,152
    Mary S.....................................149,150
    Mrs M S......................................... 151
    Raymond...................149,150,151,152
POCOCK
    C A................................................23,24
    M E.................................................. 24
POTTER
    Arbon Blackburn.......................6,8,9
    Minnie..........................................7,8,9
    Olburn............................................ 7,8
    R H................................................7,8,9

PULCHER, John..............................7,8,9
RAPPOLEE, J L..........................11,15,16
REXROAT, U T.................................... 17
ROBERT
    Litcey.............................................. 254
    Litsey.................................254,255,256
    Sudie..................................254,255,256
    Sudy................................................ 254
ROBERTS
    J J......................................99,100,115
    Sam T, Jr.................147,148,149,154
RODGERS, Geo D............................ 278
ROSE
    V W.........................................80,81,82
    Vester..........69,71,72,73,192,194,219, 237,238,249,311,312
    Vester W......2,3,26,27,30,31,32,38,40, 41,42,47,48,58,60,64,67,68,77,79,83, 85,86,99,106,107,111,112,119,125, 126,133,136,137,138,145,174,175,176 ,180,181,202,204,205,206,208,209, 210,214,224,226,227,228,230,231,232 ,241,242,245,246,250,251,252,253, 255,261,262,263,267,268,271,287,291 ,296,298,302,305,306,309,310,316, 323
SCOTT
    John...............................................34,36
    Lizzie................................................ 8,9
SCRIBNER, Carrie............................... 50
SEALE, W H........................................ 215
SHAW, Ruth ....................................... 212
SHONEY
    W A.........35,39,40,49,50,56,57,62,63, 65,66,97,102,104,107,109,110,121, 126,127,211,212,217,218,222,229,232 ,234,235,244,245,247,248,307,308, 312,313,314,315,319,324
    Wilson A ......................................... 55
SIMPSON, John..............................45,47
SPENCER, William ......................... 223
STANFORD
    Henry............................................... 49
    Henry C ...............49,50,51,97,314,315
    Maude..........................................49,50
    Maudie.....................................49,50,51
    Sallie............................................49,50

# Index

Sallie E .................................. 50,51
STEPHEN, Lamus .................. 142,143
STEPHENS, Bud ...................... 242,243
STEWART
   Anna ........................................ 56
   Annie .................. 52,53,54,55,57,58
   Ed ............................................ 53
   Florence ............ 52,53,54,55,56,57,58
   L A .......................................... 53
   Levi .............. 52,53,54,55,56,57,58,59,
   110,307,308
STOW, R J ................................. 279
STPHWN, Lamus ......................... 141
STRICKLAND
   Arcola ..................... 161,162,163,164
   C E ............................ 161,163,164
   Charles E .................................. 162
   Sarah N C ................ 161,162,163,164
STRONG, J A ............................ 150,151
TAYLOR
   Catherine ......................... 247,248,249
   Jesse ........................... 246,247,248,249
   John ............................... 247,248,249
   Lily .................................... 311,312
   R A .................................... 101,103
   Thompson .................................. 265
TENIHKA, John ............................ 213
THOMAS
   D ............................................ 154
   Markus L ................................... 147
THOMPSON
   Joe ................................ 323,324,325
   Silman ....................... 322,323,324,325
   Wacie ..................................... 123
   Wincey ..................... 192,322,323,325
   Wincy ..................................... 323
   Winsie .................................... 324
TONEHKA, Dixon ..................... 142,144
TONIHKA
   Betsy ...................................... 227
   John ................................... 216,227
   Ray .................................... 226,227
TUSHKA
   Eliza ................................... 318,319
   Impson ................................... 248
   Impson W .................. 209,210,211,212
   Joseph .................................. 209,210

Josie ................................... 211,212
Lizzie .................................. 210,212
Nellie ....................... 209,210,211,212
Simpson ................................... 247
Willis ....................................... 37
VICTOR
   Frank ............................ 117,118,119
   George ........................... 117,118,119
   Louisa ........................... 117,118,119
WADE
   Barnett ............... 141,142,143,144,145
   Claton .................................... 143
   Clayton .............. 141,142,143,144,145
   Emeline .............. 141,142,143,144,145
WALKER
   Cornelia C ........................ 20,21,22
   Rebecca N ................................. 21
   Tandy K .................................... 21
WALL, Liney ............................... 226
WALLACE
   Carlo ...................... 299,300,301,302
   Gilan ..................................... 299
   Loston ... 287,299,300,301,302,303,305
   Silan ...................................... 301
   Silean .................................. 301,302
WALLAS, Carlo ............................. 301
WARD
   Casey ................................... 26,27
   Isom .................................... 41,42
   Silena ...................................... 46
   Sillan ................................... 41,42
   W R .................................... 169,170
   W S ............. 110,126,127,247,248,308
   William S ............................... 41,42
WARREN, Jno R ....................... 150,151
WASHINGTON
   George L .......................... 311,312,313
   Laura ............................. 311,312,313
   Sally .............................. 311,312,313
WASHUBY, Williamson ................. 183
WATSON
   Allen .................................. 312,313
   Ananias ............. 176,180,238,240,241,
   242,243
   Annias .................................... 242
   Emma .................................. 129,130
   George .................................. 88,259

# Index

Johnney ............................................. 239
Johnnie ............... 238,240,241,242,243
Larsen ........................................ 89,259
Margaret ......................................... 130
Podema ..................................... 263,264
Sam .......................................... 129,130
Semi ........................................... 240,243
Semie .......................................... 240,241
Senie ............................................... 239
Sennie ............................................. 242
Thomas ..................................... 70,71,88
Washington ............................. 129,130
WELLS
   Dr A J ............................................ 163
   A J ...................................... 161,162,164
   A J, MD ................................. 162,164
WESLEY, Lenas ................................. 29
WHALE
   David ............................................. 263
   Elmira ............................................ 263
   Lindsy ..................................... 263,264
WHITE
   John R ...... 95,96,97,98,99,100,314,315
   Lena ..................... 96,97,98,99,100
   Lillian A .......................................... 97
   Lillian Aline .......... 95,96,97,98,99,100
WHITEMAN
   M J ................................................. 323
   W J ...................................... 128,129,322
WILLIAM
   Johnson .................................... 317,320
   Moses .............................................. 43
WILLIAMS
   Abner .................. 117,120,121,122,123
   Byington ................................. 121,122
   Jonson ............................................ 319
   Lucy Ann ............................... 122,123
   Moses ..................................... 121,122
   Sallie Ann ..................................... 147
   Wacie ...................................... 121,122
   Wat ................................................. 118
   Watt ............................................... 118
   Wilcey ........................................... 120
   Wilsie ................. 119,120,121,122,123
WILLIS
   Allen .............................................. 290
   John ........................................ 228,229,230
   Lottie ..................................... 228,229,230
   Sammie ................................. 228,229,230
WILLISTON, S C ........................ 126,127
WILSON
   Allie ................................... 193,194,195
   Bryant ................................ 193,196,197
   Chales ............................................ 194
   Charles .......... 68,193,194,195,196,197
   Charley ........................................ 191
   Chas A .......................................... 190
   Ed ................................................ 68,69
   Green ...................................... 191,192
   Ishtemus ...................................... 191
   Jerry ........................................ 191,192
   Kitsy ...................... 191,192,322,323
   Lucinda ................... 194,195,196,197
   Norwood ..................................... 68,69
   Reuben ......................................... 191
   Sallie ....................................... 194,196
   Simpson ................................. 73,74,76
   Taby ............................................ 68,69
   W P ................................................. 29
WINSHIP
   Anderson ............................... 203,205
   Eunittie ............................ 203,204,205
   Isaac ................................. 203,204,205
   Lincoln .................................. 203,204